S0-AFM-972

Events That Changed the World in the Seventeenth Century

Events That Changed the World in the Seventeenth Century

edited by
Frank W. Thackeray
&
John E. Findling

THE GREENWOOD PRESS
"EVENTS THAT CHANGED THE WORLD" SERIES

GREENWOOD PRESS
Westport, Connecticut • London

Library of Congress Cataloging-in-Publication Data

Events that changed the world in the seventeenth century / edited by
  Frank W. Thackeray and John E. Findling.
     p.   cm.—(The Greenwood Press "Events that changed the
  world" series, ISSN 1078–7860)
   Includes bibliographical references and index.
   ISBN 0–313–29078–4 (alk. paper)
   1. History, Modern—17th century.   I. Thackeray, Frank W.
II. Findling, John E.   III. Series.
D246.E92   1999
909.6—dc21   99–25506

British Library Cataloguing in Publication Data is available.

Library of Congress Catalog Card Number: 99–25506
ISBN: 0–313–29078–4
ISSN: 1078–7860

First published in 1999

Greenwood Press, 88 Post Road West, Westport, CT 06881
An imprint of Greenwood Publishing Group, Inc.
www.greenwood.com

Printed in the United States of America

The paper used in this book complies with the
Permanent Paper Standard issued by the National
Information Standards Organization (Z39.48–1984).

10 9 8 7 6 5 4 3 2 1

Copyright Acknowledgments

The editors and publisher gratefully acknowledge permission for use of the following
material:

Adaption from "The Tokugawa Era: 1600–1868" in *History of Japan* by Louis G. Perez,
Greenwood Press, an imprint of Greenwood Publishing Group, Inc., Westport, CT.

Contents

Illustrations

Preface

This volume, which describes and evaluates the global impact of ten of the seventeenth century's most important events, is the fourth in a multivolume series intended to acquaint readers with the seminal events of modern times. Earlier volumes covered the most important world events of the twentieth, nineteenth, and eighteenth centuries. A final volume will include the most important events of the sixteenth and fifteenth centuries. There is also a series of volumes specifically addressing the American experience.

Our collective classroom experience provided the inspiration for this project. Having encountered literally thousands of entry-level college students whose knowledge of the world in which they live is sadly deficient, we determined to write a series of books that would concentrate on the most important events affecting those students (and others as well) in the hope that they would better understand their world and how it came to be. Furthermore, we hope these books will stimulate the reader to delve further into the events covered in each volume and to take a greater interest in history in general.

The current volume is designed to serve two purposes. First, the editors have provided an introduction that presents factual material about each event in a clear, concise, chronological order. Second, each introduction is followed by a longer interpretive essay by a recognized authority exploring the ramifications of the event under consideration. Each chapter concludes with an annotated bibliography of the most important works about the event. The chapters are followed by three appendices that give additional information useful to the reader. Appendix A is a glossary of names, events, treaties, and terms mentioned but not fully explained in the introductions and essays. Appendix B is a timeline of major seventeenth-century events. Appendix C lists the most important ruling houses and dynasties of the seventeenth century.

The events covered in this volume were selected on the basis of our combined teaching and research activities. Colleagues and contributors made suggestions as well, and for this we thank them. Of course, any pair of editors might have arrived at a somewhat different list than we did; but we believe that we have assembled a group of events that truly changed the seventeenth-century world.

As with all published works, numerous people behind the scenes deserve much of the credit for the final product. Barbara Rader, our editor at Greenwood Publishing Group, has consistently lent her support, encouragement, and patience to the project. The staff of the Photographic Division of the Library of Congress provided valuable assistance. Our student research assistant, Sandra Taylor, worked diligently to fulfill our every request. Special thanks goes to Brigette Colligan, who cheerfully, speedily, and efficiently word processed what appeared to be reams of material. As always, Kirk Klaphaak applied his computer-oriented magic to the manuscript with salutary results. We also wish to thank Indiana University Southeast for supplying us with funds to hire our student research assistant. Many thanks to Roger and Amy Baylor and to Kate O'Connell for opening their hearts and their establishment to us, thereby giving us a congenial, enlightened atmosphere for wide-ranging discussions on every conceivable subject, including our manuscript, at the very time when our campus seemed less than enthusiastic about fulfilling that role. Among those who consistently supported and encouraged us are Sam Sloss, Sheila Andersen, Andy Trout, Jake Newman, Kim Pelle, Glenn Crothers, and Tom Prebys. Most important, we wish to thank the authors of the book's essays. All were cooperative, and all presented us with insightful, articulate analysis. Without them, there would be no book.

Finally, we wish to express our appreciation to our spouses, Kathy Thackeray and Carol Findling, and to our children, Alex and Max Thackeray and Jamey Findling, who nurtured our dreams, supported our work, tolerated our idiosyncrasies, and overlooked our idiocies as we grappled with our manuscript. For that we are grateful.

Frank W. Thackeray

John E. Findling

Events That Changed the World in the Seventeenth Century

The church of St. Basil the Blessed, situated on Moscow's Red Square, bore mute witness to the bloody turbulence that characterized early seventeenth-century Russia's Time of Troubles. (Reproduced from the Collections of the Library of Congress)

The Time of Troubles, 1598–1618

INTRODUCTION

In the late sixteenth century, Russia, or Muscovy, found itself in a precarious position owing to rising tensions on several fronts. Failure to resolve the problems producing these tensions led to a major crisis in the early seventeenth century known as the Time of Troubles, a turbulent period that called into question the continued existence of the young state. Writing at the beginning of the twentieth century, the great Russian historian S. F. Platonov contended that no single cause stood behind the Time of Troubles; rather, there was a confluence of crises involving complex dynastic, social, economic, and national questions.

The dynastic crisis precipitated the Time of Troubles. The modern Russian state had slowly evolved under the leadership of the grand princes of Moscow, who gradually liberated Russia from Mongol control that dated to the middle of the thirteenth century. Ivan III, also known as Ivan the Great, completed this process during his reign (1462–1505). The Muscovite princes, who under Ivan III had begun to call themselves tsars or caesars, had benefited—in their drive to oust the Mongols and increase their own authority—from a fairly smooth succession process in which the eldest son had for several generations uneventfully followed his father as ruler.

However, in the second half of the sixteenth century grave problems appeared. Tsar Ivan IV, known to history as Ivan the Terrible, was crowned in 1547 and died in 1584 after a tumultuous reign. Possessed of an uncontrollable temper, Ivan killed his eldest son and heir in 1581 during an argument. When Ivan died in 1584, the crown passed to his next eldest son, Theodore, or Fedor, who was mentally incompetent. Fedor was married to Irina Godunov, and her brother, Boris Godunov, became the power behind the throne. As uncrowned ruler Godunov proved competent, and when Fedor died in 1598 without an heir, he had himself crowned tsar. The only other possible claimant to the throne, Fedor's half brother Dmitry, had died under mysterious circumstances at Uglich in 1591.

Although Boris Godunov was intelligent and energetic, he faced serious problems that eventually overwhelmed him. His lack of a blood connection to the traditional ruling house allowed his opponents to undermine his rule. Moreover, a number of accidental occurrences, including widespread famine and epidemics that sapped his popularity and resources, bedeviled his reign. Most important, Boris inherited several major issues that defied easy solutions.

The rapid expansion of Muscovy created severe strains that the policies of Ivan the Terrible greatly exacerbated. As more land came under Moscow's control, the state struggled to administer it effectively. Bureaucracies appeared willy-nilly, leading to administrative overlap and confusion. Under Ivan the Terrible, the boyars, or great Russian aristocrats, who formerly administered much of the land, were greatly weakened as a governing elite. Ivan hated and distrusted the boyars, and he persecuted them mercilessly. The boyars who survived were made to serve the state and punished if they did not. To provide the necessary administrative and military manpower, Ivan greatly expanded the service gentry class. Drawn from all levels of society, the service gentry, or *dvoriane*, received land in return for service to the state. The *dvoriane* retained the land only as long as they and their heirs continued in state service. The boyars resented the service gentry as parvenus, and the service gentry resented the aristocratic pretensions of the boyars; both groups hated their dependence on the tsar.

While the boyars and gentry served the tsar, the Russian peasantry tilled their lands. However, for some time the free Russian peasant had been at risk due to encroaching bondage. Responding to this and to increased obligations and restrictions that both the state and the landlords placed upon them, the peasants fled the land in ever-increasing

numbers and headed for the borderlands. Peasant flight alarmed the boyars and especially the service gentry since their land was virtually
worthless without the labor to farm it. Consequently, they pressed the
tsar for even greater control over the peasants, who continued to evade
what was fast becoming for them a form of enslavement called serfdom.
With the demand for labor increasing and the supply dwindling as the
peasants fled, intense competition for labor broke out between the boyars
and the Orthodox Church—which owned huge estates—on one hand,
and the service gentry, on the other hand. With greater resources, the
former frequently won the competition, thereby further embittering the
dvoriane.

Other problems included economic stagnation in the urban centers and
a decline in their populations resulting from Ivan the Terrible's policies
of centralization and overtaxation; the presence in the southern borderlands of the Cossacks—large, armed bands of freebooters; hostile neighbors ranging from the Turks and the Crimean Tatars in the south to the
Swedes and Poles in the northeast; and the devastating effects of Ivan's
oprichnina, a sort of secret police created by and answerable solely to the
tsar that subjected Muscovy to a bloody reign of terror not unlike that
directed by Soviet dictator Joseph Stalin in the twentieth century.

Boris Godunov was elected tsar in 1598 by a *zemskii sobor*, or assembly
of the land, that included clergy, boyars, service gentry, and even some
merchants, but no peasants. Job, the patriarch of the Russian Orthodox
Church, supported Godunov, who outdistanced his closest rival, Fedor
Romanov, nephew of Anastasia, Ivan the Terrible's beloved first wife.
Nevertheless, many boyars were unhappy because Boris seemed to favor
the *dvoriane* and took a few small steps to ease the peasants' burden.
Against this backdrop, Boris' increasingly brutal and autocratic ways
provoked opposition. Widespread disease and famine also undermined
his authority.

The vehicle for those opposed to Boris' rule was a young man claiming
to be Dmitry, Ivan IV's son who had died in 1591. Rumor had it that
another boy had died and that the real Dmitry had escaped and was
now returning to claim his rightful throne from usurper Boris Godunov.
This first False Dmitry gained the support of the Polish court and its
Jesuit advisers who hoped to use him to further their interests in Russia.
Undoubtedly he also enjoyed the support of many boyars.

In October 1604 the False Dmitry invaded Muscovy with a ragtag band
of about 2,000 Cossacks, Poles, and rebellious Russians. As he moved
toward Moscow, he attracted increasing support. Every sector of Russian

society, from boyar to peasant, saw him as the solution to its particular problems. But Boris' army defeated the False Dmitry, and while the pretender escaped capture and managed to regroup, his prospects were dim. Fortune, however, smiled on this first False Dmitry. Tsar Boris died suddenly in April 1605, after which his military commander defected to Dmitry's side. In June Dmitry's army captured Moscow.

False Dmitry's reign was both tumultuous and short. All elements of Russian society expected him to act in their behalf, even though their specific desires frequently proved to be mutually exclusive. Instead, Dmitry ignored Russia's problems and, despite his obvious intelligence, acted in an erratic and irresponsible manner. He disdained traditional Russian customs and publicly insulted the Orthodox Church. His reliance on boastful Polish counselors who flaunted their Roman Catholicism infuriated Russians of all classes, and his marriage to a Catholic noblewoman from Poland further enraged them.

Muscovy's boyars now took advantage of the deteriorating situation. Led by Prince Vasily Shuisky, they denounced Dmitry as an impostor and incited the Moscow mob that invaded the Kremlin and murdered the tsar. A bloodbath followed during which several thousand Poles and Russian supporters of both the Godunovs and the False Dmitry died. With the field clear, Vasily Shuisky seized the throne.

However, Shuisky found it difficult to rule. Muscovy was in chaos, and with the exception of several boyar clans, he lacked support, to say nothing of legitimacy. The peasants' fear of serfdom led them to rebellion; the Cossacks roamed freely throughout the state, especially in the south; the service gentry gained no comfort from the prospect of boyar rule; the Moscow mob had tasted blood on two occasions; and even among the boyars there were those who rejected Shuisky.

When Shuisky moved to implement policies favorable to the boyars and especially harmful to Russia's peasants, he provoked open civil war with distinctive class overtones. From southern Russia a motley army of Cossacks, peasants, and runaway slaves moved north toward Moscow. Its leader was Ivan Bolotnikov, a former noble servitor who urged his followers to "kill the boyars." Many of southern Russia's desperate peasants joined his band. Even some disgruntled, pauperized *dvoriane* sided with Bolotnikov, but his message of class hatred eventually drove them away and into Shuisky's arms.

Shuisky's boyar army finally defeated the rebels, but only with difficulty. Bolotnikov had always maintained that he had been acting on behalf of "Tsar Dmitry," who had somehow managed to escape death and whose name galvanized large parts of a wretched and despairing population. And in fact, numerous new pretenders to the throne appeared on the scene. By far the most serious challenge to Shuisky came from the "second False Dmitry." The new Dmitry won the backing of the Polish king, Sigismund III, and his nobility, who saw a golden opportunity to despoil the weakened Russian state. The remainder of Bolotnikov's army, the Cossacks, and a horde of desperate peasants also flocked to Dmitry's banner.

Dmitry's "army" besieged Moscow but could not capture it. Consequently, Dmitry set up camp at the village of Tushino outside of Moscow and established there a parallel government. This Dmitry, often called the "Rogue of Tushino," won some support among the common people despite his avarice and heavy-handedness; however, most of the boyars and *dvoriane*, repelled by the brigands, social malcontents, Cossacks, and opportunists who supported Dmitry, sided with Shuisky.

At this juncture, the Poles, who were then besieging the important Russian city of Smolensk, began to play an even larger role in Russian affairs. When Shuisky's forces—directed by his nephew Mikhail Skopin-Shuisky and reinforced by Swedish troops sent to support Shuisky after the tsar agreed to cede Russian land on the Gulf of Finland to Sweden—began to overcome the pretender's army, some of Dmitry's aristocratic advisers decided to offer the crown to Sigismund III's son, Wladyslaw. Sigismund accepted, and the Polish army now marched on Moscow. Shuisky's army, bereft of its commander with the sudden and inexplicable death of Skopin-Shuisky, fell to the Poles in June 1610 at the Battle of Klushino. A month later, Shuisky abdicated. All semblance of order disappeared, and Muscovy disintegrated. Filling this vacuum, the Poles entered Moscow, helped to defeat a resurgent Rogue of Tushino, and laid claim to the remnants of the demoralized Russian state.

Foreign conquest sparked a Russian national revival. The Orthodox patriarch Hermogen successfully rejected Polish claims to the throne and rallied the Russians behind their Orthodox religion. Throughout Muscovy, armed forces drawn from every social class rose to drive out the Catholic Poles. Social divisions fractured the first so-called national army, but a second national army originating in the Volga River city of Nizhny Novgorod under the leadership of patriotic butcher Kuzma Minin and veteran soldier Dmitry Pozharsky soon formed and attacked the Poles. The Polish garrison took refuge in Moscow's Kremlin, but a relief column was defeated and the Poles surrendered in October 1612.

In the wake of their victory, the Russians aimed to restore political order and to end the social chaos. A *zemskii sobor*, with representatives from all social groups, selected as tsar Mikhail Romanov, a sixteen-year-old from a boyar family with ties through marriage to the old ruling dynasty. With Mikhail's coronation in July 1613, a new dynasty was inaugurated. But the Romanov government was quite weak for several years as it slowly consolidated power by defeating foreign and domestic rivals.

INTERPRETIVE ESSAY
John T. Alexander

The Time of Troubles impressed horrific experiences on millions of people during several decades. Indeed, over the centuries the impress has etched deeper as the term was applied to other national or international catastrophes. In the aftermath of the Napoleonic invasion of 1812, Russian sculptor Ivan Martos commemorated Muscovite patriotism during the Time of Troubles in a huge sculpture of Kuzma Minin and Dmitry Pozharsky, two of the "heroes" of the Time of Troubles, on Red Square in 1818. The era was dramatized in literature and opera by Russian cultural icons such as Nicholas Karamzin, Alexander Pushkin, and Modest Mussorgsky in world-famous portrayals of Boris Godunov. In a posthumously published book, the late twentieth-century Russian historian Aleksandr M. Stanislavsky underlined the Time of Troubles' allure: "threatening movements of the popular masses that shook tsars' thrones, the appearance in the historical arena of remarkable personages and brilliant adventurers, conspiracies and betrayals, incredible concatenations of circumstances, and historical enigmas still not solved by scholars. One can only be amazed at how all this fit into such a thin slice of our history."

The roots of the Time of Troubles extend deep into Muscovite history, particularly to the formative decades of its huge multiethnic empire under Tsar Ivan IV. During the sixteenth century, state territory nearly tripled and population doubled, reaching about 11 million. Muscovy turned into a sprawling "composite monarchy," with disparate parts administered by a minimalist state apparatus vulnerable to "imperial overreach" and severe inflationary pressures linked to the "price revolution" of the sixteenth century. The realm already showed signs of structural breakdown in the 1580s. These stresses intensified in the 1590s all over Europe because of famine and harvest failure from erratic weather produced by the general cooling of the Little Ice Age (1550–1700). Prolonged warfare on several fronts over four decades ended in costly defeat, state financial stringency, economic depression and population migration, state policies resulting in bondage for peasants and townspeople alike, the splintering of the boyar and gentry elites, and dysfunction in the ruling dynasty with Ivan IV's murder of his eldest (and childless) son in 1581 and his own sudden death three years later amid rumors of poisoning. The regency headed by Boris Godunov for feebleminded Tsar Fedor Ivanovich (1584–1598) was inherently unstable, the rivalry of aristocratic clans intense, and the succession questionable in view of the puzzling death at Uglich of the tsarevich, or son of the tsar and heir to the throne, Dmitry Ivanovich (1583–1591). Tsar Fedor's death without heirs ended the Danilovich dynasty, inaugurating a prolonged succession crisis that the selection of his brother-in-law Boris Godunov as tsar postponed only slightly.

In the competition to succeed Fedor, Boris Godunov bested several other aristocratic candidates, most notably Fedor Romanov (c. 1556–1633) whose clan was related to Ivan IV's first wife. Romanov was accused of sedition and banished to a northern monastery. There he was forced to become a monk (Filaret was his religious name), thereby barring him forever from secular office. Even before Godunov gained the throne, he arranged for metropolitan Job of Moscow to be elevated to the status of patriarch, or the highest-ranking official of the Russian Orthodox Church, and made peace with Sweden in 1595. As the new tsar and autocrat (or independent ruler), Godunov extended Muscovite dominion further eastward into Siberia and southward toward the Crimean khanate, or principality, with the foundation of frontier fortresses such as Tsarev-Borisov in 1600. This last step may have antagonized Cossack elements on the southern frontiers. The Cossack, free communities of escaped serfs who had intermarried with the indigenous peoples of the southern steppe and who were described as "that licentious soldiery, corrupt and wild" by Godunov's contemporary Isaac Massa, greatly valued their independence. State expansion threatened the Cossacks' freedom of action, denied them entry into frontier towns, and reaffirmed government efforts to stem the outflow of fugitives multiplying the ranks of their "military democracy." Moreover, amid the horrific famine, high bread prices, and epidemics of 1601–1603, a tide of uprooted people overran central Muscovy, sold themselves into slavery, and fled southward. According to French Protestant mercenary Jacques Margeret, "[T]hings so atrocious were committed that they are unbelievable": instances of cannibalism, tales of parents killing children, mass graves for 120,000 starving poor in Moscow, and "hungry wolves that tore people to pieces." The government labored vainly to cope with these disasters by freeing slaves released by their masters and countering banditry in the hinterland led by a former bondman nicknamed Khlopko (from *kholop*, bondman).

Amid these disasters, Boris Godunov and his family became targets for malicious gossip. His wife, the daughter of Ivan IV's henchman Maliuta Skuratov, was accused of pandering to Boris' ambitions and plotting to become empress. Both were blamed for a repressive regime that persecuted high and low alike. Suspicions of Godunov's complicity in the death of Tsarevich Dmitry may have circulated covertly for years before a Polish spy reported from Moscow in February 1598 that "Dmitry" had sent a letter to Smolensk and that Boris had a friend resembling the late tsarevich. Such tales became stronger after 1600 with the onset of the terrible famine. The first impostor claiming to be Dmitry appeared in Lithuania in 1603. Muscovite authorities denounced him as the renegade noble or defrocked monk Grigory Otrepiev.

The identity or inventor of this first impostor is controversial. One historian, Sergei F. Platonov, contended that he was a Muscovite groomed for the role by Muscovite boyars and Polish nobles, his imposture a ploy in the intra-elite rivalry for the throne. But historian Maureen Perrie thinks he was a young Muscovite disaffected from Orthodoxy and undergoing a midlife crisis who may have originated the idea himself. In any event, Dmitry of Uglich was the logical prototype for an impostor in the Muscovite monarchy, for the notion of switching or hiding true heirs to the throne was a common motif of the politics of any hereditary monarchy or aristocracy. Like circumstances gave rise to similar impostors in England, Moldavia, and Portugal in the late sixteenth century. Whatever Dmitry's origins, he wrote Russian far more freely than Polish and exhibited complete self-confidence. He may have really believed he was the true tsarevich. Margeret accepted him as miraculously saved from death, rebutted charges leveled against him of frivolity and violating Muscovite customs (lies blamed on the Shuiskys), and even doubted his assassination.

"Dmitry" appeared publicly in 1603 with support from Polish magnate Jerzy Mniszech (to whose daughter Marina he was secretly betrothed) and from Jesuits at the Polish royal court. The Polish-Lithuanian

Commonwealth was a huge composite "republic" of magnates and gentry presided over by an elected king, the unpopular Swedish-born Catholic Sigismund III Vasa, who championed the Counter Reformation in campaigns against Sweden and Muscovy. Yet his policies were opposed by Polish Chancellor Jan Zamoyski and his rule wracked by domestic division. Although Zamoyski opposed Polish backing for the impostor, Sigismund received "Dmitry" at Cracow in March 1604 and promised conditional aid.

With some 2,500 mercenaries—including Muscovites, Tatars, Turks, Poles, Lithuanians, Karelians, and Germans—the impostor invaded Muscovy in 1604–1605. Defeated several times and forced to take refuge in Putivl, "Dmitry" and his cause were reprieved by the sudden death of Tsar Boris on April 13, 1605. Mutinies in the Muscovite army quickly ensued, while new recruits from the Don Cossacks joined the revitalized impostor. His triumphant forces entered Moscow on June 1, triggering an uprising that overthrew the Godunovs and pillaged their property. Patriarch Job was also deposed and succeeded by Ignatius. "Dmitry" himself arrived on June 20, "recognized" his putative mother Maria Nagaia on July 17, and was crowned in the Uspensky Cathedral on July 21. Throughout his progress the impostor used rhetoric reflecting biblical themes of resurrection and new life.

Tsar Dmitry's reign lasted barely ten months before its violent end. He offended the boyars, many of whom knew he was a fraud, by exiling the Shuisky brothers for alleged sedition and favoring Polish servitors whose numbers swelled with the arrival of Marina's huge entourage on May 2 for her "coronation" and wedding. His "un-tsarlike conduct" also antagonized Muscovites during solemn ceremonies. He went about in public in Polish clothing, built new quarters in the Polish style, and engaged in raucous games involving a mobile fortification decorated like a dragon and snowball fights with mercenaries. He looked like a misshapen dwarf, yet he fancied himself irresistible and reputedly raped the orphaned Ksenia Godunov, among other debaucheries. He even quarreled with his Polish patrons, added "caesar" to his grandiloquent title, and boasted of inciting rebellion in Poland. Although he spent lavishly to conciliate the Muscovite service gentry and the palace guard, he seemed to shun the boyars. His wedding to Marina Mniszech on May 8 outraged Muscovite traditionalists further by infringing on a feast day, crowning her in the Uspensky Cathedral, and allowing Jesuits at the ceremony despite rumors that the Poles wished to remove the capital from Moscow.

All these discontents led to popular disturbances in Moscow, and on May 17, 1606, Tsar Dmitry was overthrown and murdered. His corpse was abused as that of a sorcerer, a Polish buffoon, or a Jew. A stake was driven through his heart, and his corpse was eventually burned on the pyre of his hellish mobile fortification. One story avers that his ashes were then fired from a cannon toward Poland. Only two days later, Vasily Shuisky was chosen tsar by an impromptu assemblage of boyars, clergy, military servitors, and townspeople. A veteran statesman from an ancient princely family, Shuisky had headed the commission that investigated the death of Tsarevich Dmitry at Uglich and also helped the impostor attain power, although he almost perished at his hands. The new government was widely seen as dominated by the boyars, to whom Shuisky made public promises of fair treatment while charging that the impostor had plotted to massacre the boyars. Like Godunov, he sent a commission to Uglich to disinter the tsarevich's remains, which were then transferred to Moscow. The tsarevich was canonized and his relics proclaimed to work miracles. His mother Maria was brought forward again to denounce the dethroned tsar as a fraud. Hermogen replaced Ignatius as the new patriarch. Filaret (Fedor) Romanov, distrusted by the Shuisky brothers, was denied the post.

Despite such propaganda, Shuisky's new regime encountered immediate resistance, especially from contingents of gentry servitors and Cossacks from the southern periphery. These forces refused to believe in "Tsar Dmitry's" death, proclaimed their allegiance to him, and produced a dozen new impostors. Leaders such as the military governor of Putivl, Prince Grigory Shakhovskoi, a former supporter of the impostor banished by Shuisky to the provinces, and two gentry servitors, Istoma Pashkov and Ivan Bolotnikov, led the anti-Shuisky forces. Bolotnikov, a former gentry servitor captured by the Crimean Tatars, had allegedly escaped Turkish captivity to join mercenaries on the Hungarian and Ukrainian frontiers, where he heard rumors that "Tsar Dmitry" had escaped death and was hiding in Lithuania. He may have visited the new impostor and been persuaded of his authenticity by a stolen state seal on an appeal for support against Shuisky. In any event, large numbers of southern gentry and Cossacks mobilized against Shuisky's government in the name of "Tsar Dmitry," whose miraculous survival they professed to champion. Astrakhan and other Volga River towns rebelled against Shuisky and opened their gates to Cossack forces rejecting Moscow's boyar government. By late summer 1606, the two motley "armies" of Bolotnikov and Pashkov, about 20,000 men strong, marched on Moscow, which they besieged on October 28, 1606.

With Bolotnikov as supreme commander, the anti-Shuisky forces assaulted Moscow in mid-November but were repulsed with heavy losses, their setback compounded by the defection of 500 gentry servitors from Riazan led by Prokopy Liapunov. Patriarch Hermogen rallied the Muscovites by branding the rebels a Godless rabble bent on bloodthirsty destruction who would spare neither women nor children. On December 2, gentry reinforcements from Smolensk helped Shuisky's new commander, his nephew Mikhail Skopin-Shuisky, defeat the besiegers, who were also betrayed by Pashkov's gentry. Many rebels were captured and clubbed to death or thrust under the ice of rivers and ponds. Bolotnikov retreated to Kaluga and then withdrew to Tula, where he was joined by a new impostor, "Tsarevich Peter," the former Cossack Ilya Korovin who engaged in piracy on the lower Volga River and then instituted a reign of terror in Putivl, where he executed many officials and nobles who had refused to recognize "Tsar Dmitry." Some were thrown from towers or dropped from bridges, a form of execution that stressed societal inversion and that may have involved some audience participation. Other victims were hung upside down, spread-eagle with arms and legs nailed to walls, and shot or their limbs disjointed and dismembered, scalded, or impaled. These ritualized executions recalled the horrors of Ivan IV's *oprichnina* with its reprisals against "traitor-boyars" and tortures inspired by notions of hellish torments.

Tsarevich Peter brought Prince Grigory Shakhovskoi and a force of Cossacks to join the drive on Moscow. Vasily Shuisky took personal command of the siege of Tula, his forces building a dam to flood the town, which finally capitulated on October 10, 1607. Prince Shakhovskoi was "liberated," whereas Tsarevich Peter was taken to Moscow, where he was executed, and Bolotnikov was imprisoned, blinded, and later drowned. Another impostor on the lower Volga, "Tsarevich Ivan Augustus," claimed to be the son of Ivan IV by his fourth wife, his unusual name recalling earlier tsarist attempts to fabricate genealogical links to the Roman emperors.

The most significant new impostor was a second Dmitry, popularly labeled the Rogue of Tushino, who declared himself in June 1607 in Starodub in the Seversk region of northwest Ukraine. Like his namesake, his actual identity is obscure. Some thought him a Pole or a Jew or a priest's son, and he lacked the first Dmitry's bombast. Even so, he denounced the plethora of rival tsareviches as renegades and executed several. He also gathered support from many different quarters, notably from Cossack leaders such as Ivan Zarutsky and, most dramatically, from the first Dmitry's widow, Marina. Released from internment, the former tsaritsa contrived to recognize her "husband" at the rebels' camp of Tushino just northwest of Moscow in September 1608.

Tushino became an elaborate rebel capital that attracted many different anti-Shuisky elements, such as Filaret Romanov, who was named patriarch and dominated the Tushino government. This second siege of Moscow by "rogue" elements led Shuisky's government to seek armed assistance from Sweden's King Charles IX against his rival and Vasa nephew Sigismund III of Poland-Lithuania. While negotiating with anti-Shuisky elements near Moscow, Sigismund sent a mercenary army under Hetman Stanislaw Zolkiewski into Muscovy in support of the Rogue of Tushino. When Sweden agreed to support Shuisky, Poland declared war on Muscovy, besieging Smolensk in September 1609. At the end of the year the Rogue suddenly fled from Tushino to Kaluga, where he mustered forces to threaten Moscow anew, but the rogues were driven away by Muscovite and Swedish mercenary forces under Mikhail Skopin-Shuisky. Shockingly, Skopin-Shuisky died in Moscow on April 23, 1610, amid rumors of poisoning. Two months later Hetman Zolkiewski defeated Shuisky's army at Klushino, a setback that prompted the tsar's overthrow and forcible tonsure as a monk on July 17. The Shuisky brothers were later taken as prisoners to Poland, where both died in 1612.

Shuisky was succeeded by a provisional government of seven boyars that agreed on August 16, 1610, to invite Crown Prince Wladyslaw of Poland to the Muscovite throne on condition that he convert to Orthodoxy and heed the boyars' advice. Filaret Romanov and Vasily Golitsyn headed the Muscovite embassy to Sigismund's camp outside Smolensk to convoy Wladyslaw, but upon arrival they were made virtual hostages. A Polish garrison was left in Moscow, and after the Rogue fled back to Kaluga he was assassinated and beheaded on December 11, 1610. The widowed Tsaritsa Marina maintained her prospects by giving birth to a son, Tsarevich Ivan Dmitrievich, subsequently known as the Little Rogue or Baby Brigand. The ambitious Cossack leader Ivan Zarutsky, a mainstay of the Tushino camp, took Marina and her son into his protection.

With Moscow occupied by foreign forces and no agreement about a new ruler, provincial towns and servitors began mobilizing against the boyar government and its Polish backers. Prokopy Liapunov, governor of Riazan, and Prince Dmitry Pozharsky of Zaraisk headed the campaign joined by Ivan Zarutsky and remnants of the Tushino camp. In Moscow under house arrest, patriarch Hermogen appealed to Liapunov and gentry servitors against Polish perfidy and tyranny while shunning the Cossacks and former Tushinites. Hermogen died on February 17, 1611. The starving populace chaffed under the Polish occupation until widespread revolt erupted on March 19, 1611. The occupation forces countered by torching the capital, and about two-thirds of the huge city burned down amid streetfighting and looting. Relief, in the form of a national militia under Liapunov, failed to arrive in time, and Pozharsky was severely wounded. Nevertheless, the occupation forces withdrew to the Kremlin, reinforcing its formidable walls with dozens of cannon.

Without siege artillery and divided internally, the national militia took two months to invest Moscow. Meanwhile, a general council issued various decrees. On June 30, 1611, these decrees were consolidated into an interim compact promising to confiscate the lands of the traitor-boyars and distribute them equitably among the militia's leaders and gentry and Cossack servitors ruined by the fighting. Liapunov invited Prince Dmitry Trubetskoi, a boyar from the Rogue of Tushino's camp, and Ivan Zarutsky, the Cossack ataman and Tushino boyar, to join him in a three-man executive overseeing gentry servitors from some twenty-five towns. The triumvirs disagreed, however, and faced constant disputes with their factious followers. They suffered further setbacks when Smolensk finally fell to Sigismund on June 3, 1611, and Liapunov's attempt to storm the Kremlin on July 5 failed. Rumors that Liapunov favored a Swedish candidate for the vacant throne, when the Swedes had just occupied Novgorod and vicinity, enraged Cossacks in the militia who seized upon a forged document purporting to show a plot to turn on the Cossacks once Moscow was taken. Unable to allay suspicions, Liapunov was murdered on July 22, 1611. The militia pressed the siege until the end of 1611 and prevented reinforcement of the Kremlin defenders, but failure of another bloody assault in early December forced it to withdraw to replenish supplies and recruit fresh forces.

What developed into the second national militia began as an outgrowth of cooperation between the Volga River towns of Kazan and Nizhny Novgorod, both of which had avoided devastation. Both had thriving commercial economies and merchant communities. The primary leader at Nizhny Novgorod was Kuzma Minin, a prosperous butcher elected to the town council in the fall of 1611. Concerned about the chaos in Muscovy and inspired by Hermogen's letter denouncing the Cossacks and Marina's son, he dreamed of saving the realm at the head of a new army. Minin proposed the formation of a new national militia to purge Moscow of traitors and to elect a lawful sovereign. He pledged all his property for the cause and urged others to join him. Minin's exhortations quickly gained local support, and the new leaders agreed to invite Pozharsky, then recovering from wounds on his nearby estate, to head the military part of the enterprise. A respected commander of great experience, Pozharsky suffered from epilepsy, probably compounded by a head wound sustained in the Moscow fighting. He agreed to captain the new effort and nominated Minin as chief treasurer. Minin accepted only on condition that he receive extraordinary powers to collect revenue to outfit and supply the new army. The Nizhny Novgorod town commune endorsed the deal with pledges to sacrifice everything for the cause. Pozharsky and Minin immediately set about mobilizing local and regional contingents, and they welcomed servitors from Smolensk fleeing from the Polish takeover. In late February 1612, the main Nizhny Novgorod militia began moving up the Volga, rallying additional forces as it went. A month later Yaroslavl became headquarters of the national campaign. A coalition provisional government emerged with numerous leaders, noble and nonnoble: a general council of about fifty men. Pozharsky assumed the title of "Steward and Commander . . . Elected by the Whole People of the Muscovite Realm and All Ranks of People, Military and Civilian." On many orders issued by the Yaroslavl Council, though, Pozharsky's signature appeared tenth and Minin's fifteenth, indicating that their dominance was not complete. The Yaroslavl government also devised a new national coat of arms: a lion, in contrast to the double-headed eagle employed by the false tsars. Crowded into Yaroslavl, their numbers growing daily, the militia began to be ravaged by epidemic disease (probably typhus) in May 1612. Protection was sought by the customary means of building a wooden votive church in twenty-four hours, the "Universal Salvation."

While the Yaroslavl provisional government took shape, developments around Moscow accelerated the rush of events. Zarutsky and the Cossack besiegers of the Kremlin faced stalemate while anticipating the approach of Polish relief forces under Hetman Jan Chodkiewicz, negotiating with the Swedes over their occupation of Novgorod, and vacillating over whom to support for the vacant throne—a foreigner or Marina's son. On March 5, 1612, Zarutsky and Prince Trubetskoi publicly swore allegiance to "Tsar Dmitry," the third impostor of that name who had appeared in the Novgorod region in early 1611, just after the death of the Rogue of Tushino. Like previous pretenders, his identity remains obscure, but he recited the standard tale of miraculous survival and resolve to regain his throne. Few paid heed at first until he was suddenly invited in December 1611 to Pskov, where he was warmly received. But he soon incited antagonism by tyrannical rule, extortion, and seduction. He contacted both Zarutsky and Pozharsky, seeking recognition, although the latter rejected the imposture and condemned all who endorsed him. Fearing capture by the advancing Swedes or betrayal by the Pskov authorities, he fled on May 18, only to be captured and taken to Moscow, where he was displayed on a chain and eventually executed.

The latest imposture further split the Cossack forces around Moscow, and just as Pozharsky's militia set out for Moscow on July 27, 1612, Zarutsky decamped to Kolomna to collect Marina and her son before fleeing southward, pillaging as he went. Seeking recognition for Marina and her son, Zarutsky was defeated at Voronezh in June 1613. The fugitives went down the Volga to Astrakhan by autumn but soon wore out their welcome there and instituted a reign of terror while attempting to contact the Shah of Persia and the Ottoman Sultan. Fleeing again before the pursuing Muscovite forces, Zarutsky and company were finally cornered on the Yaik River and surrendered. Taken to Moscow, Zarutsky was impaled, the Little Rogue was hanged, and Marina was executed or died.

Pozharsky and the Yaroslavl militia arrived before Moscow in August 1612. In several days of bloody combat, they repulsed Chodkiewicz's relief force. By late September, an alliance was negotiated with Trubetskoi's Cossack forces; the Polish defenders of the Kremlin were reduced to near starvation before surrendering on October 27, 1612. King Sigismund's forces were driven away from Tushino, and a Polish siege of Volokalamsk was also broken, leading to the Poles' withdrawal on November 27 amid severe cold. The Yaroslavl militia was quickly demobilized while its council sent out summons for the towns to send delegates to Moscow by December or January to elect a new ruler. Some 700 delegates from all ranks assembled in January 1613. They promptly rejected all foreign candidates. They needed another month to settle on the candidacy of Mikhail Romanov, the sixteen-year-old son of patriarch Filaret, who had been so prominent at rebel Tushino. Evidently Cossack opinion or pressure was instrumental in reaching a consensus. Mikhail Romanov's selection also testified to the profound conservatism of Muscovite politics, for his family was linked to Ivan IV's first wife and his candidacy had been mentioned during Shuisky's reign and later. Furthermore, his youth and inexperience promised that he would be a figurehead and likely to heed his elders. Anticipating total collapse, England, which carried on a lively trade in naval stores with Russia, considered a protectorate over northern Muscovy in 1612–1613.

The Assembly of the Land and the reconstituted Boyar Council met almost constantly during the early years of the restored monarchy. Minin played a prominent part in the new government until his death in 1616, whereas Pozharsky served with distinction for another quarter of a century. Civil discord and foreign invasion persisted for several more years, culminating in Wladyslaw's assault on Moscow on October 1, 1618, and his later failure to take the Trinity Monastery. After peace with Sweden via the Treaty of Stolbovo on February 27, 1617, Muscovy finally halted hostilities with Poland-Lithuania at the December 1, 1618, truce of Deulino that provided for an armistice for fourteen and a half years. Nevertheless, Wladyslaw retained his claim to the Muscovite throne until the 1634 Treaty of Polianovka. Patriarch Filaret returned to Moscow on June 14, 1619, becoming virtual coruler with his son until his death in 1633.

The results of this epoch of turmoil were varied. In the short run, it left Muscovy weakened and hurting, with substantial losses of western territory. The Muscovite empire gradually recouped its losses in the course of the seventeenth century. Although some elements of the boyar elite suffered a loss of prestige, the aristocracy as a whole maintained its social status, and few clans were eclipsed. In political terms the changes are controversial. Platonov believed that the concept of monarchy changed fundamentally and that the early Romanovs were not absolute sovereigns in the modern sense, their authority limited by the Assembly of the Land and the Boyar Council, and that Muscovites started to think of their realm as a commonwealth rather than the possession of a dynasty. In cultural terms the era left a legacy of greatly increased and more intimate contacts with the rest of the world. Writing and literary activity may have been stimulated as more people wrestled with the meaning of the turbulent events and how to find security and salvation amid efforts to regain peace and prosperity. In Europe the image of Muscovy as an exotic land of chaotic happenings and mysterious personages enthralled playwrights and public alike.

SELECTED BIBLIOGRAPHY

Bussow, Conrad. *The Disturbed State of the Russian Realm*. Edited and translated by G. Edward Orchard. Montreal: McGill-Queens University Press, 1994.

Eyewitness account by a Saxon mercenary who served Boris Godunov, the first False Dmitry, and Vasily Shuisky.

Crummey, Robert O. *Aristocrats and Servitors: The Boyar Elite in Russia, 1613–1689.* Princeton, NJ: Princeton University Press, 1983. Collective biography that focuses on long-term trends and the elite's dual role; questions the Time of Troubles' impact on the boyars as a social group.

Dunning, Chester. "Cossacks and the Southern Frontier in the Time of Troubles." *Russian History* 19 (1992): 57–74. Revisionist treatment of this key social group (or groups) that undercuts their revolutionary aims and totally rejects the notion of "peasant war."

———. "Does Jack Goldstone's Model of Early Modern State Crises Apply to Russia?" *Comparative Studies in Society and History* 39 (1997): 572–592. Insightful recent overview that suggests linkages between structural factors and events and the different social groups.

Emerson, Caryl. *Boris Godunov: Transpositions of a Russian Theme.* Bloomington: Indiana University Press, 1986. Applies the literary-historical theories of Mikhail Bakhtin in analyzing the different treatments by Karamzin, Pushkin, and Mussorgsky.

Freeze, Gregory L., ed. *Russia, a History.* New York: Oxford University Press, 1997. Well-illustrated overview with fine essays by Nancy Shields Kollmann, "Muscovite Russia, 1450–1598," pp. 27–54, and by Hans-Joachim Torke, "From Muscovy Towards St. Petersburg, 1598–1689," pp. 55–86, that stress territorial expansion under "minimalist," albeit ostensibly "autocratic," and militaristic government.

Got'e, Iurii V. *Time of Troubles: The Diary of Iurii Vladimirovich Got'e.* Edited and translated by Terence Emmons. Princeton, NJ: Princeton University Press, 1988. Harrowing account by an eminent historian detailing personal experiences and reflections during the Russian revolution and civil war (1917–1922), an era seen as a new Time of Troubles from which he expected nothing good.

Hellie, Richard. *Enserfment and Military Change in Muscovy.* Chicago: University of Chicago Press, 1971. Prize-winning interpretation that combines concepts of "military revolution" with a historical and sociological study of the "middle service class" and its roles in the consolidation of serfdom.

———. *Slavery in Russia, 1450–1725.* Chicago: University of Chicago Press, 1982. Densely quantitative study of the peculiar institution of limited contract slavery in Muscovy in the broad context of slave systems worldwide, with much reference to the impact of famine in forcing thousands into temporary servitude.

Kollmann, Nancy Shields. "Concepts of Society and Social Identity in Early Modern Russia." In *Religion and Culture in Early Modern Russia and Ukraine,* pp. 34–51. Edited by Samuel H. Baron and Nancy Shields Kollmann. DeKalb: Northern Illinois University Press, 1997. Revisionist reflections on how Muscovites envisioned and expressed their multiple relationships to society and state; questions stereotypes of autocracy and servility.

Margeret, Jacques. *The Russian Empire and Grand Duchy of Muscovy: A Seventeenth-Century French Account.* Edited and translated by Chester S. L. Dunning.

Pittsburgh, PA: University of Pittsburgh Press, 1983. Dramatic eyewitness account originally published in 1607 by a Protestant mercenary who believed the first False Dmitry really was the son of Ivan the Terrible and defended him against accusations of frivolity and offending Muscovite customs and morals.

Massa, Isaac. *A Short History of the Beginnings and Origins of These Present Wars in Moscow Under the Reign of Various Sovereigns Down to the Year 1610.* Translated with an introduction by G. Edward Orchard. Toronto: University of Toronto Press, 1982. Eyewitness account by a Dutch merchant who made many trips to Muscovy; Massa tended to see Popish plots everywhere and "God's wrath" as punishment for Muscovite crimes and contempt.

McNeill, William H. *Europe's Steppe Frontier, 1500–1800.* Chicago: University of Chicago Press, 1964. Broad essay expanding the concept of a Time of Troubles in space and time.

Perrie, Maureen. *Pretenders and Popular Monarchism in Early Modern Russia: The False Tsars of the Time of Troubles.* Cambridge, U.K.: Cambridge University Press, 1995. Perceptive essay with excellent maps and illustrations offering a provocative semiotic and psychological approach within a broad early modern European perspective.

Platonov, Sergei F. *The Time of Troubles: A Historical Study of the Internal Crisis and Social Struggle in Sixteenth- and Seventeenth-Century Muscovy.* Translated by John T. Alexander. Lawrence: University Press of Kansas, 1970. Lucid overview by the Russian historian whose reputation has now been fully restored; the sixth printing of this translation (1985) provides a bibliographical update of works in English published since 1970.

Rowland, Daniel. "Towards an Understanding of the Political Ideas in Ivan Timofeyev's *Vremennik.*" *Slavonic and East European Review* 62 (1984): 371–394. Insightful probe of a "remarkably untendentious" personal account—strongly shaped by biblical imagery—by a Muscovite official whose career languished under Shuisky and who spent from 1607 to 1617 in Novgorod.

Skrynnikov, Ruslan G. "The Civil War in Russia at the Beginning of the Seventeenth Century (1603–1607): Its Character and Motive Forces." Translated by Maureen Perrie. In *New Perspectives on Muscovite History*, pp. 61–79. Edited by Lindsey Hughes. New York: St. Martin's Press, 1993. Insightful reflections by the leading present-day Russian authority; repudiates the Soviet notions of class warfare and foreign intervention.

———. *The Time of Troubles: Russia in Crisis 1604–1618.* Edited and translated by Hugh Graham. Gulf Breeze, FL: Academic International Press, 1988. Detailed narrative with much attention to personalities, including church figures; questions the election of the Romanov dynasty as ending the turmoil.

Subtelny, Orest. *Domination of Eastern Europe: Native Nobilities and Foreign Absolutism, 1500–1715.* Kingston, Ontario, Can.: McGill-Queen's University Press, 1986. Broad reinterpretation of this era's turmoil, with only slight attention to Muscovy. Sees the dynamic as native noble elites opposing foreign absolutist regimes.

Tucker, Robert C. "What Time Is It in Russian History?" In *Perestroika: The*

Historical Perspective, pp. 34–45. Edited by Catherine Merridale and Chris Ward. New York: Edward Arnold, 1991. Applies the concept of a Time of Troubles to more recent developments in Russia.

Vernadsky, George. *The Tsardom of Moscow, 1547–1682*. New Haven, CT: Yale University Press, 1959. Large-scale synthesis by one of Platonov's most prominent students; sees Muscovy as a Eurasian polity and society.

Dressed in the traditional garb of the seventeenth-century samurai, the subject of this early twentieth-century photograph conveys that fearsome warrior
class' menace. (Reproduced from the Collections of the Library of Congress)

2

The Establishment of the Tokugawa Shogunate, 1603

INTRODUCTION

At the start of the seventeenth century, Japan sat at the very edge of global civilization. Consisting of an island archipelago located well off Asia's eastern coast (Japan is more than 100 miles from Korea, the closest mainland point and a rather isolated country itself) and bounded on its own east by the vast reaches of the Pacific Ocean, Japan attracted few outsiders. Nevertheless, by the middle of the sixteenth century, intrepid European sailors from Portugal, Spain, and Holland had begun to extend their operations in China to include Japan.

While Japan may have been isolated, it was neither poor nor barbaric. Its population in 1600 numbered about 18 million and lived for the most part on three major islands—Honshu, Kyushu, and Shikoku—encompassing about 113,500 square miles. The islands were mountainous but thickly wooded, and there were rich coastal plains and valleys that were good for growing rice.

Most of the population farmed, but a sizable number of fishermen and a large, vigorous urban community consisting of artisans, clerics, merchants, and landowners who preferred urban life to their detached, rural estates complemented the peasants. Prior to the seventeenth century, the Japanese economy had expanded steadily; even the sixteenth century had experienced significant economic development despite chaotic political conditions.

Life centered on the nuclear family (mother, father, and children) and the extended family or clan. Tradition played a large role in cultural life, as did religion. Surprisingly, perhaps, Japan had no national religion; rather, there were several sets of religions or ethical codes that seemed to blend well with each other. One was the traditional religion of Shinto, a uniquely Japanese product with origins in the country's misty past. Another was Buddhism, with its many variations. Buddhism, like a good deal of Japan's culture, had arrived from China a thousand years earlier. Another Chinese import that helped to form Japan's cultural life was Confucianism. So, too, was the Chinese practice of using characters to make a written language of the spoken tongue.

Despite its flourishing economy and its vibrant cultural life, Japan's political landscape at the beginning of the sixteenth century was not encouraging. Disorder, violence, and bloodshed prevailed. The origins of Japan's political problems dated back hundreds of years. In the seventh and eighth centuries, the powerful and wealthy Yamato family, which already had claimed a special relationship with the gods, began to designate its leader as emperor. At first the Yamatos extended and solidified their authority; however, decline set in when the rulers parceled out more and more land and privileges (and thus wealth and power) to religious institutions and heads of important families. Implemented to reinforce the emperor's base, this policy had the opposite effect. The beneficiaries of the emperor's largess adopted an independent stance, thereby gradually reducing the emperor to the status of revered figurehead. Meanwhile, the Japanese version of the European feudal aristocracy, competing with each other at every turn and employing ever larger bands of sometimes undisciplined warriors called samurai, brought ruin to the country.

A major crisis occurred in the twelfth century when massive civil disturbances swept the country; the aristocrats with their samurai engaged in something akin to civil war. The Minamoto family emerged victorious from the confusion and established its headquarters at Kamakura, the name subsequently used to designate this period of Japanese history. Yoritomo, the Minamoto leader, did not depose the emperor; rather, he claimed to rule in the emperor's name. Yoritomo reinforced the emperor's semi-sacred status and used his connection with the emperor to legitimize his own authority. However, Yoritomo and his successors were always careful to keep the emperor and his retinue isolated from society and far removed from real power. To cement his triumph, Yoritomo had the emperor name him shogun, or military dictator, thereby initiating the long-lasting period of shogunal government that continued until 1868.

The Kamakura shoguns never fully controlled the Japanese landed gentry, and the most important barons, or *daimyo*, remained independent of shogunal control. The gentry's position grew stronger when successive shoguns opted to buy *daimyo* loyalty through grants of land and other benefits rather than use force to curb the aristocracy's independence. Furthermore, the growth in population and the absence of a strong central authority led to the appearance and spread of local strongmen who brawled incessantly. In 1333 a successful revolt against the Kamakura occurred; but the Ashikaga family that now claimed the post of shogun could not exert much authority either. The atomized nature of Japanese politics continued: an ineffectual emperor remained on the sidelines; the shogun lacked the might and the will to assert his authority; the traditional aristocracy struggled with each other for the slightest advantage or the most empty title; and the now-numerous local strongmen, whether drawn from the ranks of commoners, priests, or samurai, challenged the prevailing order. Civil war became widespread and interminable.

This chaotic situation came to an end only in the late sixteenth and early seventeenth centuries when a series of ruthless, powerful, and determined figures brought order to Japan that was to last for two and a half centuries. The unification or pacification of Japan began with Oda Nobunaga, a young *daimyo* from central Japan who had been born in 1534. In 1560 Nobunaga's warriors destroyed an army led by another *daimyo* that was more than ten times its size. David's triumph over Goliath immediately catapulted Nobunaga into the ranks of Japan's most prominent aristocrats. Eight years later, in 1568, Nobunaga seized Kyoto, the ancient imperial capital, and forced the emperor to install Ashikaga Yoshiaki as shogun. Yoshiaki, one of several Ashikaga vying to be shogun, proved a docile tool in Nobunaga's hands and allowed Nobunaga to make all the important decisions.

Although Nobunaga clearly dominated the shogunate, he hardly dominated Japan. Resistance could be found everywhere. The religious communities, who jealously guarded their temporal powers, represented one major source of opposition. In 1571 Nobunaga attacked the famous Enryakuji monastery on Mount Hiei, the peak that overlooked Kyoto. Showing no mercy, Nobunaga's men obliterated the monastery and killed all those who fell into their hands. This was simply the first and

most famous of many attacks on religious communities that resisted Nobunaga. By the time of his death in 1582, Nobunaga had decisively broken the power of his religious rivals.

During the 1570s, Nobunaga took additional steps to bolster his
power. In 1573 he forced Yoshiaki, the shogun, out of Kyoto. While he
did not name himself shogun, Nobunaga did claim authority tantamount
to that traditionally held by the shogun. He also built a magnificent castle
in 1576–1579 on the shores on Lake Biwa at Azuchi. Designed to with-
stand firearms, which the Europeans had recently introduced to Japan,
Nobunaga's castle clearly reflected the importance of its owner.

Having secured his power base, Nobunaga then began to move against
more distant rivals. He enlisted the support of numerous vassals, one of
the most important being Toyotomi Hideyoshi, a lowborn warrior who
had risen rapidly through the ranks due to his exceptional military ability. While campaigning in 1582, Nobunaga was forced to commit suicide
by Akechi Mitsuhide, a traitorous general who held a personal grudge
against his erstwhile ally. With Nobunaga's death, Hideyoshi skillfully
maneuvered to claim his legacy.

Until his death in 1598, Hideyoshi continued Nobunaga's policy of
unification with spectacular results. Heading a coalition of ambitious
lords, he launched a series of devastating campaigns against the remaining *daimyo*. When he defeated the Hojo clan of western Japan in 1590,
Hideyoshi and his allies controlled virtually the entire country. Ruling
from his recently constructed castle at Osaka, Hideyoshi perfected a system of government that resembled a mature form of feudalism. Rather
than annihilate his enemies, Hideyoshi used a combination of threats and
favors to turn them into loyal vassals. For example, Hideyoshi pressured
the *daimyo* to send their wives and children to live at his Osaka castle, a
subtle form of hostage holding that allowed the leader to dominate his
vassals. Simultaneously, Hideyoshi favored his vassals with grants of
confiscated property and allowed them a free hand to administer their
domains as they pleased. As always, the emperor was kept in the shad-
ows, a semi-divine but totally powerless figure in whose name Hideyoshi
ruled.

Hideyoshi also took additional steps to reinforce his authority. In 1588
he issued a proclamation that required all peasants and villagers to surrender their weapons. During the incessant civil wars that had characterized Japan prior to the period of pacification, commoners had
frequently armed themselves and banded together for self-protection.
Hideyoshi now seized their weapons, thereby creating a monopoly in

arms for the *daimyo* and their samurai retainers. Two years later, he strengthened the class divisions inherent in the 1588 decree when he issued a new decree that destroyed social mobility. Henceforth, there was to be a clear distinction between peasant and samurai. According to this decree, one born into the peasantry had to remain a peasant for his entire life, whereas the samurai were now forbidden either to return to their villages to take up farming or to leave one liege lord for another. Finally, in 1598 Hideyoshi completed a series of land surveys begun in the 1580s that greatly facilitated the collection of taxes.

Hideyoshi's striking success in domestic affairs was offset by an erratic and counterproductive foreign policy. Always a warrior-conqueror at heart, Hideyoshi dreamed of subjugating China. His vision of conquest led to an ill-fated invasion of Korea in 1592. After some initial success, the Japanese encountered stiff resistance from both the Koreans and the Chinese Ming Empire. Stalemate ensued and negotiations began. However, Hideyoshi's excessive demands at the negotiating table brought about a resumption of hostilities that did not go particularly well for the Japanese. Upon Hideyoshi's death, his successors were forced to seek peace.

Hideyoshi also mishandled the matter of his succession. He chose to leave his position to a five-year-old son, appointing a regency council to rule until the child reached maturity. Not unexpectedly, this arrangement quickly broke down as the regents competed with each other for Hideyoshi's mantle. Victory went to the last of the three great *daimyo* who unified Japan, Tokugawa Ieyasu. In 1600 at the Battle of Sekigahara, Ieyasu defeated a coalition of rival *daimyo*. After his triumph, Ieyasu continued the policies of his predecessors, Nobunaga and Hideyoshi, including the earlier policy of ruling through a network of *daimyo* vassals rather than claiming absolute power for himself. In 1603, almost as an afterthought, he had the figurehead emperor appoint him shogun. This appointment marks the beginning of the Tokugawa shogunate, which lasted until 1868.

INTERPRETIVE ESSAY
Louis G. Perez

For a century after the Tokugawa government fell in 1868, it was universally castigated and demonized for all the human aspirations that it had suppressed for 265 years. It was blamed for all of Japan's real and imagined ills. Fukuzawa Yukichi, perhaps post-Tokugawa Japan's most famous and influential "modernizer" and popularizer of Western forms, claimed to hate it "like my father's murderer." The new Meiji emperor in his Charter Oath of April 1868 criticized the Tokugawa for its "evil customs of the past," which he promised to abandon and thereafter base his government on the "just laws of Heaven and Earth."

Japanese historians of the post–World War II period found the Tokugawa to be nearly as despicable and barbaric as the "Militarist Clique" that drove Japan into a brutal world war in the mid-twentieth century. Had it been the intention of the War Crimes Tribunal for the Far East in 1947, the Tokugawa *bakufu* ("tent government") that ruled Japan from 1603 to 1868 could have been convicted for "crimes against humanity" without much protest from the Japanese.

Only recently have historians examined the Tokugawa with anything but a philosophically prejudiced agenda. This is partially because the *bakufu* was an easy target: a convenient straw man to topple whenever necessary. It was economically feudal, socially stifling and misogynist, religiously repressive, philosophically obtuse, and internationally exclusivist. It fell far short of all the true and just aspirations of good men and women everywhere.

We must remember, however, that if the *bakufu* was not democratic, it never intended to be so. If it was repressive and brutal, it was decidedly less so than hundreds of contemporary governments around the world. When it was founded in 1603 it was a quantum leap improvement over the horrific civil war that had wracked Japan for nearly two centuries.

The foundation of the government that would rule Japan for over two and a half centuries was certainly no historical inevitability. The fact that it continued to rule for so long was itself an anomaly. The remnants of the previous military dictatorship had shambled on for nearly a century after its capital had been sacked and nearly ruined by its rapacious former vassals. Real power was in the hands of cruel feudal warlords (*daimyo*), who viciously fought one another for tiny scraps of land.

The last half of the sixteenth century had witnessed the very cruelest and most depraved warfare imaginable. Sons turned against fathers; brothers killed each other with numbing regularity; fathers sold and traded their daughters like cattle in hopes of transitory advantage; *daimyo* sacked and burned Buddhist temple complexes with scarcely a moment's thought; family-centered feudal governments rose and fell seemingly with the tides. Indeed, these centrifugal forces seemed more likely to tear Japan into even smaller splinter feudal holdings than lead to national consolidation.

The first two of the sixteenth century's three "great unifiers" had ruthlessly butchered, tortured, and burned their enemies with frightful inhumanity, yet neither of their governments had survived them. The ferocious military power of Oda Nobunaga (1534–1582) vanished in the flames surrounding his suicide. His successor, Toyotomi Hideyoshi (1536–1598), had seized Nobunaga's coalition and brilliantly welded it into a cohesive military machine that encompassed nearly all of Japan and even spread to Korea, with designs on China and the rest of the world. Yet scarcely months after his death, his five most trusted vassals abjured their sworn loyalty to his son, ending the century with a regression to the bloody civil war that had begun it.

The triumph of the third "unifier" was similarly no inevitability. Tokugawa Ieyasu (1542–1616) was the son of a minor *daimyo*. Ieyasu had been a hostage for his father to Nobunaga. When he succeeded as *daimyo*, he then became one of Nobunaga's vassals and generals.

Ieyasu was a pragmatist. He was not a sagacious and charismatic military leader like Nobunaga or Hideyoshi, but he was patient, observant, and quick-witted. His every action was carefully considered, and he actively encouraged constructive criticism from his men; they therefore were devoted to him. He rewarded his loyal followers well and was careful never to squander his warriors in battle needlessly. He was no more honest than necessary, having several times broken his solemn oath when he found it expedient. Once when Ieyasu's wife and son were suspected of plotting against Nobunaga, the latter demanded that Ieyasu prove his loyalty by killing them both. Ieyasu hardly hesitated in his compliance. After all, Ieyasu married many women and had several concubines, producing many sons. He could ill afford to endanger his life and career for the sake of only one wife and son.

After the suicide of Nobunaga in 1582, Ieyasu briefly was a rival to Hideyoshi as the successor to their former feudal lord. Their armies struggled momentarily without clear result. Wisely, he chose to swear loyalty and assisted Hideyoshi in extinguishing his enemies in eastern Japan. Ieyasu accepted the Kanto plain as his reward for that loyalty, giving up control over his former central Honshu domain.

Ieyasu was more an uneasy ally to Hideyoshi than a servile lackey. He was therefore able to vacillate when invited to spearhead Hideyoshi's Korean expedition, and ultimately he tarried in the Kanto, fortifying his new castle in Edo during the entire quixotic adventure. When Hideyoshi died in 1598, Ieyasu swore loyalty to his young son Hideyori but quietly bided his time until the other regents maneuvered to wrest control. He engineered a carefully timed conspiracy whereby a large portion of the enemy coalition suddenly turned against their allies at the Battle of Sekigahara in 1600. The battle turned into a rout in his favor and within months Ieyasu was the leader of all Japan.

It is truly an indication of how seriously divided Japan was in 1600 that Ieyasu was never able to completely centralize and consolidate control. He followed Nobunaga's and Hideyoshi's examples of political control by federation and vassalage. He created an elaborate system of land division; of hostages; of social, political, and economic controls; and ultimately of national seclusion. The fact that he *could* indicates the measure of his power: The fact that he *had* to do this was an indication of his weakness.

Ieyasu was neither an innovator nor a sage. But he appreciated power: He relished what he had, wielded it wisely, and craved more. Most of all, he was patient. He understood well the advice of the ancient Chinese military genius Sun Tzu who said, "If I wait patiently at the banks of the river, the body of my enemy will eventually float by." Ieyasu reasoned that if he froze the status quo, he perpetuated what he had. To change the system endangered what he had. So he risked little and refined much. He imitated Nobunaga and Hideyoshi, adapting the functional and discarding that which was not. He cared little for intellectual origins—only for efficiency.

He reasoned that nearly 1 million warriors were not necessary to keep order. Therefore, he clearly distinguished the sociopolitical division between warrior and subject. Each *daimyo* was allowed to keep a specific number of samurai, proportional to the productivity of their domains.

The common foot soldiers (*ashigaru*) were coerced into the nether world of village hereditary headmen, constables, justices, tax collectors, and petty bureaucrats. They were permitted to retain their surnames and their now largely ceremonial short swords as badges of authority and legitimacy, but they were otherwise disarmed and "demoted" to peasantry.

Similarly, Ieyasu forbade social mobility. Harsh punishments were meted out to anyone attempting to transcend social class. *Chonin* (merchants and artisans) were not allowed to acquire farmland, and peasants were forbidden to migrate to the cities or move from one domain to another. Intermarriage between classes was prohibited as well.

Obviously Ieyasu wished to freeze time. He would have preferred to have seized power from the *daimyo* and perhaps also to have trimmed the number of samurai to save expenses. But since he could not do so, he downsized as much as he could and forbade any substantive changes in the status quo. He patronized Confucian political philosophers who rationalized why a merchant should remain so and why peasants should be content with their abject bucolic lives. But what was most important to him was that they do so because it ensured his family's future and that of Japan as well.

Ieyasu was faced with a seriously divided country when he became shogun (generalissimo) in 1603. Japan had been at war for so long that no one could remember how a centralized government actually functioned. *Daimyo* had long survived by their shrewdness and by their armies; they could not be counted on to obey automatically any commands that were not in their own immediate best interests. The mere swearing of feudal allegiance was not worth the time, effort, or paper. The long history of constantly shifting military coalitions made Ieyasu's task doubly difficult because he had excelled at duplicity himself. He had to devise a method to keep the possible political powers in check.

The government of the Tokugawa lasted for 265 years and therefore must be considered a qualified success. The government was a concoction of military and civil administration. It was also a composite of private and public, regional and national administrations.

Ieyasu's most loyal personal retainers, called "bannermen" (*hatamoto*), staffed his family council. They administered the sprawling Tokugawa lands and governed the tens of thousands of vassal samurai. They served as justices, quartermasters, armorers, inspectors, spies, and all the other occupations that make any army run efficiently. During Ieyasu's lifetime there was scarcely any waste and inefficiency since he was reputed to be the "most tightfisted miser in all of Japan." He appointed competent and ethical men to positions of power regardless of their family and social station. His descendants were not so astute in promoting able men, but the system was so closely monitored and so administratively simple that it very nearly ran itself for over a century before it needed substantive reforms.

The "national" government was something of an oxymoron. It has been called "centralized feudalism" by the late historian Edwin Reischauer. Fellow historian George Wilson suggests that the crazy-quilt quality of the system was akin to a "complex parlor game." Another, more ominous characterization might be that it was "bureaucratic feudalism." It had distinctly expedient and opportunistic qualities. It seemed to have been contrived to cope with every new danger. It was very much an artificial device of political fantasy.

One council made up of senior counselors debated policy and advised the shogun before he enacted laws and issued edicts. Another council of "junior advisers" oversaw the *hatamoto*, the army commanders, and the administrators of the giant Edo castle complex. The "senior" and "junior" rankings designated not age but the size of the *daimyo's* holdings. Senior men were those with *han* (domains) producing more than 25,000 *koku* (1 *koku* = 4.98 bushels) of rice.

The most pressing danger of the time was the need to keep approximately 250 semi-autonomous *daimyo* in check. Ieyasu divided the *daimyo* into three groups. First was his own extensive family of over twenty directly related houses or *shimpan* ("collateral domain"). This group controlled about one-third of Japan's total agriculture.

The nonkinship group of over 200 *daimyo* was divided into two groups. His longtime allies called *fudai* ("house") *daimyo* were men whom Ieyasu trusted and whom he had created as *daimyo*. Their *han* were usually modest in scale but were located in strategic areas. Collectively the *fudai* controlled slightly less than 30 percent of the farmland.

Ieyasu's "new vassals," former powerful enemies, were the *tozama* ("outsider") *daimyo* who controlled nearly 40 percent of the land. Most of the *tozama* administered larger *han*. The fact that they were permitted any power is the most significant indication that Ieyasu walked a political tightrope. Any attempt to destroy them piecemeal would precipitate the others to collude together quickly despite their mutual animosities and apprehensions. And there was no guarantee that he could rely completely on the loyalty of his *shimpan*, let alone his *fudai*, if conflict ensued. Better to maintain the restive status quo than to tip the balance to an equivocal future.

He and his scions coerced every *daimyo, tozama,* and *fudai* alike to spend half their lives in his capital Edo and the other half in their domain (*han*). This system of "alternate attendance," or *sankin kotai*, served other purposes as well. This way the shogun could keep everyone under surveillance. Also, the colossal costs involved in maintaining separate residences in their *han*, another in Edo, plus the onerous travel expenditures, served as indirect taxes. Ieyasu kept their relatives hostage in Edo the entire time. Adoption, marriage, and political and economic alliances between *daimyo* were prohibited. He also employed a comprehensive and pervasive network of spies to keep many eyes on the *daimyo*.

Ieyasu used the ancient jealousies and suspicions between the *daimyo* to keep them from forging cabals. He positioned his *shimpan daimyo* astride the major routes to Edo and settled his *fudai* allies in between *tozama*. He maneuvered many of them around during the initial two decades of the period and often posted old blood enemies adjacent to each other to restrain them. He retained the right, used rarely and judiciously after the first decade of the *bakufu*, to deprive *daimyo* of their land for reasons of gross insubordination, criminally poor administration of their *han* (used only when the peasants were in full-scale revolt), or failure to produce an appropriate male heir. But these, too, he used very carefully, lest the other *daimyo* surmise that some kind of nefarious scheme was at work.

Ieyasu was forced to grant virtual administrative independence to his vassals. He interfered in their lives as much as he dared, but he had to be careful not to propel mutual enemies into alliances. He had rudimentary law codes written as models for *daimyo* to emulate, but he could not enforce compliance unless the *daimyo* showed themselves to be incompetent administrators.

Ieyasu could not tax the *daimyo* directly, but he did require them to provide, at their own expense, for the protection of the country. These indirect taxes included the costs of maintaining public roads and horse-exchange stations for the use of *bakufu* couriers. They were called upon to refurbish and safeguard the now-ancient seawall defenses in northwest Kyushu, where two Mongol attacks came in the thirteenth century. *Daimyo* dredged canals, harbors, and river ways; they forested hardwoods and bamboo; and occasionally they were forced to provide rice and other foodstuffs to alleviate famines. In short, Ieyasu, like Nobunaga and Hideyoshi before him, made the *daimyo* his public works administration and compelled them to pay for the privilege.

Despite these elaborate regimens of restraint, Ieyasu still faced three sources of mischief that worried him greatly in 1603: the imperial house, Toyotomi Hideyori, and religion. All three were potential time bombs that threatened the still restive political settlement, and all three had thousands of potential confederates. He had to tread very lightly until his position grew stronger and more entrenched.

He dealt with the imperial house immediately since he saw it as the greatest potential source of mischief. Ieyasu knew that at least three times in history an attempted imperial restoration had precipitated a change in government, so he was vigilant to constrain the emperor. In 1603 Ieyasu expropriated the office of shogun, which he turned over to his successor son Hidetada two years later. Ieyasu established a liaison bureau in Kyoto staffed by his most devoted retainers and forbade any *daimyo* from even entering the ancient capital without the express written permission of the shogun himself. He treated the emperor with great deference and respect. The court was conferred with an extensive tract of tax land, administered by the Tokugawa, and Ieyasu refurbished the palace to high grandeur. But the fact remains that the emperor and the court were hostages of the Tokugawa. Every imperial action was closely monitored. No ceremony could take place without a Tokugawa "guest" present.

Hideyori's threat was more difficult initially. Iseyau had lost direct control of Hideyoshi's son in 1598 and had to monitor his actions from afar. He had several trusted spies covertly lodged within the boy's entourage, but the child was under the control of his strong-willed mother as well as several Tokugawa adversaries in the Osaka vicinity. The boy had been permitted some 3 million bushels of his father's extensive tax land and therefore was potentially quite powerful. Ieyasu surrounded the boy with troops faithful to Tokugawa, and in fact when his son became shogun in 1605, Ieyasu made his home in nearby Sumpu to better watch over Hideyori. But the threat would remain for many anxious years until it exploded in 1614. Two years before his own death, Ieyasu personally directed the siege of the Osaka castle where almost 100,000 troops loyal to the boy were lured into revolt. Near the end of the stand-off, he managed by trickery to break the siege, and the 30,000 remaining defenders were killed. Hideyori and his mother committed suicide, and the threat from the Toyotomi force was finally over.

The threat from religion took somewhat longer because the threat was external as well as domestic and even within his own army. Ieyasu initially utilized the Christians against the powerful Buddhist temples and confraternities as Nobunaga and Hideyoshi had done. Once the military power of the temples had been broken, Ieyasu was confronted with his erstwhile Christian allies.

Like Hideyoshi, who had proscribed (but never enforced the edict) Christianity in 1587, Ieyasu feared the foreign faith that had first appeared in Japan in 1549 with the arrival of the missionary St. Francis Xavier and had enjoyed modest growth. Increasingly he started to use other Europeans against the Portuguese. The Spanish Franciscan, Augustinian, and Dominican priests were resentful of the Portuguese Jesuits. Ieyasu also used English and Dutch because they were Protestants and, unlike the Roman Catholic Portuguese and Spanish, had not tried to proselytize their faith in Japan. He conceded them trading privileges and tried to fracture the Portuguese monopoly of Chinese silk by patronizing Chinese and Korean silk traders.

The greatest threat was not from the foreign Christians, however, but rather from his own vassals who were in some cases now second- and third-generation Christians. He began to experiment in 1606 to see just how subservient they were to their God and to the Pope. He commanded a few of his vassals to renounce their faith or to leave the country. When the Christian *daimyo* chose exile rather than renunciation, he had his answer: Christians were faithful first and foremost to God. He could never trust them again.

In 1614, during the siege at Osaka Castle, he commanded that all foreign priests leave Tokugawa domains within a month. Two years later priests were prohibited from all of Japan. All Japanese Christians were ordered to renounce their faith and to become Buddhists virtually overnight. Those who refused faced death. Only about two-thirds of the some 150 priests left; the others were ferreted out, tortured, and eventually killed. Many Japanese Christians went into hiding, many more recanted, and not a few died as martyrs to their faith. But the end was very near. In 1637–1638 a Christian-led rebellion against discriminatory taxation broke out in Shimabara, close to the Christian city of Nagasaki. The Tokugawa surrounded the area, forcing Christian sympathizers into the ruined castle on that peninsula, and slowly created a hell for them there. After starving the defenders for several months, the Tokugawa marched in and butchered the remaining 40,000 defenders.

By 1640 the Tokugawa had nearly eradicated every vestige of Christianity in Japan. The Roman Catholic Church recognizes only 3,125 martyrs during this period, but there were thousands more. Only a handful escaped two centuries of persecution by hiding in remote islands and mountains. For the next 200 years *everyone* in Japan had to demonstrate annually that he was not Christian by registering with his neighborhood Buddhist temple and then performing the ritual of *fumi-e*, or "picture treading." This required that every man, woman, and child desecrate pictures or bronze replications of Christ or the Virgin Mary by walking on them to demonstrate symbolically their contempt for Christianity.

The Portuguese merchants were supplanted by the Dutch who themselves were all but imprisoned on the tiny artificial island of Deshima in Nagasaki harbor. They, too, had to perform *fumi-e* to demonstrate that they had no Roman Catholic sympathies. The Dutch had shown their animosity to Roman Catholicism by bombarding the Shimabara Christians from their ships off the peninsula. Chinese and Koreans were also allowed to ply a carefully monitored trade, but they were tested as well. The English and Spanish had left of their own accord. The next step was almost inevitable: the *bakufu* made laws to ensure a *sakoku*, or "closed country." Japanese were forbidden to go abroad on pain of death. Large oceangoing ships were made illegal. Only small coastal ships were permitted to ply Japanese waters. Unauthorized ships were fired upon. Shipwrecked foreign sailors were to be "killed in the surf," before they could hit dry land. Foreign books were now prohibited. Those brought by the Dutch for their own use were carefully searched for any references to Christianity. Without question, this seclusion served also to isolate Japan economically and technologically from the rest of the world, but the Tokugawa preferred that to foreign intervention and subversion.

The sociopolitical philosophy of Neo-Confucianism developed by the twelfth-century Chinese Confucian reformer Chu Hsi was a godsend for Ieyasu. Although more appropriate for the secular, bureaucratic Sung Dynasty in China, it suited Ieyasu's needs very well. It was based on the concept of benevolent moral administration modeled on the filial piety that governed family and other social relationships. It maintained that nature itself mandated efficient rule by the "best and brightest": the learned, ethical sages. It argued that the ethical earthly order was best served when "men of talent" governed. Four social classes based on occupational function helped to keep the society running efficiently. When used effectively, this philosophy avoided the corruption caused by nepotism and other favoritism.

In China, it allowed the replacement of evil and inefficient emperors; in Japan, it was interpreted to mean that corrupt ministers and governors of the emperor could be removed but not the semi-divine emperor himself. Not surprisingly, the Tokugawa extended this immunity to the shogun, the military deputy of the sacrosanct emperor. Since the country was officially at peace, and since Neo-Confucianism preferred an educated, civilian, cultural elite instead of the aristocratic, powerful military, or wealthy, landed leadership, the rough, uneducated samurai became administrators. It made a great deal of sense to educate them in Neo-Confucian principles of ethical administration. Those who wished to prosper under the new regime began to study seriously. For his part,

Ieyasu appointed and promoted only the ablest administrators regardless of their family backgrounds. For over 200 years the samurai continued to pride themselves on their military prowess, but their careers very much depended on their mastery of Neo-Confucianism.

Officially patronized Confucian samurai scholars incorporated the Neo-Confucian principles of benevolent and moral rule into their military code of ethics, retaining their martial virtues of loyalty, courage, honesty, selflessness, perseverance, and contempt for comfort and personal wealth. In short, they helped create a very frightening creature: the military bureaucrat.

Ieyasu set up Confucian academies for his samurai in all of the *shimpan* domains, and the other *daimyo* rushed to do the same. Within a generation there was scarcely an illiterate samurai to be found throughout the country. The schools were staffed primarily by the samurai themselves but also by learned Buddhist and Shinto priests who were well versed in the Chu Hsi doctrine. Their primers were the simplified writings of the Neo-Confucian masters. Assuredly, each samurai boy learned the various martial arts of the sword, the bow, and the horse; his status and pride demanded that. But his career and future socioeconomic station very much depended on his mastery of the literary arts as well.

At the heart of this new ethic was the idea that all people, regardless of status and social station, could fulfill their duties and obligations in an appropriate manner. This concept, called "propriety of status," found honor in proper conduct according to one's lot in life. Everyone had a place in society; everyone's duty was to behave in a manner appropriate to that place. Peasants were not to behave like samurai, and merchants were not to emulate peasants. Each class was to defer to the others, and the language even reflected the minute levels of stratification between social castes.

Even women had status—a wretched, demeaning one to be sure—but nevertheless, they were expected to fill that role. A treatise called *Onna Daigaku*, or "Greater Learning for Women," was popularized in which the "Three Obediences" were delineated. The idea was that women could have three masters in their normal lifetimes: their fathers, their husbands, and later if widowed, their sons. Women were always to obey and acquiesce to men in everything. In turn, men would protect them and treat them with consideration and benevolence. In short, women were to be treated as eternal adolescents. Girls might be sold into slavery and prostitution by their fathers and be expected to "honor" their fathers by persevering despite their miserable lives.

The samurai Confucian ethic had its counterpart among the other classes as well. The *chonin* found their own philosophy in the virtuous completion of their filial duties to their merchant and artisan families. Although not very elaborate compared to Neo-Confucianism, *Shingaku* ("Education of the Heart") demanded that the merchant sacrifice personal emotional needs for the efficacy of society. Theatrical plays were rife with the emotional tension of *giri* ("duty") versus *ninjo* ("human emotion"). The social obligations of *giri* won out at the end of each story.

The *chonin* endowed and patronized neighborhood schools called *terakoya*, or "parish schools," not because they gave religious instruction but because they were conveniently housed in neighborhood temples. The basic curriculum included the rudiments of writing and an emphasis on the arithmetic necessary to run their merchant establishments.

Chonin girls also were taught the rudiments of arithmetic, if only to help run the family business while the males were away. Often, in fact, women became highly educated almost by accident, perhaps when helping a dullard brother learn. Women entertainers—*geisha*—learned to read well enough to become familiar with the poetry and warrior tales that helped entertain their customers.

Estimates of literacy are highly suspect, but Japan has a long history of high regard for the literary arts, so perhaps a quarter to a third of all the males (certainly every samurai, and *they* were 6 percent of the population) could read, and half that number of women probably could as well.

The elite landed peasants accepted the Neo-Confucian ideas, if only because it put them just below the samurai and high above the merchant class in social status. Most peasant families possessed a highly prized "house code" of ethics that emulated those of the samurai and the rich merchant houses. These simple codes uniformly preached the virtues of honesty, frugality, hard work, and selfless devotion to the family. It would not be an exaggeration to suggest that the peasantry accepted their plebeian niche in society because the philosophy tied them to the greater and grander whole of Japanese society in much the same way that peons and serfs took pride in their place in the "chain of being" in medieval Christian Europe.

Suffice it to say that Neo-Confucianism worked very well as an instrument of social control. Everyone had a place determined by nature. Peaceful obedience and fulfillment of one's role in society contributed to the greater good. Buddhism, trying desperately to fit into this secular humanist philosophy, weighed in with a social message that agreed with Neo-Confucianism. One's place in society was determined by one's actions in previous lifetimes; one's future life could be improved by proper behavior in this life.

The political tranquillity that historian George Sansom called *Pax Tokugawa* was marred occasionally by peasant uprisings, political assassinations, and interfamily vendettas, to be sure. But the period was characterized by peace and by studious, solemn attempts by the samurai aristocracy to govern justly, benevolently, and ethically.

Perhaps because the country was at peace for nearly two centuries and certainly because the society was relatively isolated from the rest of the world, the Tokugawa era was one of conscious reexamination of Japanese culture. Without the constant influence of other cultures, the Japanese became introspective. They consciously synthesized what they considered to be the truly native arts, differentiating them from the foreign. So while Japan was almost isolated from the rest of the world and thereby missed the benefits (as well as the human excesses, one might add) of the Industrial Revolution, it did not lag behind Europe and the Americas in terms of cultural and artistic development.

The "freezing" of the social order and the seclusion of the country certainly suppressed the "natural" development and expansion of the economy. The forced urbanization caused by the Tokugawa political settlement (especially *sankin kotai*), however, helped to develop a robust and diverse national economy that was the equal of all but the most highly developed northern European economies.

The foundation of the Tokugawa *bakufu*, as socially, politically, religiously, and philosophically repressive as it certainly was, can therefore be argued to have served Japan quite well for two and a half centuries. It pacified and, one might say, civilized a society that had degenerated into the barbarism and human depravity of horrific civil war.

One is hard-pressed to find many other political systems of that era that guaranteed its subjects two centuries of peace. One needs only to compare the actions of the *bakufu* to those of imperialist Western nations of the era. The *bakufu* did not colonize, exploit, imprison, rape, and kill millions of its neighbors. And by seclusion, it protected its own people from the cultural, economic, and political genocide suffered by Indians, Filipinos, Indonesians, Africans, and Amerindians.

SELECTED BIBLIOGRAPHY

Arnesen, Peter J. *The Medieval Japanese Daimyo*. New Haven, CT: Yale University Press, 1979. A solid examination of the political and economic administration of a representative set of feudal domains.

Bellah, Robert N. *Tokugawa Religion: The Values of Pre-Industrial Japan*. Glencoe, IL: Free Press, 1957. Although dated, a provocative examination of merchant ethos.

Berry, Mary Elizabeth. *Hideyoshi*. Cambridge, MA: Harvard University Press, 1982. A sophisticated intellectual biography of this very complex man who laid the foundations for the Tokugawa *bakufu*.

Bolitho, Harold. *Treasures Among Men: The Fudai Daimyo in Tokugawa Japan*. New Haven, CT: Yale University Press, 1974. Should be used with Totman's works below to understand the sociopolitical underpinnings of the *bakufu*.

Boxer, Charles R. *The Christian Century in Japan, 1549–1650*. Berkeley: University of California Press, 1951. A masterful study of Japan's Christian experience that integrates a polyglot of primary European sources.

Dore, Ronald P. *Education in Tokugawa Japan*. Berkeley: University of California Press, 1965. Primarily focused on the Tokugawa "educational foundation for Japanese modernization."

Najita, Tetsuo. *Vision of Virtue in Tokugawa Japan*. Chicago: University of Chicago Press, 1987. A dense but very rich intellectual examination of *chonin* ideology.

Nakai, Kate Wildman. *Shogunal Politics: Arai Hakuseki and the Premises of Tokugawa Rule*. Cambridge, MA: Harvard University Press, 1988. A reexamination of the sociopolitical philosophy of the *bakufu* as perceived by the era's foremost intellectual reformer a century after its foundation.

Ooms, Herman. *Tokugawa Ideology, Early Constructs, 1570–1680*. Princeton, NJ: Princeton University Press, 1985. An essential companion to Nakai's work above in that it provides the intellectual foundation for the *bakufu*.

Sadler, A. L. *The Maker of Modern Japan: The Life of Tokugawa Ieyasu*. London: Allen and Unwin, 1937. Although quite dated, this work is an elegantly written biographical account of Ieyasu.

Sansom, George B. *Japan, a Short Cultural History*. New York: Appleton, 1943. An elegantly written intellectual tour-de-force.

Sheldon, C. D. *The Rise of the Merchant Class in Tokugawa Japan*. Locust Valley, NY: Augustin, 1958. Although Marxian in interpretation, still a solid economic history.

Smith, Thomas C. *The Agrarian Origins of Modern Japan*. Stanford, CA: Stanford University Press, 1959. Although dated, it is still the best economic history of the Tokugawa era.

Toby, Ronald P. *State and Diplomacy in Early Modern Japan*. Princeton, NJ: Princeton University Press, 1984. Brilliant in its examination of the international context of the *bakufu*.

Totman, Conrad D. *Politics in the Tokugawa Bakufu, 1600–1843*. Cambridge, MA: Harvard University Press, 1967. Absolutely essential for understanding how the *bakufu* worked.

——. *Tokugawa Ieyasu*. South San Francisco, CA: Heian, 1982. More intellectually sophisticated than Sadler's work above.

Vlastos, Stephen. *Peasant Protests and Uprisings in Tokugawa Japan*. Tucson: University of Arizona Press, 1986. Provides an elucidating provincial understanding of the era.

Webb, Herschel. *The Japanese Imperial Institution in the Tokugawa Period*. New York: Columbia University Press, 1968. Still the best examination of how the imperial house functioned, survived, and then thrived during the era.

Wigmore, John H. *Law and Justice in Tokugawa Japan*. 2 vols. Tokyo: University of Tokyo Press, 1969. Dense and intellectually challenging, it is an excellent source for the serious student.

Within the illustration: King Powhatan comands C: Smith to be slain
daughter Pokahontas beggs his life his than
and how he subiected 39 of their kings. reade

printed by Iames Reeve

Pocahontas intervenes with her father, Powhatan, to save Captain John Smith's life; native Americans in Virginia did not take kindly to the arrival of English settlers. (Reproduced from the Collections of the Library of Congress)

3

The Founding of Jamestown, 1607

INTRODUCTION

Soon after Christopher Columbus' voyages of exploration, European countries sent out expeditions to explore and later settle the New World. Throughout most of the sixteenth century, the exploration and settlement of North America remained the exclusive preserve of Spain. Nevertheless, by the end of the century France, Holland, and England had joined in the competition. The first English attempt to settle North America occurred in 1587 when the famous adventurer Sir Walter Raleigh convinced more than a hundred men and women to relocate from England to the middle Atlantic coast of North America, which he had named Virginia after the English queen, Elizabeth I, the so-called virgin queen. The expedition settled on Roanoke Island, off the coast of what is now North Carolina, and Virginia Dare, the first English child in North America, was born there. However, this bid to establish a permanent presence in North America failed when fighting between England and Spain (the famous "Spanish Armada") delayed the departure of resupply ships for three years. When the ships finally arrived in 1590, there was no trace of the colonists. It was as though they had vanished into thin air.

Several years later, after the death of Elizabeth and the accession to the throne of her cousin, James Stuart of Scotland, who ruled England as James I, the English once again tried to establish a settlement in North America. To achieve this purpose, investors formed a chartered private company, the Virginia Company of London—for the goal of the settlement was profit and not the greater glory of England or its monarch.

Founded in 1606, the Virginia Company in the following year mounted an expedition consisting of three ships and 105 men and boys with instructions to found a colony in what is now the Chesapeake Bay region. In May 1607, the ships dropped anchor in what was dubbed the James River in honor of the king, and the expedition scrambled ashore to found Jamestown, the first permanent English settlement in North America.

The Jamestown site was not an auspicious one. Although it proved easily defensible, it was located in an inhospitable malarial swamp, and its soil was not particularly fertile. Moreover, the nature of the colonists complicated matters. Most had no interest in settling permanently; rather, they were either soldiers of fortune who dreamed of finding gold or other riches, or traders looking for a quick profit through commercial exchange with the natives. Few, if any, knew anything about raising crops. Disease and malnutrition took a fearsome toll. When resupply ships arrived in January 1608, only thirty-eight of the original contingent remained alive.

Constant bickering also threatened the colony's survival. The colonists acted selfishly just when circumstances cried out for coordination and cooperation. This problem was solved when John Smith, a twenty-seven-year-old settler, took command of the colony in 1608. He organized the ragtag band, issued orders for the construction of fortifications and the plowing and planting of fields, and decreed, "He that will not work shall not eat." With the survival of the colony at stake, the men who followed Smith in leadership positions continued his authoritarian ways, even executing lazy colonists.

Smith also regularized relations with the Indians. The local natives, part of the Algonquian people, were led by a powerful chieftain named Powhatan, who did not know quite what to make of the fair-skinned newcomers. Apparently he saw them as potential allies in the Algonquians' struggle against other Indian tribes and as a source of trade. But their presence also made him uneasy since he did not trust them, and he questioned their motives for coming in the first place. Initially, Powhatan supplied the starving English with corn, but he later tried to drive them away. Powhatan's daughter, Pocahontas, befriended the colonists and on at least one occasion interceded with her father to save Smith's life.

Despite the initial help from the Indians, the colonists lived a precarious existence, and the arrival of new settlers only worsened the chances for survival. In 1608 and 1609 about 500 new colonists arrived, including the first women. However, the resources to support the newcomers were not available, and death stalked the land. Thanks to famine, disease, and the now-hostile Indians, by 1610 only sixty colonists remained. In fact, the sixty had already embarked upon the return journey to England in June 1610 when they encountered a relief expedition and returned to Jamestown.

The Virginia Company, disappointed at the colony's failure to turn a profit, now made a concerted effort to revive its fortunes. The company raised new capital and began a recruiting drive in England that netted several hundred new colonists. New leadership for the colony was found after injuries forced Smith to return to England and the colony foundered in his absence. A succession of governors—Thomas Gates, Thomas Dale, and Samuel Argall—reinforced Smith's practical but authoritarian policies. Nevertheless, disease and hostile Indians slowed growth. Despite the arrival of several thousand settlers, Virginia's population in 1619 totaled only about 1,000; in 1624, it was 1,300.

Even though growth was agonizingly slow, an economic motive for colonial expansion had appeared. While there was no gold in Virginia and the items supplied by the Indians for trade such as pelts proved disappointing, a major cash crop developed—tobacco. Tobacco was an American plant that Columbus brought back to Europe, where it was acclaimed for its medicinal qualities. Throughout the sixteenth century, the habit of smoking tobacco grew despite opposition from the likes of King James, who characterized it as "loathsome," "harmful," and "dangerous." Most tobacco was grown in the Caribbean region, but English colonist John Rolfe, who later married Pocahontas, planted West Indian seeds and discovered that they grew quite well in Virginia's soil. By 1617 Virginia was shipping ten tons of tobacco home, where English smokers eagerly snatched it up.

Tobacco is a labor-intensive crop, and with its increased popularity, the demand for labor in Virginia grew accordingly. Eventually, two sources of labor appeared to meet the demand. In 1618 the Virginia Company, disappointed at the meagre return on its capital investment, reorganized, acquired new capital, and launched an aggressive campaign to secure new settlers. To lure prospective colonists, the company promised to give each settler fifty acres of land and to give an additional fifty acres to the settler for each person whose passage he paid across the Atlantic. Thus was born the institution of indentured servitude, under which poor Englishmen migrated to Virginia, where they worked for a fixed term of years for the man who had paid their transatlantic passage. At the end of the term, they were free to pursue their own ends, which often included moving to the frontier to start their own farms. Most indentured servants volunteered to go to Virginia, seeing this as an opportunity for a better life; however, some were convicts who were forced to leave England, whereas others were kidnapped.

The second source of labor was black slaves. The first cargo of slaves arrived in Virginia in 1619 when a Dutch privateer sold more than twenty slaves to the colonists. However, evidence indicates that the Africans were treated more like indentured servants rather than out-and-out slaves, receiving their freedom after a set number of years as servants. Eventually, black slavery became established; but indentured servants significantly outnumbered black slaves.

Despite its best efforts, the Virginia Company failed. In 1624 the king gained control of the bankrupt company and transformed Virginia into a royal colony with an appointed governor to oversee the monarch's interests. Within the colony itself, a representative assembly drawn from property owners, the House of Burgesses, had existed since 1619.

Mercifully, the Jamestown colony's troubled history did not provide a model for the second English colony in North America, the Plymouth colony founded in 1620. The origins of the Plymouth colony were rooted not in a desire to make money but, rather, in the religious controversies that characterized Europe at that time. During the sixteenth century, England had converted to Protestantism. However, by the beginning of the seventeenth century, some English Protestants had concluded that the official church, the Church of England, was too corrupt. Some of these disappointed Protestants, the Puritans, elected to remain within the Church of England in order to work to purify that body; others, the Separatists, concluded that the Church of England was beyond repair, and they decided to separate themselves from that body. It was the Separatists who founded the Plymouth colony.

Early in the seventeenth century, a band of Separatists from the village of Scrooby in Nottinghamshire left England for Holland, where they settled at Leiden. However, the Separatists soon discovered that their economic opportunities in Holland were limited and that their children were absorbing Dutch culture at the expense of their English origins. Consequently, they decided to abandon Holland and to seek the isolation they sought in America. After briefly returning to England, 102 Separatists, or Pilgrims as they were later called, left for the New World from the English port of Plymouth in September 1620. In late December they established the Plymouth colony, named after the English port from which they had departed, in what is now Massachusetts.

Prior to landing in America, the Pilgrims settled the question of governance that had initially plagued the Jamestown colony. By virtue of the Mayflower Compact, named after their ship, the Pilgrims pledged their loyalty to the crown of England and swore to "covenant and combine together into a civil body politic." In other words, the Pilgrims would govern themselves. Shortly thereafter, the Pilgrims elected William Bradford as their governor.

Like their earlier counterparts in Virginia, the Pilgrims were unprepared for the hardships of life in the North American wilds, and 44 of the 102 original Pilgrims died during the winter of 1620–1621. Quite possibly the entire colony would have perished, had it not been for the generosity of the natives. Squanto, a Pawtuxet Indian who had been kidnapped by an earlier English expedition and who had spent several years in England before returning to North America, proved particularly helpful, as he taught the Pilgrims how to cultivate native crops such as corn.

Although the Pilgrims lacked practical training in agriculture, hunting, and fishing, they exhibited great determination and managed to survive, if not prosper, mainly through subsistence farming. Meanwhile, to the immediate north of the Plymouth colony, the Puritans established the Massachusetts Bay colony in 1630. The Puritans came in huge numbers (about 1,000 at first and more than 20,000 within the first fifteen years) with ample supplies. They established their headquarters at what is now Boston and rapidly spread in every direction. In 1691 the Puritan Massachusetts Bay colony officially absorbed the Pilgrim Plymouth colony.

INTERPRETIVE ESSAY
Rick Kennedy

In 1776 the great Scottish economist Adam Smith wrote: "[T]he discovery of America, and that of the passage to the East Indies by the Cape of

Good Hope, are the greatest and most important events recorded in the history of mankind." Of course, rating "greatest" events is a foolishness; but if one grants Smith his European bias, economic perspective, and emphasis on the goal of world domination, he makes a point worth considering. Certainly Western civilization never could have gained dominance over Islamic and Chinese civilization without appropriating the resources of the Americas. If the Muslims or Chinese had tried to colonize the New World, certainly the history of the balance of world power would have been altered significantly. As it was, the New World became Europe's resource, and North America, happily for Adam Smith, eventually became a cultural extension of British civilization.

The world context of the European settlement of the Americas is also entwined with a psychological and physical holocaust on three continents. For the native inhabitants of North and South America, European discovery let loose diseases that decimated the population of the two continents and destroyed flourishing economies, cultures, and governments. Africa also suffered. The demand for labor in the Americas encouraged tribal wars and the pillaging of the human resources of Africa for use in America.

Within the context of this worldwide cataclysm of colonizing America, there is a smaller question with long-term significance: How did British culture eventually win the struggle to dominate North America? Of the Europeans in the contest to colonize North America, Britain was tardy in interest and got the worst land—the East Coast. Spain focused its attention on southeastern and southwestern North America—a region we know now to have tremendous resources of gold, silver, agriculture, and tourism. France claimed the teeming fishing grounds of the Northeast and insinuated itself into the rich interior river and lake systems of North America—a region that immediately produced great wealth through the fur trade and eventually in agriculture. The British ended up sharing the rocky, marshy, and confined-by-mountains East Coast with two other latecomers, the Dutch and the Swedes. No seventeenth-century map of North America foreshadowed the eventual Anglo dominance of the whole of North America.

Given the initial weakness of the British situation, why did Britain eventually succeed over Spain and France? The simplest answer is that the British colonial strategy encouraged the creation of happy towns— well-functioning towns with families and churches, self-governing with social services. Spain and France created trading posts, forts, and missions but never succeeded in establishing towns and families in North

America. Samuel de Champlain, Pedro de Menéndez, and Juan de Oñate hoped to begin stable town life in New France, La Florida, and New Mexico; however, nothing they did ever matched the success of the British. By 1700 the British colonies were booming with towns. At the top of the population scale were Boston, New York, Philadelphia, and Charleston, each with thousands of residents. At the same time Quebec in New France, St. Augustine in La Florida, and Santa Fe in New Mexico remained underpopulated outposts.

Happiness was a key term for the British. The institutions of town life, rightly organized, were supposed to ensure the happiness of its citizens. As Thomas More wrote in *Utopia*: "Their institutions give their commonwealth a moral and social foundation for living happy lives." English political tradition was partly derived from the classical Greek ideal of the *polis* as the proper living arrangement for human beings. People, Aristotle lectured, are political animals. The *good life* could only be attained in well-functioning, self-governing towns.

In England, the typical town's government was run by local landowners who elected the "best and most honest" from among themselves to be chief burgesses (town council) and bailiffs (mayors). The church also held much civil authority. The priest ideally worked in concord with a vestry and churchwarden elected from within the parish. The churchwarden's duties usually included overseeing the needs of the poor and reporting any moral lapses among the citizens to the church hierarchy. Education was handled at two levels; indentured servanthood was a standard apprenticeship contract that included basic education, whereas those bound for college usually studied with the minister or some recent university graduate willing to teach young boys. All in all, Britain was full of well-run towns and villages where people prided themselves on their freedom and autonomous responsibility. People were happy in that they were part of a web of responsibilities where order and morality were secured by local government and church.

In colonizing America, the British colonists certainly perpetrated atrocities against humanity; however, one must not downplay the importance of their desire to create and spread the happiness of town life. In 1776 the Declaration of Independence would enshrine the right to happiness in America, a happiness that British colonists believed they had already attained and wanted to protect.

Jamestown in Virginia, founded in 1607, was supposed to transport happy town life to America, but it was a dismal failure. The stockholders of the Virginia Company who remained in England had hoped to establish towns that would support the happiness of both the natives and the immigrants. They hoped to create towns where Indians and whites would "conjoyne their labors" and "enjoy equall priviledges." The company stockholders specifically promised to create a colonial system opposite from the "raging cruelties" of the Spanish. The Indians would experience instead "fair and loving meanes suting to our English Natures."

Jamestown, ideally, was supposed to bring this type of happiness to America for both colonists and Indians. But it failed. John Smith, one of the residents of Jamestown, later wrote that the debacle of people starving, of a man killing his wife, salting her, then eating her throughout the winter, was not the weather's fault but the colonists' own. Jamestown's government never worked by "fair and loving meanes." Declarations of martial law, the execution of whites trying to escape to live with the Indians, the weak role of the church—all were manifestations of a restless bachelor-dominated culture that acted with total disregard for the ideals of town life.

Historian Edmund Morgan describes the decade after 1607 in Jamestown as a "fiasco." A high death rate from disease along with mismanagement and misunderstanding destroyed any possibility for happy town life. But it did not destroy the hope for one. The Virginia Company in London, under the instigation of its treasurer, Sir Edwin Sandys, eventually realized it needed to do something to promote stable town life in Virginia. In 1619 the company started programs to give land to settlers, encouraging especially the immigration of whole families. Sandys even put together a boatload of a hundred women willing to be sold to any colonists wanting to start families. He also wanted to introduce more self-governance; so he called for Virginia to create an elected assembly, gave the colony more governmental autonomy, and even devised a way to keep taxes low so that government officers "should not need to prey upon the people." John Smith noted that if the Virginia Company's plans worked, "then we may truly say in Virginia, we are the most happy people in the world."

But the happiness came only to the few. Town life, with its web of families, church, and elective offices, never took hold; instead, tobacco plantations, with their need to devour labor, dominated the economy. Plantation owners used the new House of Burgesses to create laws oppressing the masses and, most often, undermining the creation of towns. The immigrants rarely got their free land; family and church life found little encouragement; and the buying and selling of laborers tore the webs of mutual responsibilities.

But the immigrants continued to come. In 1622 Indians massacred several hundred white settlers, but disease killed even more. King James I took control of the colony away from the Virginia Company in an attempt to end the debacle. Edmund Morgan titles his chapter on this part of Virginia's history "Living with Death." At least a thousand settlers a year came to Virginia between 1625 and 1640, with the population only slowly increasing. The hope of stabilizing Virginia continued. Here is John Smith in *Advertisements for Unexperienced Planters*, written in 1631:

> Notwithstanding, out of the relicks of our miseries, time and experience had brought that Country to a great happiness, had they not so much doated on their Tabacco, on whose fumish foundation there is small stability: there being so many good commodities besides, yet by it they have builded many pretty Villages, faire houses, and Chapels.

The naive hope in this statement far outweighs the truth. In 1632 the Virginia legislature attempted to create a town by offering free land and tax relief, but not much happened. In the 1660s Governor William Berkeley tried to encourage town building, knowing that "only towns and cities could nourish the arts and skills that distinguished civil men from barbarians." But he failed, too.

Not until the founding of Williamsburg in 1699 did Virginia seem committed to the British ideal of town building. The British monarchs, William and Mary, desired order in their empire. They encouraged strong and conscientious military and church leaders sent from England to create a model town in Virginia. For Williamsburg, James Blair was the conscientious church leader, and Francis Nicholson was the conscientious military leader.

James Blair, one of the rare vigorous ministers of Virginia, oversaw a parish that included Middle Plantation, one of the weak attempts the House of Burgesses had made at town-founding earlier in the century. Middle Plantation had briefly served as the colony's capital when Jamestown was burned during a rebellion. In the early 1690s Blair wanted to remake Middle Plantation into the colony's religious, educational, and governmental center. In 1693 he secured a royal charter to found the University of William and Mary, and in 1699 the House of Burgesses agreed to change the town's name to Williamsburg and move the capital there. The royal governor at the time was Francis Nicholson, a career military officer and colonial official whose active participation in Britain's Society for the Propagation of the Gospel and Society for the Promotion of Christian Knowledge shows the tenor of his mind. Nicholson designed Williamsburg so that it would physically manifest the ideal English town. The capitol and college were at opposite ends of the main street, whereas the church sat at the most important cross street leading to the governor's mansion. Nicholson's plan proclaimed a new seriousness in Virginia about town life. The plantation culture of oppressed labor remained, but England had made a significant attempt to regularize Virginia life in such a way that British values were fully embodied in the colony. It took over ninety years, but Britain persevered in town planting. Spain and France never showed such long-term perseverance.

To the north in Plymouth and Massachusetts Bay colonies, the British were much more successful in quickly planting large numbers of towns and attaining the desired stability and happiness. James Blair, when arguing for the creation of Williamsburg, pointed to the New Englanders as a model where "happy government in Church and State" supported a thriving people.

Although their colonies were distinct and they derived from different branches of the Puritan movement, the Pilgrims of Plymouth colony and the Puritans of Massachusetts Bay colony shared a common rural English heritage that they wanted to bring to America. And although there was much talk of separation of church and state, the New Englanders only wanted to separate ministers from magistrates, religious leadership from civil leadership; when it came to constructing their towns, the old English ideal where town and parish were woven together prevailed.

The Puritan Westminster Confession decreed that the chief end of man is "to know God and enjoy him forever." That enjoyment began here on earth but could only happen within the happiness of well-run communities where each member participated in a web of reciprocal covenants. The 1620 Mayflower Compact affirmed the deliberate desire of the Pilgrims to "covenant and combine our selves together into a civill body politike, for our better ordering and preservation, and furtherance." Governor John Winthrop, ten years later, preached to the Puritans as they left England to found a new colony:

> We are entered into Covenant with [God] for this work, we
> have taken out a commission. . . . We must be knit in this work

as one man, we must entertain each other in brotherly affection, we must be willing to abridge ourselves of our superfluities for the supply of others' necessities, we must delight in each other, mourn together, labor and suffer together, always having before our eyes our Commission and Community in the work.

As soon as the Puritans arrived in New England, they passed a law that offered allotments of land only to people who covenanted together to form a church and a town. The Pilgrims of Plymouth colony also followed this pattern.

Both Pilgrims and Puritans well knew the weakness of humans. Neither group was surprised by the struggles, failures, and controversies that awaited their towns in New England. Twelve years after his arrival, John Winthrop noted in his diary this formula: "[A]s people increased, so sin abounded."

But what is most amazing is not the abounding sin but the abounding political success of their towns. Of course, part of this success was founded on the decimation of the Indians preceding their arrival. The earliest historians of New England, William Bradford, John Winthrop, and Cotton Mather, all praised God for sending disease among the Indians to clear the way for easy settlement. God had not cleared Virginia of the powerful Powhatan confederacy, but God had cleared New England. The Puritan historians were always quick to note God's little providences such as the demise of a scoffing and haughty sailor on the *Mayflower* whom "it pleased God" to smite with such a disease that he died and was thrown overboard. Squanto, the English-speaking sole survivor of the Patuxet tribe, was for Bradford "a special instrument sent of God for their good beyond their expectation."

Little providences may have been indicators of being blessed; however, the political success of the commonwealth is most evident in the fast production of dynamic towns throughout New England. Kenneth Lockridge's history of Dedham, Massachusetts, warns against the mythology of New England towns; however, his study and numerous other studies of New England towns all attest to the Puritan emphasis on town life and the dynamism of town development. Plymouth and Massachusetts Bay colonies went so far as to require by law that people reside in towns.

Arriving immigrants had to first join a town or participate in the organization of a town and church before the town received an allotment of land. Town grants from the Puritan legislature expected citizens to be responsible for the spiritual and physical health of their community. Education and poor relief were the responsibility of every town. Town leaders and representatives to the legislature were to be elected from among the adult male church members. Sumner Chilton Powell, who studied the town of Sudbury, noted that in the first year mutual agreement between the legislature, town, and Indians was achieved and was "orderly in the best English sense." Certainly overwhelming immigration soon caused too much vitality for things to remain as orderly as hoped; however, Powell notes that for the first forty years the minutes of town meetings never mentioned the king or English government in general. The New England towns needed no outside interference, as did Jamestown.

At the end of the seventeenth century, Boston minister Cotton Mather wrote a history of New England called *Magnalia Christi Americana*—"The Mighty Works of Christ in America." He compared New England with Israel and John Winthrop with Nehemiah, the biblical prophet who restored Jerusalem after the Babylonian Captivity. He recounted the founding of towns, churches, and a Protestant university. His most extensive praise was reserved for John Eliot, the apostle to the Indians whose principal missionary strategy was to reduce the local Indians to living in towns. Mather's book proclaimed the triumph of New England's founders. In 1700 Mather was worried about the spiritual commitment of his fellow New Englanders, but he was justly proud of the work of his grandparents' generation. Boston he called "the Metropolis of the whole English America."

But Boston would not be *the* metropolis for long. Philadelphia, a latecomer to English America, would surpass Boston's population in the first half of the eighteenth century. Pennsylvania is probably the best example of dynamic American growth in the seventeenth century that inexorably led to British domination of North America. At first the Dutch and the Swedes had begun small settlements along the Hudson and Delaware Rivers, but growth was slow. They were the first European colonies that Britain overran. By the 1660s the British controlled the land between Virginia and Massachusetts. In the 1680s Pennsylvania began its meteoric rise.

King Charles II gave Quaker William Penn a huge tract of land in 1681, asking only that English values of self-governance and religious toleration be protected. Penn then began advertising his colony to anyone and everyone, especially oppressed Protestant groups in Germany. He encouraged whole villages to emigrate from Europe to America.

Penn liked such German groups because they shared his political view that merged Jesus' Sermon on the Mount (no oaths, pacifism, and plain living) with British town values (self-governance, order, reciprocal responsibilities). Penn was legally the proprietor—the owner—of the whole colony, but he had no interest in proprietary oppression. His idealism is best evident in his *Frame of Government* for Pennsylvania, where he assumed that *all* governments strive for "happiness." He wanted to establish in America a good government founded on good people. "Let men be good," he wrote, "and the government can't be bad; if it be ill they will cure it."

Not wanting to be too restrictive, Penn did not require immigrants to live in towns; however, towns flourished. More than all others, Philadelphia flourished. Penn wrote in 1683 to prospective settlers that Philadelphia fulfilled the "expectation" of all concerned. "I will say for the good providence of God," he wrote, "that of all the many places I have seen in the world, I remember none better seated." Everything that was needed for economic and social success was there. "It has advanced within less than a year to about four score houses and cottages, such as they are, where merchants and handicrafts are following their vocations."

Philadelphia quickly became the fastest growing city in the British Empire. Twenty years later, it was clear that Boston's preeminence in North America was threatened. By that time, too, the dynamic growth of the colony and city was spinning beyond the control of Penn or the Quakers. Pacifism and the other values from the Sermon on the Mount were threatened and would eventually go. In 1708 Penn himself would be sent to debtor's prison in England, largely because the citizens of his colony had no interest in paying the nominal quitrents owed to the proprietor who had opened the land for their use. As with New England, growth eventually squeezed the higher religious ideals out of mainline government. What remained were the basic values of town and parish, self-governance, and orderly care for the needy. In the city of Philadelphia, political and cultural diversity flourished parallel to freedom and economic vitality. Philadelphia would be the home of Benjamin Franklin, the author of a tract stating that the natural increase of population in America would not long lead to England being overshadowed by its colonies.

Virginia belatedly, but Massachusetts and Pennsylvania assuredly, show the success of Britain's desire to encourage the founding of many happy townships in America. The French and the Spanish wanted to create stable towns, full of families, where religious and civil affairs mutually supported each other, but they never showed the perseverance that the British in Virginia showed in attaining them. France and Spain had a desire to have property in North America. Both moved quickly when necessary to maintain a superficial claim to territory. But in the long run, the late-starting British won control because their colonial policy supported the massive migration of people who were looking to create happy lives for themselves. One concluding example from the end of the seventeenth century can illustrate this situation.

Given the booming population growth of the British colonies, it should not be surprising that throughout the seventeenth century the Spanish and French tried to strengthen their hold in North America in an attempt to stand fast against the British. The French shored up their string of forts in the interior, extending them down the Mississippi River, eventually founding New Orleans in 1718. The Spanish tried to maintain military pressure north from Florida as first the Carolinas and then Georgia extended British dominance southward. Both the French and the Spanish had good strategies; however, they chose not to encourage their religious dissidents or economically disadvantaged to immigrate. How can any military strategy save small outposts from being overrun by a dynamic neighbor bursting at the seams with people, wealth, and optimism?

The final seventeenth-century contest for North America was a three-way race to control the Pensacola-Mississippi Delta region in 1698–1699. In the early 1690s France was moving toward creating settlements on the Gulf Coast. Spain, in response, instigated a plan to reestablish a fort at Pensacola in the hope of solidifying its claim to the area. At the same time in England, an English land speculator purchased a land grant named Carolana (different from Carolina) that included the Gulf Coast.

In the fall of 1698 the contest was afoot! In October, two brigantines left England with prospective settlers. The Spanish and the French, knowing of the English plans, already had military expeditions moving toward the Gulf Coast. The Spanish arrived first at Pensacola in November. The English ships stopped on the East Coast, and only one ship sailed on. The French military expedition, finding Pensacola occupied, moved on to what is now Biloxi, Mississippi. The British, down to one ship, arrived at the Mississippi Delta in August 1699—too late and too weak to force a claim. As at the beginning of the century, the British were tardy, and it looked as though they had forever lost the opportunity to settle.

But the story does not end there. On board the English ship were a group of French Protestants, or Huguenots, who hoped to settle in the New World as refugees from religious oppression in France. Seeing their countrymen already established in the Mississippi Valley, these French Protestants petitioned King Louis XIV to be allowed to settle under the French flag in America. The king refused. As a policy, he "had not chased heretics out of his kingdom to create a republic for them in America." The sturdy Huguenots thereupon sailed back to Virginia, where they applied to the English king for citizenship. King William not only consented but also directed Virginia Governor Francis Nicholson to give them assistance. Nicholson, the man who designed Williamsburg, settled them in Manikin Town in the foothills up the James River. The Huguenot leader gratefully wrote, "We are, thank God, in a fine and beautiful country, where, after the first difficulties, we shall live well and happy."

Meanwhile, Spain and France held the Gulf Coast. But not for long. Spain and France won the race with military expeditions, but the Spanish fort remained tiny and the French turned away the refugees who would have helped make them strong. The British lost the race but won the eventual prize. Sixty-three years later, the French ceded their American lands to the burgeoning British. In the same year, 1763, the Spanish ceded Florida to the British. In 1803, the French, having won back Louisiana from the Spanish, again had to withdraw from America. In 1848, after the Mexican War, the weak settlements of the Southwest and California Coast were deeded to the United States. The British strategy of encouraging happy townships had supported so much population growth that, even though tardy and weak at the beginning, they easily won the contest to control North America.

SELECTED BIBLIOGRAPHY

Axtell, James. *The Invasion Within: The Contest of Cultures in Colonial North America*. New York: Oxford University Press, 1985. This study of Indian, French, and British contact emphasizes how New France's better relations with the Indians long made up for the problem of few French colonists.

Bailyn, Bernard. *The Peopling of British North America: An Introduction*. New York: Knopf, 1986. Bailyn, one of the twentieth century's most important historians of colonial America, provides an overview of the immigration patterns that served to fill the towns and institutions of colonial America.

Bradford, William. *Of Plymouth Plantation, 1620–1647*. Edited by Samuel Eliot Morison. New York: Modern Library, 1967. The governor's very readable history of his colony's early years.

Breen, T. H. *Puritans and Adventurers: Change and Persistence in Early America*. New York: Oxford University Press, 1980. An excellent collection of essays comparing northern and southern town life, government, and immigration.

Bridenbaugh, Carl. *Cities in the Wilderness: The First Century of Urban Life in America, 1625–1742.* New York: Oxford University Press, 1938. An important basic study of town life in British America.

Coxe, Daniel. *A Description of the English Province of Carolana, by the Spaniards Call'd Florida, and by the French La Louisiane.* Introduction by William S. Coker. A facsimile reproduction of the 1722 edition. Gainesville: University Press of Florida, 1976. Coker's introduction and footnotes will lead readers to more information about the race for the Gulf Coast.

Fischer, David Hackett. *Albion's Seed: Four British Folkways in America.* New York: Oxford University Press, 1989. An important study of the folkways that manifested the deep social connection between Great Britain and her colonies.

Fontana, Bernard L. *Entrada: The Legacy of Spain and Mexico in the United States.* Tucson, AZ: Southwest Parks and Monuments Association, 1994. An excellent, well-illustrated overview of Spanish activities in North America.

Fries, Sylvia Doughty. *The Urban Ideal in Colonial America.* Philadelphia, PA: Temple University Press, 1977. Whereas Bridenbaugh above emphasized the nuts and bolts of city problems, Fries emphasizes the ideals involved in founding Boston, New Haven, Philadelphia, Williamsburg, and Savannah.

Goodwin, Rutherford. *A Brief and True Report Concerning Williamsburg in Virginia.* Williamsburg, VA: Colonial Williamsburg Inc., 1941. A solid but entertaining study of the founding.

Lockridge, Kenneth A. *A New England Town: The First Hundred Years.* New York: W. W. Norton, 1970. Lockridge builds up the utopianism of the Puritan settlement ideal so that he can then emphasize its fall.

Mather, Cotton. *Magnalia Christi Americana.* First published in London in 1702. Anonymously edited with translations in 1853 and reproduced in Carlisle, PA: Banner of Truth, 1979. Anyone seriously interested in colonial New England must read Mather's history.

Morgan, Edmund S. *American Slavery, American Freedom: The Ordeal of Colonial Virginia.* New York: W. W. Norton, 1975. A classic emphasizing the British idealism of the Virginia Company and the work of Edwin Sandys.

———. *The Puritan Dilemma: The Story of John Winthrop.* Boston, MA: Little, Brown, 1958. This classic study examines the Puritan governor's dilemma of how to separate without separating, how to be exclusive without being exclusive, and how to lead while encouraging self-government.

Morison, Samuel E. *Samuel de Champlain: Father of New France.* Boston, MA: Little, Brown, 1972. Champlain, the founder of Quebec, did as much as he could to encourage stable town life in New France.

Penn, William. "A Letter from William Penn, Proprietary and Governor of Pennsylvania in America . . . Containing a General Description of the Said Province." In *The Peace of Europe, The Fruits of Solitude, and Other Writings,* pp. 119–132. Edited by Edwin B. Bronner. London: Everyman, 1993.

Powell, Sumner Chilton. *Puritan Village: The Formation of a New England Town.* Middletown, CT: Wesleyan University Press, 1963. Powell fully discusses English town ideals in this Pulitzer Prize–winning study.

Smith, John. *Captain John Smith: A Select Edition of His Writings.* Edited by Karen

Ordahl Kupperman. Williamsburg, VA: Institute of Early American History and Culture, and Chapel Hill: University of North Carolina Press, 1988. An excellent short collection of Smith's writings, divided into sections on autobiography, Jamestown, relations with the Indians, and relations to the environment.

Winthrop, John. *The Journal of John Winthrop, 1630–1649*. Edited by Richard S. Dunn and Laetitia Yeandle. Cambridge, MA: Harvard University Press, 1996. A recent abridged edition of Winthrop's view of the founding years.

The "Defenestration of Prague" occurred in 1618 when Bohemia's Protestant nobles pitched representatives of the Roman Catholic Emperor Ferdinand II from the windows of Prague's Hradcany castle; this incident helped to spark the devastating Thirty Years' War. (Reproduced from the Collections of the Library of Congress)

4

The Thirty Years' War, 1618–1648

INTRODUCTION

Several decades of rising tensions in Europe's German-speaking lands—those territories that stretched from France in the west to Hungary and Poland in the east and from the Baltic Sea in the north to the Alps in the south—culminated in the Thirty Years' War. The war went through four distinct stages, and proved quite complex since it was really three wars at once; that is, three different struggles took place simultaneously on German soil.

The Thirty Years' War was a religious struggle. The sixteenth-century Reformation had shattered Christian unity in western and central Europe. The split between Roman Catholicism and Protestantism was nowhere more visible than in Germany, where about half the population remained Catholic and half embraced Protestantism. The Reformation ignited a series of quite desperate struggles known as the Wars of Religion, which pitted one form of Christianity against another. The Thirty Years' War was the last and most destructive of these wars.

The Thirty Years' War was also a civil war of sorts. Although one refers to "Germany," there was no unified, national German state in the modern sense. Rather, Germany was a collection of more than 1,000 mostly small "ministates" ruled over by local potentates. However, most of the German-speaking lands belonged to the Holy Roman Empire that had been founded in 962. But as the eighteenth-century wit Voltaire noted, the Holy Roman Empire was neither holy nor Roman nor an empire. The Holy Roman Emperor, who since the fifteenth century had come from the princely House of Habsburg that ruled Austria, had relatively little authority. Real power rested with the dukes, barons, bishops, and counts, who ruled the hundreds of principalities, duchies, free cities, and ecclesiastical units that comprised the Empire. The Holy Roman Emperors resented their lack of authority and now decided to try to concentrate power in their hands at the expense of these noblemen-rulers. The Thirty Years' War was fought to determine who would rule in Germany.

Finally, the Thirty Years' War was an international conflict involving most of the European states. By the early sixteenth century, the once obscure Habsburg family had emerged as the most powerful ruling house in Europe. Charles V, the Habsburg ruler, was concurrently Holy Roman Emperor, ruler of Austria, Bohemia, and Hungary, and king of Spain, which made him ruler not only over Spain proper and all of Spain's imperial possessions in the New World and Asia but also over the Low Countries (present-day Belgium and Holland), Franche Comté (an important province in what is now eastern France), the kingdom of Naples, and a chunk of northern Italy. In 1556 Charles divided his lands between his brother Ferdinand and his son Philip. Ferdinand received the central European holdings, whereas Philip received the Spanish inheritance. Although the Habsburg lands were now divided, the two branches of the family worked closely with each other, bound together by many interests including an intense devotion to Roman Catholicism.

Initial opposition to the Habsburgs came from the Valois rulers of France. When that house died out and the French throne eventually passed to the Bourbons, that dynasty also steadfastly opposed the Habsburgs despite its own Roman Catholicism. With the Reformation, Protestant Europe also resisted the Habsburgs out of fear that they might someday forcibly reimpose Catholicism. The Protestant powers included England, Denmark, several large Germanic states, and Holland, the northern part of the Low Countries that after decades of struggle had successfully broken away from Spain early in the seventeenth century.

At the time of the Thirty Years' War, Spain followed an expansionistic policy designed to link together all the Habsburg holdings. Working from their base in northern Italy, the Spanish Habsburgs hoped to push through eastern Switzerland in order to link up with the Austrian Habsburgs. Simultaneously, they planned to drive through western Switzerland into the Rhine River valley, thereby creating a contiguous band of Habsburg territory stretching through central Europe to the North Sea. Obviously, Spain's territorial ambitions presented a serious challenge to France. The French also opposed the creation of a unified German state under Habsburg control. Protestant states resisted the Habsburgs for both political and religious reasons.

During the first half of the sixteenth century, religious strife gripped Germany. Order was restored only in 1555 with the Peace of Augsburg that enshrined the principle of *cuius regio eius religio*, ''whose the ruler, his the religion.'' This gave to each German princeling the right to determine the religion of his subjects.

By the early seventeenth century, this settlement, which favored Protestantism and local rule over Catholicism and imperial rule, began to break down. For one thing, the Peace of Augsburg failed to consider confessions other than Catholicism and Lutheranism. During the latter part of the sixteenth century, a form of Protestantism called Calvinism had made significant gains in the German-speaking lands, thereby raising the question of how Calvinism was to fit into the Augsburg equation. Furthermore, despite the Ecclesiastical Reservation of the Peace of Augsburg that effectively forbade Catholic churchmen from converting to Lutheranism and taking their lands with them into the Protestant fold, Protestantism had continued to eat away at Catholic holdings in Germany. Finally, to counter the spread of Protestantism the Roman Catholic Church had despatched to Germany a large contingent of the Society of Jesus, or Jesuits, a militant Catholic religious order dedicated to the destruction of Protestantism. In response to the growing tension, the Protestant princes created the Protestant Union in 1608; in 1609 the Catholic rulers followed suit with the Catholic League.

Actual hostilities began in 1618, initiating the so-called Bohemian phase of the Thirty Years' War that lasted until 1625. In 1617, Ferdinand of Styria became king of Bohemia, a state of the Holy Roman Empire that included Bohemia, Moravia, and Silesia, with Prague as its capital. Ferdinand was a Habsburg, the cousin of the reigning Holy Roman Emperor, Matthias, whom he succeeded upon the latter's death in 1619 as Ferdinand II. He was also a devout Roman Catholic, but the Bohemia he ruled over had a Protestant majority. When the emperor took steps that threatened Protestantism in Bohemia, the Protestant-dominated Estates of Bohemia confronted his representatives on May 23, 1618. In the course of what can be described as a riot, the representatives were thrown from a window of the Prague castle. Their injuries were not fatal, as they fell into a pile of refuse, although Catholic legend has it that angels intervened to break their fall. The Bohemian Protestants followed this "Defenestration of Prague" by deposing Ferdinand and proclaiming the head of the Protestant Union, Frederick of the Palatinate (a principality situated in the middle Rhine valley), as their king. War ensued, and in the 1620 Battle of White Mountain outside of Prague, the Protestant forces were crushed. In the aftermath, Protestantism in Bohemia was extinguished, Frederick's Palatinate was given to Roman Catholic Bavaria, and Spain, which had aided the victorious Ferdinand, improved its position in the Rhine valley.

By 1625, the Bohemian phase of the war gave way to the Danish phase that was to last until 1629. Christian IV, the Lutheran king of Denmark, who feared that a resurgent Roman Catholicism and an enhanced imperial power threatened the German lands he had recently acquired, now headed the Protestant and princely cause. He had the misfortune to face one of the seventeenth century's great military figures, Albrecht von Wallenstein. Wallenstein, a Protestant converted to Roman Catholicism, supported Ferdinand in his struggle with Frederick and acquired considerable holdings in Bohemia as a reward. Ferdinand now called upon him to raise an army to confront Christian. Wallenstein assembled a force of about 50,000 mercenaries. This was virtually a private army, loyal to Wallenstein and no one else. Wallenstein was a complex and secretive man, but it seems as though he was angling to increase his own holdings and stature. In any event, he threw his army into the fray on the side of the emperor and was chiefly responsible for administering a series of defeats to Christian that startled Protestant Germany and brought imperial Roman Catholic forces to the southern shore of the Baltic Sea.

The Danish phase of the Thirty Years' War ended in 1629 with the Edict of Restitution. Issued by the emperor, the edict returned to the Roman Catholic Church all lands that it had lost since the Peace of Augsburg. As a result, a considerable amount of territory, much of which had been Protestant for generations, reverted to Roman Catholicism. The Edict of Restitution not only outraged the terrified Protestants, but it also represented a signal triumph for a resurgent Roman Catholicism and a high-water mark for imperial power. Consequently, the Protestant world now focused its attention more closely on Germany, and many German princes, regardless of their religious affiliation, began to worry seriously about the emperor's waxing strength. Furthermore, France, up to now nervously watching from the sidelines as Spain and the Habsburgs advanced, began to play a more active role.

The Swedish phase of the war began in 1630, when the king of Sweden, Gustavus Adolphus, arrived in Germany. A devout Lutheran, the Swedish king hoped to stem the Catholic tide. In this cause he received considerable support from France, which bankrolled his army, a well-equipped, well-trained, and well-led force of about 40,000. France's power behind the throne, Cardinal Richelieu, also used his influence with Germany's Catholic princes to prevent them from rallying to the emperor's side. In 1631 the Swedes won the Battle of Breitenfeld and in the following year triumphed at the Battle of Lützen, although this latter victory was tempered by the death of Gustavus Adolphus. As the Swedes advanced, Wallenstein, the great Catholic champion, behaved erratically. Having been dismissed by the emperor after the Danish phase of the war, he had been called back to service to block the Swedes. However, the ambitious Wallenstein seemed more intent on extending and consolidating his own power than in serving the emperor, who once again dismissed him. Two years later, in 1634, Wallenstein was assassinated.

With the death of Gustavus Adolphus, the defeat of the Swedes at the Battle of Nördlingen in 1634, and the 1635 Peace of Prague, which secured the withdrawal of the large Protestant state of Saxony from hostilities and prompted other Protestant states to rethink their support of Sweden, France decided to enter the war, thereby initiating the conflict's French or international phase. As always, France wanted to prevent the consolidation of the emperor's power in Germany and to defuse the threat posed by Spain's presence on the Rhine. Although France had worked to achieve these goals through third parties—by supporting the German Protestants, subsidizing the Swedes, and courting the German Catholic rulers—its success had not been complete. Hence, Richelieu in 1635 decided to involve France directly by declaring war on Spain. This time the war spread beyond Germany proper, although that unhappy land bore the brunt of the fighting as it had previously. After enduring a Spanish invasion, France took advantage of difficulties on the Iberian Peninsula where Spain faced rebellion in both its Catalan province and its recently acquired (1580) Kingdom of Portugal.

Peace negotiations eventually opened in 1644, but they dragged on until late 1648. Finally, two treaties, collectively known as the Peace of Westphalia, were signed at Münster and Osnabrück, bringing to an end a conflict that some historians regard as the first world war.

INTERPRETIVE ESSAY
Garrett L. McAinsh

By 1624 the war that had been wracking much of Germany for six long years had come to Hesse. Conditions there soon grew so intolerable that the Estates of Hesse wrote in pitiful desperation to their ruler, "What God . . . threatened his disobedient people through the prophets, such [we have] experienced for some time now, with . . . extreme melancholic pain, misery and sighs, yes with the loss of everything that belongs to [us]. . . . It is as if God wished to overturn our land and people and remove us from his sight, because the sword reaches to the soul and there is no one who can save us from the hand of calamity." Little did they know that the horrors that war would rain down upon them had barely begun.

Warfare inevitably produces suffering, and the people of seventeenth-century Europe were no strangers to its anguish. The misery of Germany's Thirty Years' War, though, appeared to contemporary observers to go far beyond the normal toll of war, and it remains distressingly vivid to this day. Military casualties were enormous, as the tactics of the day left soldiers terribly exposed to enemy fire. At the Battle of Breitenfeld in 1631, some 20,000 Imperial troops, two-thirds of their total number, were lost. Some were captured, but few compared to those who perished from hunger and cold, from plague and other epidemics, and—due to the virtual nonexistence of medical services in the various armies—from the effects of even trivial wounds.

Nor, as the pitiful plaints of the people of Hesse remind us, were suffering and death confined to those who actually fought the war. Indeed, the civilian population of Germany was far more vulnerable than the soldiers and underwent even more horrors. Whenever a body of troops occupied an area, villagers could expect that their hard-earned food and other supplies would be requisitioned by its commanders and that they would be forced to share their homes with often brutal soldiers. Worse, as the war progressed the increasingly undisciplined troops would use torture to force people to reveal where they had hidden their livestock, money, or other valuables. Women were seized and raped by soldiers, often kept until their desperate families could ransom them back. Retreating armies, to prevent the land they were abandoning from supplying the needs of their advancing foes, would destroy crops in the fields, slaughter all livestock they could not take with them, and burn houses, barns, and equipment. The peasants who survived such atrocities were left bereft of food, homes, and fuel. Many, in desperation, simply fled their holdings, abandoning everything they had. Comparison of the number of households in various Hessian villages before the war (1583) and during it (1639) tells a grim tale. Berneberg went from twenty-four households to eight, Königswald from fifty-eight to fourteen and Alten-burschla from forty-nine to just seven.

Townsfolk, protected by the strong walls that girdled their cities, gen-erally fared better. Particularly the larger towns, even when they were conquered, were usually spared the outrages inflicted on rural popula-tions. After all, their new rulers would want to use them as fortresses and as cash cows generating regular income. Smaller towns with just a few thousand inhabitants, though, and on occasion even major cities, could be subjected to incredible horrors. The worst example came in 1631, when Protestant Magdeburg was taken by storm after months of siege. Count Johannes Tilly and the other Catholic commanders were unable to prevent a frantic scramble for plunder and vengeance on the part of their victorious troops. They were equally helpless against the fires that, fanned by high winds, spread with terrifying rapidity through-out the doomed city. Within a few days, one of Germany's finest cities had been reduced to a burned ruin, useless to friend and foe alike. Its entire garrison, some 4,000 troops, had been put to the sword, and as many as 15,000 civilians—three-quarters of the city's population—had perished as well.

Although the armies of the seventeenth century lacked the weapons of mass destruction that have made the warfare of our own age so lethal, the war left so many people hungry, homeless, ill-clad, and vulnerable to disease that its death toll has a sickeningly modern ring to it. The extent of the carnage becomes apparent when we look at demographic figures. Germany probably contained 18 million inhabitants when the war began, but fewer than 12 million remained when it ended three decades later. While much of northwestern Germany and the Austrian lands in the southeastern corner of the Holy Roman Empire were but lightly touched, other regions were horribly devastated. Northeastern Germany lost more than half its population, and areas along the Rhine River saw declines as great as 70 percent. Some places did not begin to approach their prewar population levels again for over a century, al-though Germany as a whole recovered with gratifying rapidity in the decades following the war. Still, the war was the greatest demographic catastrophe central Europe had seen since the Black Plague three centuries earlier, and proportionately it dwarfs anything since, including the world wars of our own era.

Why should this particular conflict have been so lethal? After all, armies had traditionally tended to "live off the land," that is, off of plunder and rapine, throughout all Europe throughout all history. The most obvious factor in the uniqueness of the Thirty Years' War is seen in its name. Thirty years is a long time to fight. Year after bloody year, the sort of decisive victory that could force one side or the other to abandon the conflict, thus restoring peace, remained maddeningly elusive. Both sides were composed of uneasy, constantly shifting alliances rather than tightly disciplined units. All participants were almost as suspicious of their allies as of their enemies, remaining ready to withdraw or even change sides if the fortunes of war threatened to bring those allies too decisive a triumph. This virtually guaranteed that the war would be indecisive and prolonged, that many regions would be hit again and again and again by marauding troops. In addition, the ruinous tax burdens that the war entailed, by lasting for decades, sapped people's abilities to support themselves far more than those of briefer conflicts.

A second factor in the war's destructiveness is that the armies involved were significantly larger than Europe had ever seen before. In previous centuries, battles rarely involved more than a few thousand men on each side. Europe had never seen anything to compare with such clashes as Breitenfeld in 1631, where more than 40,000, troops led by the Swedish king Gustavus Adolphus defeated over 30,000 Imperials. Almost as large was the Battle of Nördlingen in 1634, where 33,000 Imperials beat 25,000 Protestant troops. All told, perhaps a million men fought at one time or another in this interminable war.

A third factor is the role religion played. While political interests were of growing importance in determining when various states entered the war and on which side, religious passions also played a significant role. In Germany and throughout Europe the war kindled hopes that God's truth would emerge gloriously triumphant; that God's enemies, the Protestants or the Roman Catholic Church, depending on one's point of view, would be fatally humbled. Chilling fears that unless the godly struck quickly, hard, and often God's truth might be horribly wiped from the face of the earth joined these exalted hopes. The feeling that victory would produce happiness and virtue, while defeat would involve cataclysmic horrors, roused passions to dangerous levels. The stakes were high enough to justify even extraordinary cruelty, particularly since the enemy was God's foe; he deserved to suffer. It would be an over-simplification to argue that religious passion alone started the war, or made it last as long as it did, or provoked its innumerable atrocities, but it must be acknowledged that religion was involved in all of these things.

While the effects of the war on those who lived—or failed to live—through it must never be forgotten, we must also examine the long-term significance of this brutal conflict to the culture, society, and institutions of Germany and of Europe. The war's economic effects on Germany have been extremely difficult to assess. It is easy enough to establish that population, trade, and production were all at significantly lower levels following the war than they had been in 1618, but were these drops necessarily all caused by the war? The problem is complicated by what historians have come to call "the general crisis of the seventeenth century." All over Europe populations that had expanded during the sixteenth century were by 1600 brushing up against a ceiling. Europe as a whole had become overpopulated, unable to produce enough food for all with consistency. Thus nearly all of Europe—not just war-torn areas—suffered from economic and demographic stagnation or decline during the seventeenth century. Indeed, figures indicate that in several German areas the economic decline had begun well before the outbreak of the war.

Many other German cities, regions, and trades, though, apparently continued to prosper in the early seventeenth century, a prosperity that vanished as they were sucked into the maelstrom of war. The weight of contemporary scholarship indicates that the war was an economic disaster for Germany. Skilled workers were scattered or killed, investment capital disappeared into the bottomless pit of military costs, trading routes and relationships were hopelessly disrupted, and much of Germany's infrastructure was dashed into utter ruin. At the least, the war deeply intensified economic problems that were already becoming apparent at its outbreak, and in more cases still, it replaced prosperous growth with precipitous declines. Indeed, many scholars argue that it took the German economy more than a century to recover fully from the war. In western Europe, they point out, the population pressures of the seventeenth century gave people an enormous incentive to instigate economic changes. Landlords, peasants, merchants, and craftsmen were ultimately forced to seek more efficient and rational ways to produce and distribute goods. These western European economies, particularly those of England and Holland, were put on the path of modernization by the problems of the seventeenth century. In Germany, on the other hand, war's carnage eliminated the overpopulation that served as a catalyst for change in the West. Thus the old, inefficient ways that were being scrapped or streamlined in the West were allowed to continue on into the eighteenth century in Germany.

Here again, though, reality is perhaps not so simple. Germany was already economically backward compared to the West even before the war began. Certainly the war played a significant role in delaying its economic modernization, but it would be an exaggeration to lay the exclusive blame for Germany's economic backwardness on the Thirty Years' War.

The war appears to have deepened the divisions and inequalities that had long marked German society. At its end, many peasants found themselves without the capital needed to restock their herds and flocks or to rebuild the fences, barns, tools, and buildings that had vanished during the war. Large numbers were hopelessly in debt, to boot. Trying to farm their land often held little promise for them. Meanwhile, wages were high, as the bloodshed of war had caused a labor shortage. Many peasants simply sold their ancestral lands, descending socially from independent farmers to hired hands. Throughout much of eastern Germany, particularly in Hohenzollern lands such as Brandenburg, the peasant descent was even more extreme. In return for noble acceptance that they could levy taxes without the consent of the estates, the Hohenzollerns conceded that nobles could treat the peasants on their lands as serfs, virtually their private property. Serfdom, dying out in western Europe, was given a new lease on life in many areas of Germany owing to the Thirty Years' War.

At first glance, the war's effects on Germany's political organization may be difficult to discern. When the war began, the Holy Roman Empire was little more than a hollow shell. Its Habsburg emperors exercised real power only in their family lands, such as Austria and Bohemia. Elsewhere within the Empire, hundreds of territorial rulers governed their own duchies, counties, bishoprics, and cities with little regard for the emperor's wishes. At the war's end, little had changed here. The Habsburgs still held the imperial dignity, and the various territorial states continued to function as virtually independent entities. Indeed, the Peace of Westphalia gave their rulers the right to conduct their own foreign policies, making them, in theory, more independent than ever. In practice, however, they had already been pursuing their own foreign policies without regard for imperial restraints, so the war and the treaty made little difference to their status.

In a very real sense, the war's importance to German political and constitutional development lies chiefly in what did not happen, rather than what did. The Habsburgs had long sought to increase their effective power over the vast expanses and resources of the Holy Roman Empire. Ideally, they would have liked to convert the Empire into a unified monarchy along the lines of England and France. The Thirty Years' War was to be their last real attempt to achieve this goal of unifying Germany politically, and they failed.

By the end of the 1620s, it appeared that the attainment of genuine power throughout Germany was within the grasp of the Habsburgs. The most powerful Protestant states in Germany, particularly Saxony and Brandenburg, had tended to remain warily on the sidelines rather than risk military disaster by rushing to the aid of their beleaguered coreligionists. Emperor Ferdinand II's armies had marched from victory to victory, bringing ever more lands under his control. With brilliant generals such as Count Tilly and Albrecht von Wallenstein serving under his banners, continued military triumphs seemed assured. Ferdinand's confidence and ambition can be seen in his seizure of the Duchy of Mecklenberg from its feckless Protestant dukes and his granting of this large, important territory to Wallenstein, his favorite general. It can be seen even more in the Edict of Restitution that Ferdinand issued in the spring of 1629. This edict ordered the return to the Catholic Church of all those lands that had been held by prelates who had converted to Protestantism since 1552. If enforced, it would cripple many Protestant states by removing some of their most valuable lands from the control of their princes, thus leaving them ripe for future takeover by the emperor. In addition, the edict would enormously increase imperial power throughout Germany because the emperor would effectively appoint many of these newly wealthy and powerful prelates. Surely he would appoint loyal friends.

The fall of Habsburg power from the heights of 1629, though, was swift and irreversible. The Catholic princes on whose support imperial success depended were becoming increasingly worried that if the Habsburgs did succeed in gaining full control over Germany's Protestant states, their own independence would be extremely difficult to maintain. They began to back away from the struggle and successfully insisted that Ferdinand dismiss Wallenstein, his greatest military asset. Meanwhile, the Edict of Restitution was confronting previously neutral Protestant states with the highly unpleasant prospect of losing vital territories and revenues, and of having virulent new centers of Catholic propaganda and agitation established within their borders. Many of them determined to join the fight, a decision stiffened by the Imperialist's brutal sack of Protestant Magdeburg in 1631.

Nor was it only the Germans who worried about the continued growth of Habsburg power. In 1630 Sweden's able king, the Lutheran Gustavus Adolphus, marched his well-disciplined and well-equipped troops into northern Germany. Gustavus was motivated partly by sympathy for his fellow Lutherans in Germany, but even more by hope of gaining lands and power for himself there and by hopes that he could block the emergence of a strong, unified Holy Roman Empire on the southern shores of the Baltic Sea. Meanwhile, France's Cardinal Richelieu, who had long been convinced that breaking the power of the Habsburgs must be his country's primary goal, also decided to intervene on the Protestant side. Although France would not actually declare war and send troops into Germany until 1635, Richelieu began financing the Swedish army with generous subsidies in 1631. The revitalized Protestants, led by Gustavus Adolphus, smashed the Imperial forces at the Battle of Breitenfeld in the autumn of 1631 and swept deep into southern Germany. Not until the Swedish king's death at the Battle of Lützen late in 1632 was the power of the Protestant offensive broken. Ferdinand then conceded defeat, buying off many Protestant German states by agreeing to abandon the Edict of Restitution. While this was enough to stave off total ruin for the Habsburgs, never again would they be able to contemplate ruling Germany as anything but figurehead emperors. When the war ended, the traditional rights and liberties of the German princes were confirmed and even expanded by the Peace of Westphalia.

The impact of the war on German political development, while significant, should not be overemphasized. After all, the Empire on the eve of the war was already much more a confederation of effectively independent states than a real nation in the modern sense. The war, then, did not create the politically fragmented Germany of the eighteenth and early nineteenth centuries; it merely confirmed that decentralization.

The political and constitutional development of the individual states within the Holy Roman Empire was profoundly affected by the war. When the conflict began, the power of virtually all of the rulers of these states was quite limited. Their ability to tax, to raise troops, to intervene in the lives of their subjects, and to pursue policies of their own devising was usually circumscribed by laws and traditions, by representative assemblies, by churches anxious about their independence, and by nobles who were fiercely determined to maintain their traditional rights and liberties. Typically, a precarious balance existed between the power of the rulers and their subjects' ability to resist that power. The war, in almost every case, helped to upset that balance and left Germany's princes well on their way to becoming absolute monarchs within their domains.

The constant military dangers presented by the war left people with little choice but to support the creation of large armies under their princes' control. Such armies, of course, could be used to crush internal resistance as well as foreign invasion. These armies also necessitated much higher tax burdens than people were accustomed to paying. Throughout much of Germany, princes during the war were able to raise taxes to levels that had usually provoked rebellion in prewar years, then raised them even higher. By the end of the war people had grown accustomed to these new levels of taxation, giving their rulers the money to maintain armies and bureaucracies that vastly increased princely power. The princes were also helped by the widespread belief in strong and stable government that grew out of the chaos and insecurity of the war. Most people were now willing to give their loyalty to a leader who could protect them, rather than risk descending once again into the maelstrom of disorder by opposing him, even if he was cutting into their traditional liberties.

Churches, Catholic and Protestant alike, tended to become more dependent on the territorial princes during the war. Only the prince could assure that their flocks would be protected from the insidious blandishments of rival faiths; only the prince could maintain the church's status and prerogatives. Churches, by war's end, had ceased to be significant factors limiting princely power. Much the same can be said of Germany's nobles as well. The war was extremely hard on this proud and turbulent class. They saw the peasants whose dues supported them decimated by the conflict, reducing their income significantly. The disruption of trade routes further diminished their ability to sell their crops profitably, and often they saw their own estates occupied by hostile troops, their homes burned, their property looted. Not surprisingly, many turned in desperation to their prince. They strove to get themselves and their sons commissions in the prince's army or positions in his bureaucracy. Increasingly, their incomes and their status came to depend on cooperation with and service to their prince. By war's end, absolute monarchy was becoming the dominant political system within Germany. Again, we must be careful not to exaggerate the effects of the Thirty Years' War, as the roots of this authoritarianism go far back in German history. The war, though, certainly intensified the tendencies toward absolutism there and played a significant role in entrenching it throughout Germany.

While most of the Thirty Years' War's fighting took place within the Holy Roman Empire, it is important to remember that this was a great international conflagration. Nearly every state in Europe was involved in the Thirty Years' War in one way or another, and it had profound and lasting effects on several of them. From its very beginning, the conflict in Germany was inextricably tangled with the older struggle between Spain and the Dutch Republic. When the war broke out in 1618, the Spanish Habsburgs had immediately leaped to the aid of their Austrian cousins with troops and financial support. Much more was involved in their decision than family loyalty or support for Catholicism. The Spanish were looking forward to 1621, when their truce with the Dutch was due to expire. Central to their plan for reconquering the Dutch was their ability to move troops and supplies overland from northern Italy to Holland, up the Rhine River through the western part of the Holy Roman Empire. Spain's own ambitions committed it to support the growth of Habsburg power and Catholic resurgence within Germany.

Spain sunk an enormous amount of treasure, energy, and manpower into its military efforts in Germany and against the Dutch. Nevertheless, implacable French hostility, Dutch resistance, and the failure of the Imperialists to maintain control over the Spanish land routes through Germany doomed these efforts to failure. With the Peace of Westphalia in 1648, Spain was finally forced to concede formal recognition of the Dutch Republic's total independence. Acceptance of Holland's loss, though, was far from the most important impact the war had on Spain. The military efforts Spain had committed itself to in this conflict were simply beyond its capabilities. When the Count-Duke of Olivares, Spanish monarch Philip IV's great war minister, tried to reform and rationalize Spain's government and tax system to enable Spain to wage war more effectively, he was met with violent revolution. Particularly serious was the 1640 rebellion in Portugal, which ground brutally on until Portuguese independence was conceded nearly thirty years later. Less successful but equally traumatic was the rebellion in Catalonia, on the other side of the Iberian peninsula. This raged from 1640 until 1652, further tearing Spain apart. Nor did making peace with the Dutch at Westphalia and withdrawing from Germany in 1648 end Spain's agony, for the French continued to fight the Spanish on a variety of fronts. This conflict lasted until 1659, when an exhausted and demoralized Spain accepted defeat with the Treaty of the Pyrenees.

If the Thirty Years' War was a major factor in Spain's decline as a great power, it was no less a factor in France's emergence as Europe's most formidable state. Ever since the early sixteenth century, France had been troubled by the rise of the Habsburgs, whose power in Spain, northern Italy, the Holy Roman Empire, and the Netherlands threatened to encircle it. Cardinal Richelieu, who directed French policy for Louis XIII from 1624 until his death in 1642, held firmly to the belief that the struggle against the Habsburgs must take precedence over everything else. Neither religious considerations nor the need to reform France's ramshackle government nor the groans of an overtaxed populace could distract him from this task. As early as the 1620s, Catholic France had given financial and diplomatic support to the "Protestant" or anti-Habsburg side in the Thirty Years' War. This escalated to open backing of Swedish invasion in the early 1630s and to open intervention with French troops beginning in 1635.

France not only humbled and weakened Habsburg Spain, its most dangerous rival; it also played a key role in frustrating Habsburg hopes to dominate Germany and regain control over the Dutch Republic. All this tremendously heightened its own security by breaking the threat of Habsburg encirclement. In addition, the Peace of Westphalia recognized French rule over most of Alsace and strengthened its position in Lorraine; the Treaty of the Pyrenees eleven years later added still more territory wrested from the Habsburgs. It is true that at the close of the Thirty Years' War France was in the throes of a major domestic upheaval, the Fronde, similar to those that had bedeviled Spain; however, the French monarchy was able to overcome this domestic unrest. It emerged from its struggle with the Habsburgs as the strongest power in Europe. France would maintain this status without serious challenge until Germany finally achieved political unification, more than two centuries after the Peace of Westphalia.

Space does not permit the examination of the war's consequences on every country affected. Suffice it to say that virtually no European state could boast that it was unscathed by this mammoth and protracted conflict. Germany during the war decades promiscuously exported fears of persecution and disorder, as well as the need for larger armies and higher taxes. Everywhere, these helped to create social, religious, and political pressures similar to those evident in Spain and France, with their attendant riots and rebellions.

Even England, which cautiously remained on the periphery of the conflict, was deeply affected. King James I, chronically short of money, held back when the war broke out in Germany even though many of his subjects urged him to save the true faith by championing the Protestant cause there. Not until 1624 did he agree to declare war on Spain, but alas, England's hapless armed forces fared embarrassingly badly. James' successor, Charles I, backed out of the European conflict with an ignominious peace in 1630. This lack of royal enthusiasm for defending beleaguered Protestantism fueled English Puritan fears that their kings were lacking in proper piety, even giving rise to suspicions that they might be secretly in league with Rome. These suspicions did not by themselves create the spiral of distrust that led to England's civil war in the 1640s, but they were certainly contributing factors.

Assessing the impact of the Thirty Years' War on European culture and values is even more difficult than measuring the extent of its effect on political and social developments. One area worthy of examination is the place of religion in European civilization. Religious passion was on the wane nearly everywhere in Europe during the seventeenth century. The increasingly secular outlook that had come to dominate modern Western culture was beginning to take shape. Many factors contributed to this phenomenon, but our understanding of it would be incomplete without an examination of the part played by the Thirty Years' War. It appears that on both sides of Europe's greatest religious divide the indecisive nature of the war helped to convince many people that it was impossible to root out the other faith, to restore Europe's religious unity by force. Both the great hopes of religious reunification and the great fears of the persecution that this would entail became increasingly unrealistic as the war ground on. Grudgingly, the idea that religious pluralism would have to be accepted won increasing acceptance. The Peace of Westphalia reflects the change. It stated that both Lutheran and Catholic states could continue to go their own way religiously, thus confirming the religious diversity that had been unacceptable to so many before and during the war. In addition, the treaty went further in several respects. Calvinism, illegal everywhere in the Holy Roman Empire before the war, was now to be officially tolerated on the same basis as Lutheranism or Catholicism. The treaty also set January 1, 1624, as a "normative date." People who had been free to worship as Calvinists, Lutherans, or Catholics at that time would keep or regain that right, even if they lived in states ruled by princes of another faith. Thus, while the Thirty Years' War did not produce full religious liberty in Germany, it took several significant steps in that direction.

In addition, the horror and misery of the Thirty Years' War produced a backlash throughout all Europe. Many people grew disgusted by such suffering being inflicted on people in the name of a loving God. Religious persecution, once almost universally accepted as a necessity by Catholics and Protestants alike, was subjected to more critical scrutiny. Few were yet ready to embrace the idea of religious toleration as a positive good in the middle of the seventeenth century, but the seeds for this momentous development had been sown and were beginning to sprout. The Thirty Years' War, in the long run, played a significant role in making the West more tolerant.

The idea of the seventeenth century as a time of general crisis in Europe has gained common acceptance among historians in the closing decades of the twentieth century. The seventeenth century was a time of war, famine, rebellion, fear, and uncertainty. It was a time in which authority of all kinds—religious, political, social, traditional, and intellectual—was under unprecedented challenge. The Thirty Years' War, which kept much of Europe in chaos for several decades and which helped produce tension and struggle in much of the rest of the Continent, was unquestionably a major factor in this crisis.

SELECTED BIBLIOGRAPHY

Asch, Ronald G. *The Thirty Years' War: The Holy Roman Empire and Europe, 1618–48*. New York: St. Martin's Press, 1997. Brief but scholarly and up-to-date account by a leading German scholar; skimpy on military narrative but good on social, economic, and diplomatic aspects.

Cooper, J. P., ed. *The New Cambridge Modern History*. Vol. 4: *The Decline of Spain and the Thirty Years' War, 1609–48/59*. Cambridge, U.K.: Cambridge University Press, 1970. Chapters by a number of scholars give in-depth analysis of the war itself and the various individual countries involved.

Elliott, J. H. *Richelieu and Olivares*. Cambridge, U.K.: Cambridge University Press, 1984. This fascinating study ably contrasts the aims, resources, and fortunes of the successful Richelieu with those of his less fortunate Spanish counterpart.

Evans. R.J.W. *The Making of the Habsburg Monarchy, 1550–1700: An Interpretation*. Oxford, U.K.: Clarendon Press, 1979. Arranged topically rather than chronologically, this work stresses cultural factors, particularly religion, in creating the Habsburg Empire that grew out of the Thirty Years' War.

Kamen, Henry. "The Economic and Social Consequences of the Thirty Years' War." *Past & Present* 39 (1968): 44–61. A useful synthesis of recent research.

Knecht, Robert J. *Richelieu*. London: Longman, 1991. A judiciously sympathetic account of the goals and achievements of France's war leader.

Langer, Herbert. *The Thirty Years' War*. New York: Hippocrene Books, 1980. More concerned with social developments than narrative political history, this sumptuously produced volume contains a number of beautifully reproduced illustrations.

Maland, David. *Europe at War, 1600–1650*. London: Rowman & Littlefield, 1980. Focusing on the conflict between Spain and the Dutch, the author skillfully ties together the tangled web of conflicts and alliances wracking Europe in the first half of the seventeenth century.

Mann, Golo. *Wallenstein: His Life Narrated*. New York: Holt, Rinehart & Winston, 1976. A massive and well-written account of one of the war's most enigmatic and fascinating personalities.

Parker, Geoffrey, ed. *The Thirty Years' War*. 2nd ed. London: Routledge, 1997. The most comprehensive recent account in English, featuring interpretive chapters by a number of leading scholars and a massive bibliography.

Rabb, Theodore K. "The Effects of the Thirty Years' War on the German Economy." *Journal of Modern History* 34 (1962): 40–51. Still the best approach to the basic issues and controversies involved.

Rabb, Theodore K., ed. *The Thirty Years' War*. Lexington, MA: D. C. Heath, 1972. This slim volume contains brief excerpts from a variety of scholars illustrating their continuing disagreements over the war's nature and significance.

Roberts, Michael. *Gustavus Adolphus*. London: Longman, 1992. This brief admiring biography, the synthesis of decades of study, will remain the definitive work on Gustavus for some time to come.

Steinberg, S. H. *The Thirty Years' War and the Conflict for European Hegemony*. New York: W. W. Norton, 1966. This controversial interpretation attempts to debunk the idea that the war was a catastrophe for the German population and society.

Theibault, John C. *German Villages in Crisis: Rural Life in Hesse-Kassel and the Thirty Years' War, 1580–1720*. Atlantic Highlands, NJ: Humanities Press, 1995. The author's meticulous research provides a gripping picture of the war's disastrous effects on the rural populations of this hard-hit region of central Germany.

Wedgwood, C. V. *The Thirty Years' War*. New York: Doubleday, 1961. Though dated, this remains the most vividly readable introduction to the events and personalities of the war.

Louis XIV and the Grand Monarchy, 1643–1715

INTRODUCTION

The story is told that when King Louis XIII of France lay fatally ill in 1643, his aides brought his young son Louis to his bedside. The dying monarch asked his son to identify himself, and the four-year-old child boldly announced that he was Louis XIV. While the story is most certainly apocryphal, it does provide an important clue about the man who would be Europe's most important figure for more than half a century. From an early age Louis was keenly aware of his importance, and he devoted the bulk of his reign to enhancing his majesty. This objective was not as frivolous as it might seem at first glance, for Louis was the quintessential product of the Age of Absolutism.

Thanks to a combination of economic, administrative, and technological advancements, from the late Middle Ages onward Europe's monarchs had steadily gained ground against their rivals, the nobility. The monarchs also benefited from the sixteenth-century Reformation that not only destroyed Christian unity in western and central Europe but also diminished the Church as a serious threat to royal authority. As monarchs concentrated more and more power in their hands, it became necessary to explain and to justify their ascendancy. The theory of divine right monarchy, or absolutism, provided an explanation.

The elegantly regal Louis XIV epitomized divine right monarchy, or absolutism, at its zenith. (Reproduced from the Collections of the Library of Congress)

According to divine right theory, God is the source of the monarch's power. God in His infinite wisdom (a wisdom that no mere mortal can hope to comprehend) has selected the eldest legitimate male in the ruling house to act in political matters as His agent on earth. Since the monarch has been selected by God and is obviously charged with doing God's will, he cannot be restrained in his legal authority by any mortal man, by any collection of mortal men such as a parliament, or by any document or institution created by mortal men such as a constitution. Under divine right theory, to challenge the monarch is tantamount to challenging God Himself. This is not to say that the monarch is free to act in an arbitrary and capricious manner, as twentieth-century dictators do. Rather, his actions must be good and just, reflecting the nature of God Himself. Nevertheless, Bishop Jacques Bossuet, a leading advocate of absolutism in Louis XIV's France, considered royal authority in its proper sphere as a manifestation of God's will and wrote that "royal power is absolute. . . . [T]he prince need render account of his acts to no one."

Louis XIV was the epitome of an absolute monarch. Born in 1638, Louis grew to only five feet four inches, but he had a regal bearing and always conducted himself with the utmost charm and dignity. Louis did not receive a comprehensive education, but he was methodical, hard-working, and purposeful. He was also blessed with an excellent memory and a good deal of what might be called common sense.

With the death of Louis XIII in 1643, a regency headed by Louis' mother, Anne of Austria, ruled France. However, Cardinal Mazarin, a protégé of Cardinal Richelieu, the power behind the throne throughout Louis XIII's reign, exercised real power. During Louis' minority, Mazarin continued Richelieu's policy of making the king supreme in France and France supreme in Europe. When Mazarin died in 1661, a mature Louis took the reins of government and held them until his death fifty-four years later.

The France that Louis inherited was Europe's richest and most populous country. It also boasted a long cultural tradition. Beginning with the reign of Henry IV in 1589, royal power in France had been waxing, as successive kings and their advisers worked to subordinate all of France—but especially the nobility—to the monarch. Within Europe, France was a major power and would grow stronger under Louis XIV. Both the Spanish and Austrian branches of the House of Habsburg, France's traditional enemy, had been defeated in the recently concluded Thirty Years' War. For the rest of the century, poor leadership plagued a rapidly declining Spain, and threats from the Ottoman Turks preoccupied the Austrian Habsburgs. Revolutionary England's affairs were chaotic, and the Dutch, Louis' most persistent foe, lacked the population and territorial base to challenge France alone. The German-speaking lands were fragmented.

Louis' domestic policies always had one overriding goal—to enhance the absolute power and prestige of the monarch. To this end he built Versailles, a magnificent palace truly fit for a king chosen by God. Located eleven miles southwest of Paris on swampy ground, Versailles began as a hunting lodge for Louis XIII. Its transformation into the most famous and imitated European palace began in 1669 and continued for several decades. As many as 35,000 laborers worked on the project, many dying because of unhealthy conditions. The cost of building Versailles was great, and legend has it that Louis XIV burned the bills. But the end product was majestic. The largest building in all of Europe, the palace sat in the middle of hundreds of acres of manicured lawns, formal parks, walkways, statuary, fountains, and lakes. Its salons were adorned with the finest tapestries, inlaid woods, mirrors, and paintings. Versailles was (and is) an awe-inspiring site. Monarchs throughout Europe scrambled to copy it, giving rise to a flurry of palace building. Versailles added luster to Louis' stature and helped to justify his nickname, the "Sun King." Most important for Louis, Versailles validated his majesty. Certainly only a prince chosen by God could live in such splendor.

Versailles served as Louis' headquarters in his ongoing struggle to control the French nobility. Louis worried most about the high nobility and the so-called princes of the blood (members of his extended family) who seemed intent on ignoring or even subverting his divinely granted authority. Although Richelieu and Mazarin had taken important steps to curb the nobility's power, the Fronde, an aristocratic rebellion of such dimensions that in 1649 the young Louis had to flee Paris in the middle of the night, demonstrated that unruly and restless noblemen could still threaten the monarch's authority. Despite their rebelliousness, many French noblemen depended upon the king for gifts, offices, honors, and other perquisites that ensured their social standing and provided ready cash. Louis, who always respected the social prerogatives of the nobility, used this dependency to his advantage. He employed what might be called a giant patronage operation. The king manipulated the nobility, giving and taking away as it suited his purposes. In doing so, he brought the nobility closer to him. This was literally true, as noblemen sometimes sought the king's favors at Versailles, where they usually got caught up in the social whirl. The court ritual at Versailles was typical of the seventeenth century; that is, it was complex, arcane, and time-consuming. Louis thought it quite natural that visiting noblemen would follow this ritual. If in the process they became distracted, so much the better for the king.

The king also initiated a cultural policy of sorts that enhanced his prestige. During Louis' reign, French cultural figures, including the dramatists Molière (Jean Baptiste Poquelin), Jean Racine, and Pierre Corneille, the painter Charles Le Brun, the architect Jules Mansard, and musicians Jean-Baptiste Lully and François Couperin, received substantial subsidies. In turn, these creative figures produced masterpieces that reflected the glory of their patron and enhanced his prestige.

Louis XIV was a devout Roman Catholic who attended Mass almost daily. His country was also overwhelmingly Roman Catholic; but an important minority comprising about 10 percent of the population embraced Protestantism. Louis was not a religious bigot per se, but he saw things in terms of his divine mandate. Consequently, the king concluded that the mere existence of a Protestant minority threatened the principle of royal absolutism. Louis' goal was "one king, one law, one faith." Accordingly, in 1685 Louis revoked the Edict of Nantes (1598) that had extended religious freedom to French Protestants, or Huguenots as they were called. Many Huguenots converted to Roman Catholicism, others emigrated to Protestant countries, and still others were arrested and sent to the galleys.

The king's ire also fell on dissident Catholics. Louis attacked the Jansenist movement, which consisted of Roman Catholics whose theology was more rigid and severe than the norm, and closed its headquarters at Port Royal in 1660. Simultaneously, however, Louis vigorously defended the "Gallican liberties" that gave the Roman Catholic Church in France (greatly influenced by Louis) a substantial degree of independence from Church authorities in Rome, including the Pope. The need for conformity and control always informed Louis' decisions.

While Louis himself knew very little about economics, he selected as his controller-general of finances Jean-Baptiste Colbert, an ambitious and energetic man who provided the expertise necessary to keep the regime solvent. Colbert embraced mercantilism, the dominant economic practice of the seventeenth century and a vital component of absolutism. Mercantilists aimed to make the monarch and his domain economically and financially independent. To achieve this, mercantilists interfered in the market economy. They regulated business activity, dispensed economic subsidies, levied selective taxes, imposed a tariff policy designed to discourage imports and stimulate domestic production, and accumulated gold bullion. They also encouraged the growth of empire as a way to secure a guaranteed supply of inexpensive raw materials and to acquire a reliable market for surplus domestic production.

In his defense of absolutism, Louis reformed France's administration. In particular, he brought France's heretofore virtually independent armed forces securely under state control. He strengthened the idea of the chain of command (with himself at the head of the chain), expanded the army's size, and successfully melded various military units such as the infantry and the artillery into a single coherent force.

Louis based his foreign policy on equal amounts of vanity and realpolitik. Louis was a vain man, who saw conquest as the road to glory. At the same time, he wanted to expand France's frontiers, thereby buttressing French security and establishing France as Europe's dominant power. Louis' desires brought a series of conflicts that eventually pitted France against most of Europe. The War of Devolution (1667–1668) was followed by the more serious Dutch War (1672–1678), which ended with France gaining the prosperous Franche-Comté and several important towns in the Spanish Netherlands. However, Louis' aggressiveness had alienated much of Europe, which now viewed the French king with growing suspicion. Louis' next war, the War of the League of Augsburg (1688–1697), did little to enhance Louis' glory or to augment France's territory. It was followed by the War of the Spanish Succession (1701–1714), during which French forces fared poorly and the country itself experienced severe deprivation. No wonder that on his deathbed Louis XIV warned his heir to avoid war, noting that he had "loved war too much."

Louis XIV's death on September 1, 1715, brought an end to the Grand Monarchy. During his reign, however, Louis had gone far to justify his reputed boast, "L'etat c'est moi" (I am the state). Nevertheless, it is noteworthy that during Louis' funeral procession in Paris the common people threw rocks and bottles at his coffin.

INTERPRETIVE ESSAY
Andrew P. Trout

Louis XIV, the legendary king of France, was never quite so secure or so powerful as he would have us believe. Royal propagandists plastered his name, his image, or the sun, emblem of the Bourbon family, for everyone to see. For a long time historians took much of this at face value, portraying the Sun King as the very essence of absolute monarchy. There is some truth in this. Louis XIV's lengthy reign saw an expanding bureaucracy and greater exploitation of the power of the monarchy. To discourage possible rivals, Louis shut his own family and the high nobility out of his supreme council; in other words, they could no longer aspire to be ministers. Moreover, the king appointed no first (or principal) minister, as his father had done; he made it clear that he intended to be his own first minister, especially for war and diplomacy.

No formula as succinct as absolute monarchy summarizes what it meant to be king of France in the seventeenth century. For one thing, the king's authority differed from one French province to another. In a few provinces the king's representatives had to bargain with elected assemblies that controlled taxation; in others the government exercised direct authority over taxes. In Paris, the king's capital, royal authority was much more in evidence than in faraway provincial cities. In fact, the authority exercised by the king over his own officials varied markedly. A great number of them, civilian or military, actually owned the positions they held—meaning that the officeholder had purchased it from the crown or another owner or had inherited it. These positions are called *venal*, implying purchase and sale but not suggesting incompetence or corruption. Purchase of office amounted to a loan to the government in return for annual interest in the form of salary. But officeholders were not amenable to direct control by the crown—as were the king's ministers, whom Louis could hire and fire at any moment. The crown would have liked to abolish venality of office but could not—not as long as a war persisted or another was in sight. For warfare was the most expensive pastime of monarchs, exhausting tax revenues and forcing the king to borrow and create more offices to sell. Abolishing the system of officeholding would have meant huge expenditures to redeem these posts. Sale of office limited the supposedly absolute authority of the king. It was not enough for Louis XIV simply to command; sometimes he had to resort to persuasion or negotiation with his officeholders.

The crown had better control over the intendants, men directly appointed to represent the royal government in the provinces. Some historians have rejected the old notion that intendants were practically kings in their own domain. For example, Peter Campbell concludes that they were "far from being the virtual administrators of France." Answering demands for information coming from the desk of an important minister like Jean-Baptiste Colbert was perhaps as important as anything they did. Rather than simply dictate to other authorities, such as the provincial governors, intendants were instructed to work with them.

Lack of speedy communications made it difficult for the king's ministers to control events and to govern without resistance from provinces located hundreds of miles from Paris. Local authorities were known to side quietly with a populace rioting against taxes. Legally, it was not enough for the king simply to issue commands, for many laws were not binding until law courts known as *parlements* had registered them. If a *parlement* refused, the king could command registration. Most of the time, however, they did not directly defy the king, and Louis was usually careful not to encroach on the courts' prerogatives.

More and more, historians see absolute monarchy as applicable only in its proper sphere, and that sphere was narrower than a twentieth-century government's. Much day-to-day judicial business was outside that sphere. Any attempt by a king of France to name his own successor would be contrary to the fundamental law, or constitution, of France. Although appointment of Roman Catholic bishops was the king's prerogative (subject only to a papal veto), the bishops knew how to stifle enforcement of royal policy if they deemed it necessary.

War with Spain dominated Louis XIV's early years. What proved to be a forty-year struggle among various European powers had originated in 1618, but not until 1635 did France enter to strike a blow against its old enemy, Spain. Louis XIV inherited his throne in 1643, but since he was only four years old, a regent would rule in his name. That person was his mother Anne, assisted by a first minister, Jules Cardinal Mazarin. Between 1643 and 1661, Mazarin, a former Italian diplomat (but not a clergyman) made policy much of the time, for he had the confidence of Anne and her son Louis. It was Mazarin that tutored Louis in the art of government.

Equally instructive for the young king was his experience during the Fronde, or civil wars (1648–1653), when he and his mother had to flee their residence in Paris. The occasion for the turbulence was an unpopular war with Spain and the taxes, high-interest loans, and state bankruptcy that flowed from it. The violence originated in a revolt by the judges in the Paris *Parlement*, supreme law court for one-third or more of France. These judges belonged to the highest rank of the newer nobility of the robe, men holding important judicial and financial offices. Before long the revolt entered a new phase as princes of the blood (the king's relatives) and some of the greater nobility took control of it. These nobles, or nobility of the sword, were the most prestigious of their class, with titles of military origin and pedigrees quite ancient (or so it was claimed).

For Mazarin and the royal family, the Fronde meant exile from Paris. From bitter experience the king would learn the lesson that an unruly nobility needed to be curbed and that an isolated tax riot might lead to something much worse. Some of Louis' decisions of a later date, such as creation of that huge complex known as Versailles, can be seen as insurance against renewal of the Fronde.

As public opinion turned against the violence of the Fronde, Mazarin's government was able to restore a semblance of order by 1653. But the conflict with Spain begun in 1635 continued until the Treaty of the Pyrenees (1659). Although the Pyrenees settlement implied French predominance in Europe, it was less onerous for the defeated power than one might expect after a quarter century of hostilities. France acquired a few territories along its Pyrenees mountain border with Spain and in the Spanish Netherlands (an area roughly equivalent to modern Belgium and Luxembourg). The two governments agreed that Louis XIV would marry a Spanish princess—supposedly a guarantee of harmony between the two powers. Significantly, the marriage would place the French royal couple's heirs in line to inherit the Spanish throne if no direct heir to that throne materialized.

Equally important, Mazarin bequeathed to Louis XIV a security system. France was the predominant power in Europe. Spain was defeated, and along France's eastern border some German provinces had united in a Rhine League friendly to France. (Germany was not a unified state but a collection of states known as the Holy Roman Empire.) In brief, when he died in 1661 Mazarin left Louis XIV a stable government in France and no excuse for a another war abroad. As we shall see, the king would find a pretext anyway.

For the moment, peace had a chance. It seemed crucial to reform the finances, which were a shambles after decades of high taxes and deficits. Reform turned out to be an unpleasant experience for government creditors because Jean-Baptiste Colbert, soon to become finance minister, was as ruthless as he was competent. During the wars, it appeared, crown lenders had defrauded the government; now that peace had returned, the crown would retaliate. In the 1660s a special court known as a chamber of justice tried hundreds of creditors and fined great numbers in what amounted to repudiation of certain government debts—partial bankruptcy, in other words. The trials were the talk of Paris, disturbing no doubt for those high aristocrats who had lent funds secretly to the crown through financiers, the men who managed the king's money. If discovered, the loans would prove embarrassing to a class who wished to appear untainted by commerce or moneylending. The financiers, many of them on trial before the chamber in peacetime, and their accomplices were an integral part of the state machine in wartime.

The main event of the early 1660s was the trial of Nicolas Fouquet, finance minister held over from the Mazarin era. As far as fraud or other illegalities were concerned, there is no reason to think he was worse than Mazarin or Colbert, both of whom had taken great liberties with the king's money. In an era when public funds and private wealth were easily commingled by higher authorities, it was no secret that a king let his ministers get rich. Maintaining an expensive residence was one way for a minister to impress the public, thus an instrument of governing. Even for a minister, however, Mazarin's holdings exceeded the norm. He became the wealthiest of Louis XIV's subjects, but when at his death he promised his fortune to the king, Louis declined. Perhaps it was a king's gratitude to the man who apparently had saved Louis' state for him in the face of war and rebellion.

As for Fouquet, he actually had spent a good deal of his own money in the king's service and, unlike a number of other aristocrats, had proved loyal during the Fronde. The trouble was that he flaunted his wealth and acted as if he expected to succeed Mazarin as first minister. This apparently too-powerful subject must have frightened a young king who obviously had not forgotten the Fronde. The king, with much encouragement from Colbert, dismissed and arrested Fouquet in September 1661 and ordered him tried for treason and fraud before the chamber. If Fouquet had not sold his office in the Paris *Parlement* at the king's behest, he could have demanded trial there by the judges, his peers, and almost certainly escaped with a light sentence or none at all. The king and Colbert wanted the death penalty and had packed a chamber of justice to that end; nonetheless, that court rejected the treason charge, sentencing the ex-minister to exile for fraud. The final result was a sort of compromise. Rather than simply throwing out the court's verdict and insisting on the death penalty, the king sentenced his former minister to permanent exile and, worse, imprisonment in Italy. Louis apparently had acted as much out of fear as anything, although the sentence may also have amounted to a search for a scapegoat for the financial chaos of the past. Today Fouquet appears not as a dangerous would-be Frondeur but as a muddled, indiscreet politician. Louis' conduct was not typical of the Sun King, who ordinarily would let the law take its course.

The main trials wound down in 1665, as the government assessed heavily the crown lenders it considered the most guilty; Colbert made sure that his friends were spared the worst. Meanwhile, he emerged as a minister of all sorts. Within his portfolio were not only finance and commerce but the navy and certain fortifications, not to mention the king's buildings and the modernization of Paris. The latter process would endow the capital with the best urban police in Europe, an increased water supply, wider streets, and annual paving subsidies from the crown. But the king disliked his capital, eventually vacating it to take up permanent residence (1682) at a newly expanded royal palace at Versailles, a few miles from Paris. The fact that paving expenditures in Paris reached their peak in 1671 says something about Louis XIV's priorities. From that point on, war would frequently interfere with Colbert's plans for urban improvements, subsidies to industries, and balanced budgets.

The government that Louis XIV introduced in 1661 commenced the king's personal reign, meaning that Louis was, in today's parlance, a "hands on" ruler. He paid close attention to government, particularly foreign and military policy. No longer was there a first minister to make decisions. In Louis XIV's reign the typical minister was a member of the lesser but by no means unimportant nobility known as the robe for its judicial connections. It included in its ranks ministers of state such as Colbert and some of his relatives, Michel Le Tellier, and a son known as the Marquis de Louvois. These were not merely middle class, or bourgeois; these were noblemen whose families the king might encourage to marry into the old military nobility. But, unlike certain greater nobles with ancient titles, these ministers knew that the king had elevated their families to power, and they were not about to bite the hand that fed them. They were very loyal to Louis XIV and often quite proficient on the job.

As for the high nobility, Louis rarely appointed them ministers but did not deprive them of rank and titles and a share in government. It is true that to prevent them from fomenting trouble in the provinces he encouraged them to come to live at Versailles. Only the wealthy could afford that, but Versailles dwellers were the ones likely to benefit from royal largesse if a position was vacant. Most noblemen remained at home. Versailles, a small "company town," could never have housed them anyway. At Versailles some of the most important and noble names

in France became household servants. To understand this we must remember that such service to the king was not considered demeaning and
that Versailles was both the king's residence and a court, or center of
government. (Paris, a day's journey away, remained the capital and
headquarters for much of the royal administration.) Thus it should not
surprise anyone if a gentleman who handed the king his shirt or his wig
in the morning was also informally and secretly consultant to Louis XIV
on matters of state. Louis has been described as "first gentleman" of
France; as such he respected the rank and social distinctions that divided
other gentlemen from the common herd. Moreover, military and diplomatic posts were open to the great nobles, as were governorships of
provinces.

The notion that the great nobility merely vegetated at Versailles is
misleading, as is the view that the great building complex was inordi-
nately expensive. Estimates are that it amounted to no more than 3 to 5
percent of royal expenditures in the 1660s and 1670s. It was war rather
than palaces that so often kept the government in tow to the money-
lenders. But Colbert was probably right in insisting that the king would
have done far better to reside in Paris, home for several hundred thousand people, rather than relocate in a rural resort.

King's court and residence, Versailles in its enormity and magnificence
signaled to foreign visitors and ambassadors what a mighty prince the
occupant was—someone the foreigner should be careful not to offend.
To the king's subjects it was continual theatrical display but also a site
for an outing. Versailles was more open to the public than the modern
White House. The properly attired visitor could mingle with the aristocracy and possibly rob one or two of them. It could be worse. Colbert
once ordered the Paris police to look among the crowd at Versailles for
an escaped murderer—sunburned and disguised with a blond wig.

Neatly drawn tables of organization might suit the twentieth-century
bureaucratic mind, but they hardly apply to Louis XIV's France. Obviously the king was at the top of the social and political pyramid as
supreme legislator and supreme judge. Next in political power were the
ministers, members of a supreme council, who advised the king and
wrote correspondence. But once Louis made a decision, councilors did
not argue with him; whoever chose to do so could be dropped quickly.

Farther down the political ladder was the intendant, serving the crown
in the provinces by supervising tax collection and gathering information.
But he also served his own community by reporting local opinion to his
correspondent at Paris or Versailles. In government circles it was feared

that he, and particularly his assistant, was becoming too identified with his own locality. Intendants were not numerous, varying anywhere between twenty-three and thirty, while in Colbert's time fourteen inspectors aided them in publicizing regulations. Whatever bureaucracy Louis had consisted of ministers, intendants, councilors, and several hundred others. Apart from these, of course, hordes of venal officials, some of them useful, some ornamental, were scattered throughout the realm; and their numbers expanded with each wartime financial emergency.

Parallel governing mechanisms in the form of patronage networks existed alongside the intendants and councilors and the like. A great personage, such as a minister, might have dozens of clients strategically placed in certain districts to serve the court at Versailles or the minister's personal interests. (Some ministers did not carefully distinguish between the two.) Historian Sharon Kettering has concluded that for the purpose of strengthening royal control throughout France, distributing patronage to well-connected people was as effective, especially in frontier provinces, as dispatching intendants.

A minister-patron had various perquisites to offer a client, such as a prestigious job. In return his client would render services, such as reliably reporting to Versailles news from the province where he resided— for example, information as to who could be trusted and who could not. The client could use his influence to put in a good word for the minister among the families who counted most in his locality.

To bring together prospective patrons and clients, there was a broker— perhaps a governor of a province occasionally traveling to and from Versailles bringing a minister, say, into correspondence with a prestigious gentleman in the governor's province. There were few rules and little formal structure to all this. Patrons were by no means limited to the ministerial class. One patron might claim dozens of clients, and a client could serve several patrons at once and hope there was no conflict of interest. Indeed the system (for lack of a better word) was fluid; when a patron's influence at court was declining, a client might desert him and his family for a rival. To understand a given person's place in society it helps to know how many clients he could count on. For patronage was at the center of a system in which a king governed not as an oriental despot but with the consent and cooperation of elite groups. A royal edict on its face might seem to be an isolated act of an absolute monarch; in reality, it might be the end result of a complicated negotiation among patrons and clients.

Louis XIV took charge of military and diplomatic policy, and left to

Colbert the money grubbing that made the king's foreign policy feasible. The mid-century years were important for the French military, as the war minister Michel Le Tellier turned what had amounted to private armies controlled by various commanders into a national army. Nevertheless, it is easy to exaggerate the king's control over it. Officers continued to swindle the government by demanding money to pay troops existing only on paper and by ignoring desertions. Nor were inspections by intendants the perfect antidote; rather, according to historian Nicholas Henshall, some were a "foretaste of Laurel and Hardy" in that men were enlisted simply to be counted before disappearing. Two centuries before the telegraph and telephone revolutionized communication, there were occasions when troop movements were so rapid that an intendant could, quite mistakenly, count the same force twice. Nor were royal armies necessarily reliable in maintaining internal order, since noble captains might refuse to discipline other nobles. It is easy to understand a captain who would not unleash his own troops for fear they might pillage the countryside. Yet, after all is said, Louis XIV had the most effective army in Europe.

The nearest thing to a theme in the French king's foreign policy was a preoccupation with the Spanish Empire and its eventual fate if King Carlos II should die without heirs. But Louis' policy can just as well be seen as no more than a series of ad hoc, counterproductive, incoherent measures for military glory or some momentary territorial gain. In the 1667 War of Devolution, Louis invaded the Spanish Netherlands—a move that prompted England, the Dutch Netherlands (Holland), and Sweden to form a Triple Alliance to compel France to make peace with Spain. In the face of a threat to intervene, Louis concluded the war with the Treaty of Aachen (1668) that yielded him a bit of territory in the Spanish Netherlands. More important in the long run, a coalition had forced Louis to make peace while his overbearing stance caused the dissolution of the friendly Rhine League of German states.

It is easy to exaggerate Louis XIV's ambitions as his enemies did. He may have aspired to be the dominant power in Europe, but he was no Napoleon seeking to conquer it or even to annex the Spanish Empire. Nor was he seeking the "natural frontiers," such as the Rhine River, staked out in the 1790s by revolutionary France. Nonetheless, the course he pursued beginning in 1667, and especially from 1672 on, frightened his neighbors and led them to form anti-French coalitions to contain the Sun King.

Checked but not defeated in 1667, Louis conspired with King Charles

II of England to wage war against the Dutch. Louis' real object in the Dutch War (1672–1678) was to induce Spain to enter the conflict as apparent aggressor and then to seize the Spanish Netherlands. The capture of a few Dutch forts was something of a feint; the French had no intention of marching to Amsterdam.

French planning went astray in 1673 as Louis' forces made a preemptive strike into Germany, only to be checked by the army of Holy Roman Emperor Leopold I (1658–1705), ruler of Austria and member of the latest anti-French coalition. The diversion into Germany seems pointless. Not only that; Louis' ally Charles II wanted no quarrel with Spain, so he bowed out. Although Louis got the war with Spain that he wanted, unrest at home in the form of tax riots and the threat of an Anglo-Dutch coalition were pushing him to the peace table. The Dutch War concluded with the Treaty of Nijmegen (1678–1679), compelling the French to repeal an anti-Dutch tariff and allowing Louis to annex the Franche-Comté from Spain—but not Belgium, the apparent object of Louis' war. The conflict proved costly: six years of hostilities, borrowing by finance minister Colbert for a war he really opposed, and the permanent enmity of William of Orange, Dutch ruler and future king of England. For his part, the king declared victory. A fireworks display in Paris in 1679 portrayed the monarch as the mythological Hercules standing on a pedestal, dictating peace to Europe.

The notion that powerful rulers necessarily knew what they were doing merits reexamination. The 1680s would see a continuation of that "confusion" on the king's part that influential scholar Andrew Lossky has identified. Louis apparently never abandoned the idea that the Spanish inheritance or part thereof would fall to a Bourbon relative of his if Carlos died without heirs. But he was pursuing policies bound to antagonize the Spanish, the very people whose friendship he would need if the succession opened up. To the east, Louis had not only alienated the erstwhile Rhine League; in the 1680s he would continue to accumulate enemies through intimidation or subversion short of protracted war. Among his acquisitions were the cities of Strasbourg and Luxembourg. In 1684 Emperor Leopold and the French concluded the truce of Regensburg, allowing Louis to hold for twenty years certain gains along that eastern frontier.

As German emperor Leopold had a great interest in this frontier question, but as Austrian ruler he was even more distracted by a war inflicted on him by the Ottoman (Turkish) Empire. The Turkish siege of Vienna in 1683 had brought an international army to the rescue; after raising the siege the Christian forces continued to chase the Muslim Turks out of Austria and Hungary. Meanwhile, Louis XIV was watching events in eastern Europe. Although not actually allied with the Turks, he viewed with equanimity the prospect of a Turkish army defeating Leopold and his allies—after which he, Louis, would come to rescue Europe, drive the Muslims out, and win great acclaim for his trouble. As we have seen, the Christian forces upset Louis' game plan. So Louis sought other means to win acclaim as a crusader. To him the time seemed ripe to revoke the Edict of Nantes, which had guaranteed toleration to France's Calvinist minority since 1598. At home, many of the king's subjects applauded the revocation.

Abroad, the reaction to the revocation from the Protestants, some German Catholics, and the Pope was negative. Louis' position in Europe continued to deteriorate as Spain, the Holy Roman Emperor, and some other German states formed a League of Augsburg (1686) to curb the territorial ambitions of the French king. Not long after that, Louis' most persistent enemy, the Dutch ruler William of Orange, gained the throne of England in 1688 and prepared to utilize England's naval and financial power in any war with France. Meanwhile, Louis launched a preemptive strike at the fortress of Phillipsburg in Germany, a prelude to a war he actually did not want and for which France was unprepared. As usual, a coalition formed—this time to include Spain, the Holy Roman Emperor, the Dutch, and the English. In 1697, after nine years of inconclusive struggle, the parties negotiated the Treaty of Ryswick.

By 1697 everyone knew that the major issue confronting Europe was the question of the Spanish succession; with no direct heir to the sickly Carlos II in sight, partition of Spain's empire seemed inevitable if the European balance of power was to be maintained. So William of Orange, now William III of England, and Louis XIV agreed on the First Partition Treaty (1698), which conceded most of the Spanish Empire to a Bavarian prince; the rest would go to the Bourbons and the Austrian Habsburgs. All three families were related to the king of Spain. Selecting a Bavarian prince made sense because a candidate to the kingship from a minor German state was unlikely to destabilize Europe. A candidate from France or Austria might have seemed menacing to neighboring powers.

Unfortunately the Bavarian prince's death in 1699 negated the first treaty. Thereupon the two kings, Louis and William, negotiated a Second Partition Treaty (1700), this time awarding Spain, Spanish America, and Belgium to an Austrian candidate and reserving compensations for France. But neither Carlos nor Emperor Leopold would agree to this.

The Spanish were determined that their empire remain undivided, and it seemed to them that a Bourbon could best preserve it intact. So when Carlos died in 1700, his will left the entire inheritance to Louis XIV's grandson Philip. Should Louis as head of his family refuse the inheritance, it would go to an Austrian Habsburg. Whether Louis adhered to the Second Partition Treaty or accepted Carlos' will, the Austrians were likely to launch a war, for neither document offered them the foothold in Italy that they desired.

Although the will offered no territory to France, the king decided to accept it. If there was to be a war, it seems clear now that wise diplomacy could have limited it. England's reaction was crucial, and for many members of the English Parliament a Bourbon Spain was no threat. But Louis behaved rashly. Abroad the idea circulated that the crowns of France and Spain could eventually be united in one person. For some reason Louis never explained that this was not to be; the Spanish people would never have tolerated it. Louis made a bad impression when, with Philip's consent, he dispatched troops into the Spanish Netherlands, which the Dutch considered a barrier against France. He also secured for France trade privileges in the Spanish Empire. The Dutch and English replied by forming a Grand Alliance, which the emperor eventually joined.

The War of the Spanish Succession (1701–1713) differed markedly from what had gone before. This time it was the emperor, not Louis, who opened hostilities; this time it was a preemptive strike in Italy. In this war the Alliance powers took greater chances and marched greater distances to win bigger battles and suffer greater losses. Quite thoughtlessly, the English, who had already recognized Philip as king of Spain, reneged and expanded their war aims by agreeing to place the emperor's younger son on the Spanish throne.

Military reverses left Louis prepared by 1709 to make genuine concessions, but the English refused to negotiate seriously, insisting that Louis drive his grandson from the Spanish throne. Fearful that he might even lose his own throne, Louis called upon his people for help. The English broke the deadlock by electing (1710) a Tory party majority in Parliament to replace the warlike Whigs. Anglo-French talks led eventually to the Peace of Utrecht (1713), with terms close to those of the partition scheme the English and Dutch had agreed to in 1701. Spain and its American possessions remained with the Spanish monarch Philip V, while Austrian acquisitions included the former Spanish Netherlands and Milan. Louis XIV's judgment of himself will have to stand: "I have loved war too much." With foreign policy in mind, contemporary historian Paul Sonnino summarized it well: The Sun King could never "leave well enough alone."

SELECTED BIBLIOGRAPHY

Campbell, Peter Robert. *Louis XIV, 1661–1715*. London: Longman, 1993. An informative but compact summary of recent research on how Louis XIV's government actually worked.

Cole, Charles Woolsey. *Colbert and a Century of French Mercantilism*. 2 vols. New York: Columbia University Press, 1939. An important work about an important minister; well worth consulting for any research project.

Dent, Julian. *Crisis in Finance: Crown, Financiers, and Society in Seventeenth Century France*. New York: St. Martin's Press, 1973. Interesting trip through the bizarre world of financial officials and lenders to the French kings; it explores the connection between war and money.

Frey, Linda, and Marsha Frey, eds. *The Treaties of the War of the Spanish Succession*. Westport, CT: Greenwood Press, 1995. Its scope is wider than the title might indicate. More than forty specialists contribute several hundred entries in a wide-ranging volume.

Goubert, Pierre. *Louis XIV and Twenty Million Frenchmen*. Translated by Anne Carter. New York: Pantheon, 1970. General account of the reign with considerable emphasis on economic history.

Henshall, Nicholas. *The Myth of Absolutism: Change and Continuity in Early Modern European Monarchy*. London: Longman, 1992. Revisionist, controversial, and at times amusing summary of recent scholarship.

Kettering, Sharon. *Patrons, Brokers, and Clients in Seventeenth-Century France*. New York: Oxford University Press, 1986. An important book on political connections and manipulation beneath the surface of the "absolute" monarchical administration.

Lossky, Andrew. "The General European Crisis of the 1680s." *European Studies Review* 10 (1979): 177–197. Of particular interest for Louis XIV's confused diplomacy.

———. *Louis XIV and the French Monarchy*. New Brunswick, NJ: Rutgers University Press, 1994. An important biography with particular emphasis on foreign policy and religious history.

Louis XIV. *Mémoires for the Instruction of the Dauphin*. Translated by Paul Sonnino. New York: Free Press, 1970. Louis XIV's view of himself and his politics in the early phase of the personal reign.

Mettam, Roger. *Power and Faction in Louis XIV's France*. New York: Basil Blackwell, 1988. Of particular relevance for the author's treatment of the higher nobility's retention of power during the Sun King's reign.

Mettam, Roger, ed. *Government and Society in Louis XIV's France*. London: Macmillan, 1977. Well-edited collection of documents with informative notes.

Mousnier, Roland. *The Institutions of France Under the Absolute Monarchy, 1598–1789*. 2 vols. Translated by Brian Pearce and Arthur Goldhammer. Chicago: University of Chicago Press, 1979–1984. Encyclopedic work by an esteemed French historian; a mine of information.

———. *Peasant Uprisings in Seventeenth-Century France, Russia, and China.* Translated by Brian Pearce. New York: Harper & Row, 1970. Louis XIV's government, far from being perfectly secure, experienced a number of riots and civil disturbances usually directed at tax collectors.

Ranum, Orest. *The Fronde: A French Revolution, 1648–1652.* New York: W. W. Norton, 1993. A good guide to the complexities of mid-seventeenth-century French politics and war.

Rowen, Herbert. "The Peace of Nijmegen: DeWitt's Revenge." In *The Peace of Nijmegen 1676–1978/79: International Congress of the Tricentennial, Nijmegen 14–16 September 1978.* Edited by J. H. Bots. Amsterdam: Holland Universiteits Press, 1980. An authority on French and Dutch history deflates Louis XIV's pretensions to success in the Dutch War.

Rule, John C. "Louis XIV, Roi-Bureaucrate." In *Louis XIV and the Craft of Kingship*, pp. 3–101. Edited by John C. Rule. Columbus: Ohio State University Press, 1969. Useful as a general account of administration during Louis' reign.

Sonnino, Paul. "The Origins of Louis XIV's Wars." In *The Origins of War in Early Modern Europe*, pp. 112–131. Edited by Jeremy Black. Edinburgh: John Donald Publishers, 1987. This informative chapter on Louis' diplomacy notes the king's inability "to leave well enough alone."

Symcox, Geoffrey. "Louis XIV and the Outbreak of the Nine Years War." In *Louis XIV and Europe*, pp. 179–212. Edited by Ragnhild Hatton. Columbus: Ohio State University Press, 1976. This essay does much to clarify a subject not easily clarified—diplomacy and war in the 1680s.

Trout, Andrew. *Jean-Baptiste Colbert.* Boston, MA: Twayne/G. K. Hall, 1978. Introductory account of the great minister's career.

Wolf, John B. *Louis XIV.* New York: W. W. Norton, 1968. This remains a standard biography.

In 1644 the Qing dynasty succeeded the Ming dynasty on Beijing's famous Dragon throne, symbolic of rule over China. (Reproduced from the Collections of the Library of Congress)

6

The Manchu Conquest, 1644

INTRODUCTION

At the start of the seventeenth century, the Ming dynasty that had ruled China since 1368 appeared secure on the throne. Arguably, Ming China was the wealthiest, most populous, most powerful, and most sophisticated state on earth. The Mings reigned over approximately 120 million people, and their empire encompassed most of present-day China. The Mings ruled through a well-developed professional bureaucracy that featured a large cadre of intelligent, highly educated officials operating within a well-defined chain of command not unlike that of a modern state or multinational corporation. Moreover, a huge body of statutory law covered every conceivable variation in Chinese life. Taken together, the bureaucracy, the legal code, and the longevity of the Ming reign gave China great stability.

Economic life in late Ming China also flourished. Towns and cities prospered, thanks to bustling commercial and administrative activity. In the teeming countryside, millions of peasants enjoyed a measure of prosperity, although the extent and degree of this prosperity varied from region to region and even from farmstead to farmstead.

Finally, Chinese cultural life was rich and vibrant. Chinese culture, based on a Confucian foundation dating back 2,000 years, was admired and emulated throughout the Orient. At the beginning of the seventeenth century, Chinese literature experienced a period of noteworthy productivity, as did Chinese painting, drama, and handicrafts such as porcelain production and silk weaving. The literacy rate—at least among the well-to-do—was also high owing to education's traditionally revered position and movable type that facilitated the availability of the printed word.

However, despite this bright picture, the Ming dynasty faced a growing number of serious problems that it failed to solve. In terms of leadership, the Ming dynasty began to show signs of exhaustion. This became evident during the long reign of Emperor Wanli. With the death in 1582 of Zhang Juzheng, Wanli's chief adviser, the young emperor turned inward and spent the remainder of his life in virtual seclusion behind the walls of Beijing's Forbidden City. With the emperor effectively ignoring his duties, governance of the realm fell to the eunuchs, the castrated male servants who oversaw day-to-day life in the royal palace.

Although supposedly chosen for their loyalty and ability, the eunuchs ill-served their master. They were corrupt and decadent and wasted the empire's resources through incessant competition with the empire's bureaucrats for power and wealth. Under their influence, the empire's affairs fell into disrepair. The most notorious of the eunuchs, Wei Zhongxian, controlled court life after the death of Wanli in 1620. Wei squandered tax receipts and raised taxes to cover the ensuing deficit. He further aggravated Chinese society and depleted the treasury when he ordered the construction of temples in his honor.

The weakness in Ming leadership and the scandalous behavior of the eunuchs provoked a reaction among some scholars and administrators who gathered together to reflect on China's problems. The most important of these groups was the Donglin Society that met in the city of Wuxi. The Donglin supporters and their friends urged reform and renewal, a suggestion that brought them into conflict with the dominant eunuchs. In the years immediately after Wanli's death, it appeared as though the reformers would carry the day. However, Wei and the eunuchs successfully resisted the reformers, many of whom were executed between 1625 and 1627. Although the arrival of a new emperor, Chongzhen, in 1628 resulted in the death of Wei, the back of the reform movement had been broken, and the Ming dynasty continued to drift toward its ultimate demise.

Economic and financial difficulties aggravated the breakdown of effective leadership. The dynasty spent money indiscriminately on such things as the construction of sumptuous imperial tombs and maintenance of the large but essentially useless imperial family. The eunuchs' greed and the costs of warding off external threats also drained the treasury. The resulting deficits led to a significant tax increase for the peasantry and a series of revenue-raising measures that harmed trade and commerce. The influx of silver that accompanied the arrival of European traders who, indirectly, had access to the fabulously rich silver mines then being exploited in the New World also harmed the country's finances. As was the case in Europe, an abundance of silver in China led to disruptive inflationary pressures.

Economic difficulties paralleled financial ones. Millions of Chinese peasants had always lived on the edge of survival; even very small changes in the country's production and consumption patterns could push them into not only hopeless despair but also outright rebellion against their fate. Thus, the increase in taxes on the peasants, something that the Ming decreed seven times between 1618 and 1639, virtually guaranteed rural unrest. Moreover, the Ming abandoned almost all public works projects, thereby depriving China's poor of desperately needed employment opportunities. In the cities, poor job prospects, declining wages, and high taxes spurred discontent. Early in the seventeenth century miners, weavers, and porcelain makers went on strike, rioted, lynched local officials, and generally made known their unhappiness with prevailing economic conditions.

The Mings also faced external pressures that weakened the dynasty. In 1592 a resurgent Japan invaded Korea, a Chinese vassal state. China came to Korea's aid and at great expense helped to push the Japanese out in 1598. While militarily successful, the Korean operation drained China. There were additional problems in the north and northeast with the Mongols, who frequently breached the Great Wall, and in the South China Sea with increasingly bothersome bands of pirates who raided the coast. Finally, Europeans began to arrive in some numbers, presenting at least a potential threat to Ming stability.

A series of internal disturbances and rebellions gave to the Manchus, a foreign people, the opportunity to topple the Ming dynasty. Throughout the first decades of the seventeenth century, anarchy took root in some of the empire's more remote districts. Incidents of lawlessness, revolt, and banditry spread steadily as economic and financial conditions deteriorated and weak leadership created a power vacuum. The largely mercenary Ming army failed to restore order. By the middle of the 1630s, two rival rebel leaders had consolidated their power and led imposing bands of insurgents. One was Li Zicheng, whose forces eventually dominated the provinces of Shaanxi, Henan, and Hubei and who proclaimed himself head of a new kingdom called Dashun, or "the Region of Grand Obedience." Li's main rival, with whom he alternately cooperated and feuded, was Zhang Xianzhong, who controlled much of prosperous Sichuan province.

Unable to suppress either Li or Zhang, the Mings also faced a growing threat in the extreme northeast of the country. There a tribal people called the Jurchen predominated. During the twelfth and thirteenth centuries, the Jurchen had established their own dynasty called the Jin, which included much of northern China. However, the Mongols had destroyed their empire, and in the sixteenth century, the Jurchen were vassal peoples of the Ming dynasty.

At the beginning of the seventeenth century, Nurhaci, a powerful Jurchen nobleman, began to unite and organize his people. Ironically, he was aided in this course by the Mings, who used Nurhaci's embryonic Jurchen army to help defeat the Japanese in Korea and rewarded him with the title "Dragon-Tiger General." He was also aided by a number of ethnic Chinese who either defected or surrendered and were treated with honor and respect. Like many Jurchen, Nurhaci had been widely exposed to Chinese culture and the Chinese administrative system. He is perhaps best known for creating the "banner system," a form of military organization that grouped his warriors into units distinguished by colored banners. Virtually all those living under Nurhaci found themselves enrolled in a banner. The banner served civil and administrative purposes as well as a military one.

Slowly but surely, Nurhaci nibbled away at the Ming presence in the northeast. He also swept up the Mongols who were numerous in the region and who acknowledged his leadership. In 1616 he declared himself the khan, or ruler, of a new Jurchen dynasty called the *Chin*, later changed to *Qing*, which means "pure" or "clear." Later, also, the designation *Jurchen* was dropped in favor of *Manchu*. From 1616 until his death in 1626, Nurhaci challenged the Ming presence, winning a number of battles and seizing the important city of Mukden, which he then made his capital. At Mukden the Manchus established their own administration modeled after that of Ming China.

Nurhaci's successor, Hongtaiji (sometimes known as Abahai), continued his policies. The Qing brought Korea under their control, and their raiding parties breached the Great Wall. One group of Qing raiders even penetrated as far as Beijing, which it looted. During this period, the Ming system once again served as the model as the Qing refined their administrative practices. Hongtaiji was careful to appoint Chinese and Mongols as well as Manchus to high administrative posts, thereby blurring ethnic lines. The Manchu successes stood in stark contrast to the Ming failures and convinced many ethnic Chinese—but especially military figures—to join the Manchu cause. When Hongtaiji declared himself emperor in 1636, the threat to the Ming dynasty intensified, and by the time of Hongtaiji's death in 1643, the Manchus held virtually all of Manchuria and the province of Heilongjiang. Hongtaiji's brother Dorgon and his cousin Jirgalang now directed Manchu fortunes as regents for the late emperor's five-year-old son.

The final Manchu victory over the Mings owes much to the rebel Li Zicheng. In April 1644 Li led his forces into Beijing. The Ming garrison fled, and the last Ming emperor hanged himself. At this very time, Wu Sangui, one of the few remaining competent Ming generals, was defending the strategic pass at Shanhaikuan against a possible Manchu drive on Beijing. When news of Li's advance reached him, Wu abandoned his position in order to return to Beijing to defend the emperor. Beijing fell before Wu could arrive, and with no resistance before them, the Manchu armies streamed through Shanhaikuan Pass. Wu now faced a difficult choice: He and his army could either side with Li or join the invading Manchus. Despising Li, Wu chose the Manchus. On June 6, 1644, the combined forces of the Manchus and General Wu entered the capital. Li fled, and the Manchu boy ruler was now crowned as Emperor Shunzhi.

All that remained to make the Manchu triumph complete was the elimination of the leading Chinese rebels and the dispersion of forces that remained loyal to the Ming dynasty. The rebels were pursued relentlessly. Li died in the summer of 1645, and Manchu forces killed the other rebel chieftain, Zhang, in January 1647. Subduing the remnants of the Ming dynasty took a bit longer, especially in southern China, which had been a Ming stronghold. At various times several Ming princes claimed the throne; however, the Manchus methodically hunted them down and eliminated them. The last Ming claimants to power were captured by General Wu in 1661 and executed the following year. The Qing dynasty, which was to last until 1911, now ruled China.

INTERPRETIVE ESSAY
Yu Shen

The Qing dynasty was formally established in Beijing in 1644, having driven out the rebels who had occupied the capital and attempted to set up a new dynasty to replace the Ming (1368–1644). The Qing was one of the two non-Chinese dynasties (the Yuan, 1279–1368, was the other) that successfully governed the whole of China for an extended period of time. Under the Manchus, who had developed on the fringe of Chinese culture in the country's northeast, the Qing dynasty spanned more than two and a half centuries; yet it did little to change with the tide of history. No wonder the Qing Empire was to be the last imperial power in China's long process of dynastic transition. When the last Qing emperor fled Beijing's imperial palace in 1911, the long history of imperial China went with him. A republic was established in its place, marking the beginning of a new era in China.

What permeates the study of the Qing dynasty is the "alien" origin of the Qing rulers. *Manchu*, the name given to these people, described a nomadic tribal folk on China's northeastern frontier. How did this non-Chinese minority reign over China, or rather, how did these "barbarians" rule the "civilized" Chinese? What did they contribute to Chinese civilization, and what accounted for their failure to modernize in the face of the Western challenge in the nineteenth century? Ironically, the Qing has been described as the most successful dynasty of conquest in Chinese history, even though most people remember it as a corrupt and weak regime powerless to resist nineteenth-century Western intrusions. Frederic Wakeman, a well-known historian, said of the Qing: "The Qing period saw both the zenith and the nadir of the traditional Chinese state." During the seventeenth century, the early Qing intensified their drive for national unification and expansion, culminating in the establishment of a Manchu dynasty that would preside over China between 1644 and 1911. This was the "zenith" part of the story. However, the success of the early Qing may have contained the seeds for its later collapse.

Scholars argue over the key to the Qing's success. Did the dynasty flourish because of its adaptation of Chinese ways, or did it prosper because of its ability to maintain its ethnic identification and to exploit its non-Chinese roots? On the surface, there appears a dichotomy between the two assessments—between becoming Chinese and remaining Manchu. At a deeper level, the dichotomy turns into a complicated history that combined both ethnic assimilation and cultural preservation. A main characteristic of the Manchu experience in China was its ever-existing deep-rooted ambiguity over the treatment of the Han Chinese and the Chinese position in the Manchu system. In their early contact with the Chinese, the Manchus quickly realized that the Chinese could improve the Manchu way of life because of their knowledge of and skill in agricultural production, manufacturing, and trade. Consequently, the invading Manchu aristocrats captured and enslaved many Chinese who helped their captors to develop a more efficient and profitable economic system.

But the value of the Chinese was not limited to material progress only. For those Manchus who hoped to conquer China, the Chinese offered an opportunity to learn and to prepare for the day when the Manchu minority would sit on the dragon throne in Beijing's imperial palace. To reach that goal, the Manchu empire builders consciously appeased the Chinese and enlisted their support. Manchu military leaders often re-tained Chinese advisers who rendered valuable services. However, this approach to state building provoked strenuous opposition that resulted in serious compromise. Manchu leaders were deeply divided on the ul-timate goal of ruling over all China. Many did not see a future in that direction for their people who were accustomed to a life on horseback. They wanted to continue the Manchu way of life and to blunt Chinese influence. They lost ground once a unified Manchu state was established, which put the Manchus on an irreversible course leading to the conquest of China. Still, the debate over the role of the Chinese in Manchu life continued. During the dynasty's long reign in China, the Manchus, as minority rulers, struggled to reach a balance between adopting Chinese social and political systems and maintaining Manchu cultural traditions and between sharing power with the Chinese and preserving their own authority. This, in essence, is the core of the Qing experience in China.

The Qing dynasty was a success: it nearly doubled the size of the Ming Empire, thereby creating the largest empire in China's imperial history; it more than doubled China's population, thanks to long stretches of peace and prosperity; and it successfully brought together the Manchus, Mongols, and Chinese in a multiethnic society. The eighteenth-century Manchu emperors elevated China to a high point of traditional Chinese civilization. These Qing accomplishments owed a great deal to its martial supremacy and to its ability to adopt the cultural and political systems of the conquered. At the same time, the Manchus failed to resolve the tension between these two elements—tradition and sinicization.

The Manchu success story began with Nurhaci (1559–1626), a warrior born into a family whose members had been in service to the Ming. The Ming dynasty had always paid a great deal of attention to its northern frontier, having gained its power from the Mongols who had originated from and fled back to the north. Over time, the Ming policy of main-taining a large defense force on the frontier resulted in its frontiersmen merging with the local population, the Manchus. Those Chinese who adopted Manchu customs and even names lost their Chinese identity. Even though the majority of Chinese living with the Manchus resisted assimilation, its presence and participation in industry and commerce in Manchuria enriched and empowered the Manchus. Chinese and Manchus interacted; Chinese ways combined with the Manchu fighting strength to contribute to the rise of Manchu power.

The Ming dynasty closely watched this worrisome development on its frontier. In order to prevent any single Manchu tribe from gaining supremacy, it stimulated tribal competition and conflict. It relied on a variety of approaches, ranging from direct military intervention to bestowing Ming titles upon tribal leaders. During one such intervention, Chinese troops killed—probably by mistake—Nurhaci's father and grandfather. The young warrior vowed revenge, and he targeted the tribal leader who had aided the Chinese military operation. He mobilized his family and tribe, conquered and absorbed other tribes in his region, and in 1586 killed the rival tribal leader. It was the first step in building his hegemony. During the next twenty years he brought Manchuria under his control, uniting the major tribes and rising to the position of indisputable Manchu leader.

In 1601 Nurhaci devised a new system to organize his people and consolidate his power. Based on the Mongol model, Nurhaci instituted the banner system. Originally he established four banners; by 1615 there were eight. According to the system, every 300 warriors/farmers were to form a company; every five companies constituted a battalion; and every five battalions came under one banner. Each banner was identified by a colored flag and was under the command of a chieftain. Three banners were directly under Nurhaci's personal command; the rest were under his sons' and a nephew's. Banner leaders were the highest military commanders under Nurhaci. However, the banners were not merely a military organization; they functioned as administrative units as well. Registration, taxation, and other civil matters were conducted under the banners. The banners were thus a civil-military as well as political organization, which effectively enrolled and unified the Manchus from different tribes. The banner system also absorbed non-Manchus, an advancement from the old tribal relations based on blood or marriage. The transition from tribal to bureaucratic organization was thus under way for the Manchu state.

Driven by his imperial ambitions, Nurhaci continued to build the Manchu state. He reshaped clan government into a new administrative institution where five imperial clan leaders formed a state council. This state council met every five days to discuss state affairs. Together with the banner officers, the members of the council formed the state's power center. Nurhaci himself made all final decisions.

Other developments toward state building included the creation of a writing system, using Mongolian alphabets aided by dots and circles to denote Manchu pronunciations. This creation met the administrative needs of the state and enabled the Manchus to record their history in writing. With this development, translations of Chinese works—Confucian classics as well as Ming regulations and law codes—flowed into Manchu society.

Nurhaci's expansion of power in Manchuria in the early seventeenth century brought him into direct confrontation with the Ming. In fighting against Ming forces, the Manchu commander relied on his banner troops for military conquest. At the same time, he tried to win over the Chinese without a fight. He would send messages to Chinese commanders assuring them that in their inevitable defeat the cities they were trying to defend would face ruthless massacres and total destruction. However, if they chose to surrender without fighting, the Manchu commander would guarantee not only their lives but also their Chinese customs. The city would be spared a bloodbath. Furthermore, Nurhaci held out the possibility of promotion to a higher position for those who would cooperate.

This approach suggested that the Manchu leader did not believe in converting the Chinese to the Manchu way of life and intended to treat the Chinese who would heed his advice as equals. At the same time, it also implied that Nurhaci could be very tough with those who resisted his power. On two occasions in the 1620s, Chinese living under Nurhaci rebelled. The Manchu leader put down the rebellions and executed many educated Chinese whom he suspected of having instigated the uprisings. He then instituted stricter separation of Chinese and Manchus. While realizing the importance of the Chinese for his imperial ambitions, he did not fully trust people who might turn against him if given the opportunity. He therefore alternatively applied policies of equal treatment and racial discrimination toward the Chinese. Compared with later Qing rulers, Nurhaci's policy toward Chinese proved to be harsh.

Like Chinggis Khan, Nurhaci failed to achieve his goal of conquering China in his lifetime. One of his sons, Hongtaiji (r. 1626–1643), succeeded him and quickened the pace of conquest. Hongtaiji was a banner leader and had sat on the state council; his succession represented continuity. However, he went further than his father in adopting Chinese institutions and relying on Chinese adherents.

The Manchu advance toward Beijing coincided with the Ming dynasty's internal decline. A "general crisis" weakened the once glorious Ming civilization. An incompetent emperor, political collapse (as indicated by the fierce struggle between the Donglin Academy literati and the court eunuchs), and natural disasters such as climatic cooling that decreased agricultural yields undermined the Ming. The final blow was an anti-Ming rebellion led by the Chinese rebel Li Zicheng. While Li and his forces were strong enough to overpower the Ming, they lacked the strength to establish their own state. The Manchus took advantage of the chaos and, with the help of a Chinese general, drove out the rebels and founded their reign in China.

Before entering Beijing, Hongtaiji's Manchu Empire had already developed a state structure modeled after the Chinese example. The Manchus named their state *Qing*, meaning "pure." In the course of consolidating his power, strengthening the Manchu state, and preparing for the conquest of China, Hongtaiji took a more conciliatory approach toward the Chinese in exchange for their support. He gave the Chinese more protection and opportunity in the Manchu system than Nurhaci had, and he improved the social status of the Chinese and treated them as equal (though separate) members of society. He included former Ming officials and Chinese literati in his government and added Han banners to the Manchu military system. He admired Chinese civilization and ordered his officials to register their sons for study so that future generations would better understand Chinese ways. One of his sons, later to become Emperor Shunzhi (r. 1644–1661), traced his partiality to Chinese culture to this early exposure.

The Manchu seizure of the throne was not the final phase of the conquest; the new rulers had to consolidate their authority. Immediately the new Beijing government restored order to the capital, thereby presenting a good image of the new state to Chinese elsewhere. By choosing Beijing as their imperial residence, the Manchus validated themselves as the heir to the Ming and demonstrated that they would continue the Ming rule. To legitimize their succeeding the Ming, they claimed to have come to rescue the Chinese from the miserable and illegitimate rule of the anti-Ming rebels. To win Chinese allegiance, they conducted an imperial burial of the last Ming emperor, observing the Confucian rituals and procedures. To prevent discontent and resistance, they assured former Ming officials of their safety and of their positions in the new government. The new rulers even allowed the former Ming officials to continue to wear the Ming-style official attires. There would be no disruption in the lives of scholars who had devoted themselves to Confucian classics and government service. The new government followed the long-established Chinese tradition of giving civil service examinations and recruiting bureaucrats from among the successful candidates. To pacify landlord-gentry families, the Qing dynasty soon abandoned its initial policy of redistributing land among its own people. The Qing's policy of "soothing" rather than harsh extermination aimed at securing the allegiance of the northern Chinese and setting a good example for Chinese elsewhere. It effectively persuaded most local officials in the north to accept the new dynasty. But winning the south would take a much longer time, and the Beijing government had to use its military might to wipe out the resistance. Its comparatively easy conquest of the north provided it with Chinese officials who contributed tremendously to the pacification of the south.

As in the earlier conquest, the Manchus relied on both brute force and appeasement. The Yangzhou massacre in 1645 illustrated the Qing dynasty's determination to destroy Chinese resistance. After that city's defense collapsed and its top Ming commanders died, Manchu troops inflicted severe punishment on Yangzhou's survivors. At first, the Qing soldiers simply looted the homes of the wealthy, then systematic executions followed. When people in hiding responded to a proclamation promising life, they were herded in chains and massacred. Fires spread, and those who tried to hide in their homes were burned, or when they staggered out, they were killed. Women were raped and mutilated. No one was spared. The slaughter went on for days, with an estimated 800,000 victims.

Advancing into the south, the Qing troops massacred thousands, thus crushing any resistance and showing the new dynasty's resolve to rule the whole empire. But the Manchus knew that they needed to win over the Chinese. Killing would not gain support for the Manchu rule. Days after the Yangzhou massacre, an imperial edict was promulgated that denounced the "crimes" of those who did not submit to Qing rule immediately and justified the butchery. However, the same edict—in the name of the "Mandate of Heaven"—granted amnesty and promoted those civil and military officials who ceased resistance. With the north mostly pacified and the new government firmly established, it did not take long for the resolute new rulers to persuade most southern elites to surrender.

The early Qing dynasty steadily consolidated its rule, although it was not until the 1680s that it finally brought all China under its control. Taiwan, the large island off the southeastern coast, was the last bastion of resistance. Under the Ming, Taiwan was not officially part of China although it enjoyed close ties with the mainland through trade. The Dutch East India Company had a strong presence on the island between 1624 and 1662. In the 1640s and 1650s, the island attracted many Ming loyalists. In 1662 the last surviving force of anti-Qing resistance established its base in Taiwan. During the next two decades, Zheng Chengong (also known as Koxinga) and his successors expelled the Dutch, ignored the Qings, and created a community with over 100,000 Chinese emigrants. Up until the early 1680s, the Chinese on Taiwan refused to recognize Qing authority. Finally the Qing emperor sent a naval expedition to Taiwan that subjugated the island. Within a century, the Qing Empire had grown from an unorganized nomadic tribal structure to a centralized power that controlled an expanded China.

After 1644, two major tasks confronted the Manchus: consolidating their power and tightening their grip on China. Under two capable emperors, Shunzhi (r. 1644–1661) and Kangxi (r. 1661–1722), the Manchus achieved these goals by the end of the century.

The Manchus are said to be good inheritors, and they were. Because their culture lacked an ideology and system of government, and because they were surrounded by Han Chinese, the Manchus had to rely on the Chinese and to adopt Chinese institutions. Both Shunzhi and Kangxi realized the need to sinicize their people in order to stay in power despite opposition from those who were deeply committed to sustaining Manchu supremacy over the Chinese. In the years between the death of Shunzhi and the personal rule of Kangxi (who was only seven when the emperor died and did not rule in person until he was thirteen), regents who disliked Shunzhi's sinicization policies held sway. Shunzhi's success in rapidly adopting Chinese institutions alarmed them, and they found it particularly disturbing that he had entrusted significant administrative responsibility to Chinese instead of Manchus. With a concerted effort, they revived a few Manchu institutions and appointed Manchu officials. For example, they replaced the Grand Secretariat—a Ming institution that allowed the grand secretaries to advise and assist the emperor in governing the country—with a Manchu organization called the Three

Inner Courts. Outnumbered by the Chinese in the Grand Secretariat, Manchu appointees occupied six out of nine positions in the Three Inner Courts.

From Nurhaci to Kangxi, in a span of less than a century, Manchu leaders steadily moved away from clan rule based on collective leadership to imperial rule with power centralized in the hands of emperors. Nurhaci's successor, Hongtaiji, set the process in motion. After a decade of repeatedly stripping power from the Manchu nobility who were part of the collective leadership, he enlarged his own power and increased the bureaucracy. At his death, the Manchu princes' political power had been greatly reduced, and a Ming-style bureaucracy was taking shape.

From the beginning of Qing rule in China, the emperor sought greater authority over state affairs. Both Shunzhi and Kangxi worked long and hard at the art of governing. Aided by confidants beyond the bureaucracy, they gathered for themselves decision-making authority. On the one hand, this reflected the Manchu's determination to control the inherited administration; on the other hand, it indicated its willingness to sinicize.

The Manchu emperors set up their government in a dyarchical balance, with equal numbers of Chinese and Manchu officials holding office. For example, each of the six ministries that handled government business at the capital was headed by a Chinese and a Manchu. At the provincial level, typically the governor was Chinese, whereas his supervisor, the governor-general, who usually administered more than one province, was a Manchu. At the local level, almost all the county magistrates were Chinese. Following the established Chinese tradition, recruitment of Chinese bureaucrats occurred through civil service examinations that were not much changed from the Ming era. The Qing emperor was present at the palace examination—the highest level after the local and provincial ones—rewarding a small number of the most diligent and loyal scholars with the highest title.

The Manchus thus inherited the political structure without making any fundamental change. This arrangement allowed the Manchus to retain large numbers of former Ming officials and continue to recruit more Chinese, while the Qing court relied on the large staff that served the Manchu Empire before it conquered China to control the higher levels of the bureaucracy. The Manchus added this distinctive feature to the government—multiplication of layers and structures. But this layered hierarchy was not meant to create two separate structures within the government. Qing rulers had decided early on that Manchu nobles and bannermen would not be placed over and above their Chinese allies. Rather, they preferred to merge their control with a bureaucracy styled after and run by the Chinese.

Kangxi, in his sixty years on the throne, made lasting contributions to the Qing Empire and left an enduring mark on Chinese culture. He retained Manchu martial spirit; but at the same time, he also acquired a high degree of Chinese learning. Being a warrior himself, the young emperor led effective military campaigns to crush anti-Qing resistance. He enjoyed riding and hunting, and he cherished Manchu customs. Fearful that Chinese civilization might overtake Manchu tradition, he closed off part of Manchuria to the Chinese to preserve that land for the Manchus. There they could revitalize their warrior spirit and relax in a familiar environment. For a long time the Manchus controlled the military, with all banner commanders being Manchus. Kangxi was not only a very capable Manchu military and political leader; he also received high marks from Chinese intellectuals for his achievement in Chinese scholarship. He was well versed in the Confucianist classics and actively sponsored intellectual endeavors. Important works were produced with his support, some of which he prefaced such as the famous *Kangxi Dictionary* and a massive, multivolume *Synthesis of Books and Illustrations of Ancient and Modern Times*.

Kangxi's intellectual interests also drew him to Western science, brought to China by Jesuit missionaries who arrived during the late Ming period and remained at the Qing court. The Jesuits were good astronomers, and after Kangxi was convinced of their more accurate way of making calendars, he appointed a Jesuit director of the Imperial Board of Astronomy, a post occupied by Jesuits into the nineteenth century. Kangxi admired their scientific knowledge, and in 1692 he issued an edict relaxing restrictions on the Jesuits and allowed them to reside in Beijing, where he maintained personal contact with them.

Entering Beijing amid chaos, the Manchus appealed to the Chinese desire for a unified and strong empire. They advertised their rule as a restoration of order and strength. To gain support for their claims to the Mandate of Heaven, Manchu leaders had to prove their government morally superior to that of the late Ming. Both the Manchus and the Chinese agreed that one of the Ming evils had been the empowerment of eunuchs in the court and the government. Confucian scholars despised the eunuchs, although eunuch power in imperial China reached its zenith under the Ming. There were thousands of eunuchs, and they became a separate administrative echelon. Although eunuchs were not official members of the bureaucracy, they moved themselves to the center of power through their loyal and intimate service to the emperor's personal needs. They inserted themselves between the emperor and the bureaucracy, becoming the emperor's eyes and ears. They kept secret files on officials, accessible only to the emperor. Their close interaction with the emperor jeopardized the bureaucracy's rule. The Manchus, realizing the danger of Han eunuchs, worked to limit eunuch power at the court. By the time of Kangxi, eunuchs were under tight control. The Qing dynasty's ultimate solution to this persistent problem that had demoralized so many Chinese courts was the creation of an Imperial Household Department, staffed mostly by bondservants, to take charge of the emperor's daily life. These bondservants were of Han origin, but they had been incorporated into the Manchu households before the Manchu conquest of China. The new department effectively dealt with the eunuch threat for a long time.

Because of their non-Han origin, Qing emperors took a greater interest in minority affairs and policies than their Han predecessors. In the agency that dealt with Inner Asian matters, the staff was exclusively composed of Mongols and Manchus. The Qing worked to integrate all the conquered minority peoples into the polity they had adopted. By expanding Chinese territory to include twice as much as that under the Ming, the Qing succeeded in creating a multiethnic empire. This helped to reinforce China's confidence in its ability to absorb alien cultures. However, the resultant complacency proved to be a mixed legacy for the future.

The Manchus also needed a strong tax system to support the empire's stability. An ineffective and unfair tax system had hastened the collapse of the Ming dynasty. However, the Qing dynasty found itself in a dilemma. On one hand, it committed itself to maintaining the Chinese social structure, thereby gaining the gentry support that it considered vital for the new empire. On the other hand, it knew that the gentry had the ability to pay more taxes and that tax evasion by the wealthy had led to government deficits. Initially the new dynasty extended tax exemptions to the gentry, but as the Qing took root in Beijing, it began to target the gentry who abused the exemption system. It prosecuted thousands of gentrymen, many of whom were jailed, beaten, and humiliated. Their will crushed, the Chinese gentry left jail more willing to cooperate with the government in its effort to reform the tax system. The new system was called "equal fields, equal labor services," and for many years it provided the Qing dynasty with a treasury surplus.

The Qing dynasty, for all its accomplishments—expanding China to include Taiwan and Inner Asia, perfecting China's bureaucratic system, maintaining peace and prosperity for much of the dynastic reign, and stimulating the development of art and literature—was blamed for China's later collapse in the face of Western challenges in the nineteenth century. Drawing a lesson from the fall of the Ming and always guarding its authority, the Qing, a minority ruling over a growing multiethnic population with an absolute majority of Han Chinese who outnumbered the Manchus many times over, discouraged any innovations in either government or society. For example, law remained modeled on the Ming codes, and rigid control continued to characterize social expectations for women. Under the Qing rule, more widows than before refused to re-marry, and for this display of social conformity their communities erected memorial arches as an honor for, and a public endorsement of, their loyal submission.

It is in this context that the Qing dynasty failed. It spent a great deal of its energy and resources on keeping traditional order and, with the assistance of the Chinese, the power of the central government was re-inforced. Because its rule was so effective, it could resist early blows from the West; but this delayed any meaningful reform for a long time. Once the dynasty could no longer maintain its traditional ways, it went down quickly and sank to the bottom.

SELECTED BIBLIOGRAPHY

Cao Xueqin. Honglou Meng, *The Story of the Stone (Dream of the Red Chamber)*. 5 vols. Translated by David Hawkes and John Minford. Harmondsworth, U.K.: Penguin, 1973–1982. China's greatest novel describes the decline of Qing society.

Chang, Chun-shu, and Shelley Hsueh-lun Chang. *Crisis and Transformation in Seventeenth-Century China: Society, Culture, and Modernity in Li Yu's World*. Ann Arbor: University of Michigan Press, 1991. A famous contemporary man of letters explores various aspects—state, society, economy, and cul-ture—of the Ming-Qing transition.

Ch'u T'ung-tsu. *Local Government in China Under the Ch'ing*. Cambridge, MA: Harvard University Press, 1962. The most comprehensive analysis of the Qing government at local levels.

Esherick, Joseph W., and Mary Backus Rankin, eds. *Chinese Local Elites and Pat-terns of Dominance*. Berkeley: University of California Press, 1990. This col-lection of essays examines elites in Ming, Qing, and Republican China, and challenges the common image of a uniform national gentry class.

Harrell, Stevan, ed. *Cultural Encounters on China's Ethnic Frontiers*. Seattle: University of Washington Press, 1995. Explores the effects of the "civilizing project" on the peripheral peoples; in the case of the Manchus, the conquerors of China and emperors of the Qing absorbed much Chinese culture while struggling to maintain their Manchu origins.

Huang, Liu-Hung. *A Complete Book Concerning Happiness and Benevolence: A Manual for Local Magistrates in Seventeenth-Century China.* Translated by Djiang Chu. Tuscon: University of Arizona Press, 1984. Offers a unique insight into the job of a magistrate under Qing rule.

Johnson, David, Andrew J. Nathan, and Evelyn S. Rawski. *Popular Culture in Late Imperial China.* Berkeley: University of California Press, 1985. This volume probes the interaction of official culture and popular culture, and examines the development of mass culture during the Qing era.

Kessler, Lawrence D. *K'ang-Hsi and the Consolidation of Ch'ing Rule, 1661–1684.* Chicago: University of Chicago Press, 1976. Studies Kangxi and his successful effort to consolidate the empire in China.

Leonard, Jane Kate, and John R. Watt, eds. *To Achieve Wealth and Security: The Qing Imperial State and the Economy, 1644–1911.* Ithaca, NY: Cornell University East Asia Program, 1993. A collection of eight articles describing the Qing's economic policies and practices.

Rigger, Shelley. "Voices of Manchu Identity, 1635–1935." In *Cultural Encounters on China's Ethnic Frontiers,* pp. 186–214. Edited by Stevan Harrell. Seattle: University of Washington Press, 1995. Repudiating the image of a consistent and unitary identity shared by all Manchus, Rigger presents various voices, including those of Hongtaiji, the Qianlong emperor, the frontier men, and even the Han, in construing their separate identities.

Spence, Jonathan. *The Death of Woman Wang.* New York: Viking, 1978. With "Woman Wang" as the most interesting portrait among others in the collection, Spence's social history describes the life of a Shandong village between 1668 and 1672.

———. *Emperor of China: Self-Portrait of Kangxi.* New York: Alfred A. Knopf, 1974. A self-portrait based on the public and private writings of the Kangxi emperor that offers insight into his reign.

———. *Ts'ao Yin and the K'ang-hsi Emperor: Bondservant and Master.* New Haven, CT: Yale University Press, 1966. The personal and political relationship between the Manchu emperor and his Han servant who became a government official.

Spence, Jonathan, and John E. Wills, Jr., eds. *From Ming to Ch'ing: Conquest, Region, and Continuity in Seventeenth-Century China.* New Haven, CT: Yale University Press, 1979. While focusing on the fall of Ming, this book shows the ramifications—military, institutional, economic, intellectual, and political—of the seventeenth-century transition.

Struve, Lynn A., ed. *Voices from the Ming-Qing Cataclysm: China in Tigers' Jaws.* New Haven, CT: Yale University Press, 1993. Eyewitnesses from the Ming-Qing transition tell their stories.

Taisuke, Mitamura. *Chinese Eunuchs: The Structure of Intimate Politics.* Translated by Charles Pomery. Rutland, VT: Tuttle, 1970. Although written for a general audience, this anecdote-filled volume places eunuchs in a political environment and explains why they could take advantage of their position.

Wakeman, Frederic, Jr. "China and the Seventeenth-Century Crisis." *Late Imperial China* 7 (1986): 1–23. Focuses on the Ming dynasty's economic decline and social disintegration.

———. *The Fall of Imperial China.* New York: Free Press, 1975. An excellent introduction to the Qing period.

———. *The Great Enterprise: The Manchu Reconstruction of Imperial Order in Seventeenth Century China.* Berkeley: University of California Press, 1985. The definitive account of the "most dramatic succession in all of Chinese history" and the Qing's early experience.

Wu, Silas. *Passage to Power: K'ang-his and His Heir Apparent, 1661–1722.* Cambridge, MA: Harvard University Press, 1979. Focuses on the political struggle in Kangxi's court.

Zelin, Madeleine. *The Magistrate's Tale: Rationalizing Fiscal Reform in Eighteenth-Century Ch'ing China.* Berkeley: University of California Press, 1984. Although focusing on the eighteenth century, Zelin's work discusses a very important aspect of the early Qing dynasty's accomplishment that ensured the empire's later survival.

7

The Scientific Revolution, c. 1650

INTRODUCTION

The Scientific Revolution was hardly a revolution in the conventional sense of the word. There were no pitched battles; no crowds in the streets mounted barricades; no crowned heads rolled in the dust. Nevertheless, the Scientific Revolution changed the way the world thinks, solves problems, and goes about its business.

Although the Scientific Revolution began in the sixteenth century, it reached maturity only in the seventeenth. It was a uniquely European event, but it proved so important that it subsequently spread throughout the rest of the world. During the Middle Ages (roughly A.D. 500 to A.D. 1300), science did not figure prominently in European life. The vast majority of Europeans labored mightily to eke out a bare subsistence; the extremely small minority that had the leisure time to think often focused its energies on spiritual matters such as the meaning of God and the nature of heaven and hell.

Change came slowly, but the growth of a more stable society, exposure to the learning of the Arabs, a revived interest in secular life, and the formation of universities in western Europe by the thirteenth century laid the groundwork for the Scientific Revolution. Nevertheless, science in the late medieval world differed dramatically from modern science.

The brilliant Italian astronomer and physicist Galileo often clashed with the hierarchy of the Roman Catholic Church; nevertheless, his research significantly advanced the cause of modern science. (Reproduced from the Collections of the Library of Congress)

Although science had entered the universities as part of the discipline of philosophy, it was held in lower esteem than both the other disciplines—theology, law, and medicine—and the other branches of philosophy, where the study of logic reigned supreme and a burning question of the day was, "How many angels can dance on the head of a pin?" Furthermore, late medieval science encompassed a curious mishmash of the real and the illusory. Astronomy and astrology, chemistry and alchemy, mathematics and magic—all were accorded the same level of legitimacy.

The Renaissance helped to usher in the Scientific Revolution. Renaissance fascination with Antiquity led to the uncovering of many ancient Greek and Roman works. Unlike their counterparts in the Middle Ages, Antiquity's scholars tended to focus on the secular—the earthly here and now—rather than the spiritual, and their writings reflected this. Europeans now encountered a number of fresh and important ideas about their physical world. Especially significant were the advances in the field of mathematics, where the ancients had made great strides. Sophisticated mathematics proved to be modern science's most effective tool.

The Scientific Revolution also benefited from Europe's long-standing interest in technology and its need to solve pressing practical problems. A receptivity to technological innovation merged with a desire to find solutions to immediate issues such as making ocean voyages safer and more certain. This union resulted in the invention of instruments such as the telescope, thermometer, barometer, and microscope. Technicians rather than scientists usually invented these tools, but the latter employed these instruments to further scientific inquiry. Over the centuries a relationship grew up in which practical problems demanded new tools; the new tools or instruments aided in the advancement of scientific knowledge; and the advanced knowledge was used to solve ever more complicated practical problems.

The Scientific Revolution was the work of many men over several centuries. Not all of these pioneers fully understood what they were accomplishing, but collectively their achievements remade the world. While the Scientific Revolution touched many branches of what today is called science, activity tended to concentrate on three specific areas—anatomy, astronomy, and physics.

Medieval anatomy relied almost entirely upon the work of Galen, a second-century (A.D.) scholar. For centuries Galen's views were considered unimpeachable. However, Andreas Vesalius, a faculty member of the University of Padua in Italy, challenged this orthodoxy. Vesalius noted that some of Galen's ideas failed to conform to data gained from dissecting cadavers. In 1543 he published *The Structure of the Human Body* in which he proclaimed that the study of the human body should be based on the gathering of data through the dissection of cadavers rather than blind acceptance of any prevailing view. William Harvey, an English doctor, pushed this line of reasoning and type of methodology even further. In his 1628 book, *On the Motion of the Heart and Blood in Animals*, Harvey cited his careful collection of data through dissection to conclude that the heart is similar to a pump and that the blood circulates through arteries and veins.

In the same year that Vesalius published his groundbreaking work, a Polish cleric named Nicolaus Copernicus, who had also studied at Padua, published *On the Revolutions of the Heavenly Spheres*. As was true of anatomical studies, medieval students of astronomy relied almost exclusively on the writings of the ancients. In the case of astronomy, the fourth-century (B.C.) Greek philosopher Aristotle and the second-century (A.D.) Greek astronomer Ptolemy dominated. Both proclaimed that the earth was the center of the universe. Copernicus, however, found that his mathematical calculations concerning the planets and the stars produced results that set him at odds with the ancients. His data seemed to indicate that the sun, and not the earth, was the center of the solar system. Thus was born the modern heliocentric, or sun-centered, model of the universe.

It took some time, however, before Copernicus' conclusions were accepted. Tycho Brahe, a late sixteenth-century Danish astronomer, took an important, if unwitting, step in that direction. Working in a state-of-the-art observatory funded in large measure by the Danish king, for more than twenty years Tycho made and recorded detailed observations on the movements of the stars and planets. However, because of insufficient mathematical skills, Tycho failed to develop a set of coherent conclusions from his data. That task fell to his assistant, a mathematician named Johannes Kepler who applied his mathematical skills to Brahe's data to confirm Copernicus' heliocentric theory. Kepler also solved a problem that had troubled Copernicus and others when he used advanced mathematics to prove that the orbits of the planets around the sun were elliptical rather than circular. His subsequent laws of planetary motion loomed large in the thinking of Isaac Newton, the late seventeenth-century genius whose work seemed to explain the universe.

However, before examining Newton's contribution to the Scientific Revolution, one must consider another major figure, the Italian Galileo Galilei who lived from 1564 to 1642. Like many other important figures of the Scientific Revolution, Galileo was born into the lesser nobility. However, his mathematical ability led him in a different direction. He was particularly interested in motion, and over the course of his lifetime, he clearly demonstrated the nature of earthly motion, developing the principle of inertia along the way. He also turned his attention to the heavens. Using a new piece of technology, the telescope, Galileo quickly discovered the first four of Jupiter's moons, sun spots, and the craggy nature of our own moon. Not only did he reinforce the Copernican hypothesis, but he also seemed to prove that the sun and planets were not simply points of light but that they had substance—and in the case of our moon, a substance not unlike that of the earth itself. Furthermore, since stars remained points of light even under telescopic examination, Galileo suggested that the universe was much larger than anyone had imagined and, perhaps, might be infinite.

It fell to Isaac Newton to unite all the strands of mathematical, astronomical, and physical knowledge that the Scientific Revolution had generated to produce a comprehensive explanation of the universe. Newton, the son of a small English landowner, was born in 1642. Sent to Cambridge University for schooling, he was such a brilliant student that he remained on as professor after his graduation. His greatest work was *Mathematical Principles of Natural Philosophy*, published in 1687 and generally known as the *Principia* from its Latin title. In the *Principia*, Newton merged Kepler's ideas about planetary motion with those developed by Galileo to explain terrestrial motion, demonstrating that both sets of ideas were part of a single set of principles governing motion both on earth and in the heavens. Relying on advanced mathematics to make his point (both Newton and the German Gottfried Wilhelm Leibniz, working independently, developed calculus at about this time), Newton unveiled his law of universal gravitation. The entire universe now seemed to be a gigantic, but scientifically understandable, machine. The English poet Alexander Pope captured this sentiment when he wrote in 1730, three years after Newton's death, "Nature and nature's laws lay hid in night; God said, 'Let Newton be!' and all was light."

The Scientific Revolution gave rise to new methods of inquiry, which, in turn, further stimulated the development of science. Basically, the new methodology rejected all "given" knowledge, such as knowledge about the physical world obtained from the Bible, and substituted in its place knowledge gained from observation, experimentation, and reason. Two philosophers of science stand out. The first was the Englishman Francis Bacon, who lived from 1561 to 1626. He insisted that the only valid knowledge is that gained from inductive reasoning. In other words, in order to have a true understanding of something, one must observe and experiment ceaselessly in order to amass data from which one can draw a logical conclusion. Bacon also envisioned great practical benefits derived from knowledge obtained in this manner. His posthumously published *New Atlantis* (1627) forecast an almost utopian world in which scientists, working collaboratively, would discover the mysteries of the universe and thereby allow all humankind to achieve a large measure of progress.

The second philosopher of science was the Frenchman René Descartes, who was a great mathematician in his own right and the inventor of analytical geometry, a mathematical tool of profound importance for modern science. Like Bacon, Descartes, who was a contemporary of Bacon, Kepler, and Galileo, also rejected "given" knowledge; and like Bacon he endorsed inductive reasoning. However, Descartes found greater value in deductive reasoning, or the process of employing general principles to deduce the laws that govern science. Furthermore, Descartes employed the language of mathematics to express his ideas. To a large extent, modern science represents the fusion of Bacon's inductive method with Descartes' deductive reasoning.

The seventeenth century's Scientific Revolution did not go unnoticed. Several of its major figures, such as Galileo and Descartes, wrote in the vernacular, or language of the people, rather than Latin, the universal language of the time and the language of the specialists. Galileo, in particular, wrote clear, witty prose and adopted a polemical style that assured a broad audience for him and his ideas.

While these writings popularized the scientific method and the results that it produced, formal organizations sprang up to act as clearinghouses of scientific knowledge. The short-lived Lincean Academy of Rome (1603) and Florence's Accademia del Cimento (1657–1667) were probably the first examples of a learned society. More permanent were the Royal Society of London, established in 1660, and France's Royal Academy of Sciences, founded six years later. These learned societies conducted experiments and published results in the first scientific journals. They also kept scientists in touch with each other and abreast of the latest discoveries. The publicity that they generated helped to ensure the lasting success of the Scientific Revolution.

INTERPRETIVE ESSAY
Robert K. DeKosky

The Scientific Revolution of the sixteenth and seventeenth centuries profoundly transformed the ideas, method, and social organization of western European science. The conceptual foundations of astronomy and physics changed dramatically. Other fields of science such as chemistry, biology, and the earth sciences would await revolution until the late eighteenth and nineteenth centuries. The experimental method (defined as the imposition of artificial or controlled conditions in order to test an idea) emerged to alter the sciences of physiology and optics, usher in new sciences such as electricity and pneumatics, yet remain largely irrelevant to the sciences of astronomy, mechanics, and botany/zoology. Acceptance of the experimental method linked as well to a critical change in the Western view of the science-technology relationship. Perceived previously as independent departments of life, science and technology were increasingly regarded as affiliated, mutually supportive activities by the end of the seventeenth century. By the latter 1600s, novel forms of scientific organization in London and Paris had surpassed universities as centers of scientific communication. Moreover, the new "scientific societies" reflected national conditions of organization and financial support. In contrast, most universities continued to express a medieval concept of European rather than national identity that they signified by their predominant use of the Latin language. These developments vaulted Western science from previous mediocrity to clear superiority compared to impressive scientific traditions of Native America, China, India, and Mideastern Islamic culture. The early modern ascendancy of Western science has dramatically influenced world history ever since.

Some time between 1508 and 1510 in Poland, a cleric named Nicolaus Copernicus (1473–1543) embraced a sun-centered cosmology and system of astronomy. In the accepted system of Aristotle and the astronomer Ptolemy, the earth lay unmoving at the center of the universe, and all the stars and planets orbited the earth. Copernicus knew that the sun-centered arrangement, in which the earth rotated daily and moved about the sun once per year, had been conceived by Aristarchus, an ancient Greek astronomer, but Copernicus was the first astronomer since the ancient period to accept it despite its obvious disadvantages. For one thing, certain biblical passages literally implied that the sun moved about the earth on the daily motion. Furthermore, stars should exhibit "stellar parallax" if the earth moves about the sun (that is, appear at slightly different angles relative to each other over the course of the year), but none did. Finally, to put the earth in motion demanded rejection of Aristotle's concept of "natural places" for each of the four traditional elements: earth, water, air, and fire. Thus Aristotle's "natural motion," in which an element sought its natural place in order to achieve rest, could no longer explain the spontaneous fall and rise of heavy and light bodies.

Copernicus did not reveal to us in his writings why he accepted the new system. But he probably recognized that it accounted for relationships between planets and the sun that in the traditional earth-centered arrangement required physically implausible assumptions. The fact that Venus and Mercury always appeared around dawn or dusk—never at midnight—was demanded by the Copernican system but not by the Aristotelian-Ptolemaic arrangement. Likewise, the fact that Mars, Jupiter, and Saturn always appear "in opposition" (180 degrees) from the sun when each undergoes periodic temporary reversals of motion against the stars ("retrograde motion") was expected in the Copernican system but not in the traditional arrangement. In addition to these considerations, Copernicus also favored the sun-centered system because it allowed the determination of relative planetary distances from the central sun, thus establishing the order of the planets. The Aristotelian-Ptolemaic arrangement provided no means to calculate the planetary order strictly on the basis of observational data.

Yet Copernicus could not and did not claim that the sun-centered system was superior to the traditional system for predicting positions of any planet. Nor were the technicalities of sun-centered calculations any less complex than those of the rival arrangement. Although imbued with the Pythagorean faith that planets and stars move according to exact mathematical relationships, Copernicus came no closer to demonstrating this than had his predecessors. In the decades following publication of the Copernican system in 1543, very few people accepted it.

The most eminent astronomer of the late 1500s was the Dane Tycho Brahe (1546–1601). Traditionally underrated in popular histories of astronomy, Tycho contributed monumentally to Western astronomy in three ways. First, he accumulated very accurate data of planetary positions over several decades of dedicated observation—a necessary precondition for the discovery of exact mathematical relationships in planetary motions. Next, Tycho determined that a comet showed a smaller parallax than the moon (displayed a smaller difference in position when viewed from two remote locations at the same moment). This demonstrated that the comet was farther from the earth than was the moon. But the movement of the comet in the region of the planets meant that solid transparent spheres previously invoked as movers of planets fixed within them did not exist. By discrediting solid transparent spheres as planetary movers, Tycho threw open the question of what moves the planets. A satisfactory answer would not emerge until Isaac Newton's work of the 1680s. Finally, Tycho advocated a third system of the world that came to bear his name. This "Tychonic system" maintained the traditional ideas of an immobile earth at the center of the universe and a solar revolution about the earth. But it embodied the Copernican notion that the sun served as the orbital referent for the planets ("carrying" the planets as it moved about the earth). Indeed, this system included all of the advantages of the Copernican system but none of its disadvantages, since all disadvantages of the Copernican system stemmed from the hypothesis of the earth's motion.

The immediate beneficiary of Tycho's data was the young German astronomer Johannes Kepler (1571–1630), who was one of very few astronomers believing in the Copernican system at the turn of the seventeenth century. In that century's first decade, he discovered that Tycho's data on the motion of Mars matched an orbit that was elliptical and a movement in which an imaginary line linking Mars and the sun swept equal areas in equal times. This constituted both a technical revolution in astronomy and a stunning confirmation of Pythagorean faith that nature displays exact mathematical relationships. By 1627, Kepler showed that predictions of planetary positions based on the elliptical orbit and the "area law" were anywhere from 20 to 100 times more accurate than any previous set of planetary tables.

Kepler and his Italian contemporary Galileo Galilei (1564–1642) were the two pivotal figures in the revolution engulfing astronomy and physics in the seventeenth century. Galileo's forte was the physics of motion and simple machines. He was not an astronomer, and he was not actively involved in discussions about the systems of the world until the newly invented telescope changed his life in 1609 at the age of forty-five. Constructing and improving his telescope, Galileo turned it toward the heavens with astonishing results that induced him to embrace the Copernican system publicly by 1612. His observations of the moons of Jupiter and the motions of sunspots supported the Copernican system. The most significant revelation was that Venus exhibited the full range of phases from crescent to full. This meant unquestionably that Venus orbited the sun. By his telescopic observations, therefore, Galileo narrowed the competition among world systems to the Copernican versus the Tychonic. Interestingly, in ensuing years he would virtually ignore the Tychonic system when discussing the issue of planetary arrangement—notably in his famous *Dialogue on the Two Chief World Systems* (1632) in which he shaped the competition in terms of the Copernican versus the traditional Aristotelian-Ptolemaic systems. In so doing, Galileo was unspokenly conceding that no definite advantage existed for either the Copernican or Tychonic system in the early to mid-seventeenth century. By the middle of the first decade of the seventeenth century, Galileo had introduced two novel ideas into speculations about the physics of motion. First, he noted that a body moving at constant speed in the absence of resistance will continue to move at that speed without cessation. Next, he observed that any heavy body will fall with constantly increasing speed (uniform acceleration) in the absence of resistance. All heavy bodies regardless of size, weight, density, or shape will fall with this identical uniform acceleration. An equivalent way to express this is that the distance increases as the square of the time.

Frenchman René Descartes (1596–1650) became the most influential natural philosopher of the mid-seventeenth century. He presented a clear program for science and natural philosophy that posited mathematical relations as the organizing principles of nature and mechanical agencies (material movements, collisions, and aggregations) as causes of all phenomena. Barred from Descartes' natural philosophy were any explanations in terms of goals or ends (e.g., natural motions of the four elements). Unacceptable as well were immaterial forces that were "occult" (incomprehensible to the human intellect)—for example, the mysterious planetary forces that magicians and alchemists had invoked to explain the development of metals and minerals under the earth's surface.

Descartes sharpened Galileo's speculations about motion at constant speed. He claimed that a body moving without resistance at constant speed in a straight line will continue that motion without need for causal maintenance. This was a revolutionary step. It redefined uniform linear motion as a state analogous to rest in contrast to the Aristotelian view that any motion is an effect requiring a cause.

Unfortunately, Descartes failed to accommodate mathematical description (e.g., Kepler's laws and Galileo's law of falling bodies) to mechanical explanations involving impacts by moving streams of matter. His successor in England, Isaac Newton (1642–1727), conceded around 1679 that solely mathematical description and mechanical explanation would not account satisfactorily for a multitude of natural phenomena. Newton reintroduced the concept of "force" into physical science and natural philosophy. Although immaterial and occult, Newton's force carried an explicit definition that linked essentially to Descartes' new concept of motion. While uniform linear motion required no causal maintenance (Descartes' and Newton's "first law" of motion), "force" as a causal agent would be associated with change of motion (Newton's "second law" of motion). Armed with this concept, Newton proceeded to unify celestial and terrestrial physics by identifying the force causing the (accelerated) fall of a heavy body and that causing orbital motions in the heavens. Adding his own concept of a universal gravitational force, he showed the intimate relationship between Galileo's law of falling bodies and Kepler's planetary laws. By 1700, Newton's masterful theoretical achievement convinced most educated people in Europe to accept the Copernican system.

At about the same time that Copernicus was developing a public statement of his new planetary system in the 1530s, two other men were engaged in activities that represent to us transitions to experimental methodology. Philippus Aureolus Theophrastus Bombastus von Hohenheim, or "Paracelsus" as he dubbed himself (1490–1541), was challenging the idea of disease associated with the greatest medical and anatomical authority of the ancient world, Galen. Galen's medical theory had exerted enormous influence on university medical faculties since the inception of universities in the 1200s. Galen taught that disease resulted from an imbalance in the four bodily humours (blood, phlegm, black bile, and yellow bile). Remedies included alteration in diet, herbal medicinals, and if necessary, more extreme measures to induce sweating, vomiting, or bleeding. Opposing this, Paracelsus believed that something foreign to the body seized control of a physiological function. The solution was to produce an agent that could subdue the cause of the disease. Paracelsus felt that these dynamic medicinals were of metallic and mineralogical origin, and he urged physicians to isolate them in the laboratory using the techniques of alchemy and metallurgy. Paracelsus' vision of a chemically based medical tradition and emphasis on laboratory operations to extract potent curatives from metals and minerals encouraged links among medicine, pharmacy, and alchemy. This was an important transitional stage leading to the concept of an experimental chemistry advocated by Andreas Libavius (c. 1540–1661) and later Robert Boyle (1627–1691).

While Paracelsus was challenging the Galenic concept of disease, Andreas Vesalius (1514–1564) submitted Galen's anatomical writings to the test of direct experience. While at the University of Padua in the late 1530s, Vesalius broke with tradition by conducting dissections on human cadavers as he lectured. Many professors of anatomy contented themselves with reading from Galen's writings while a barber-surgeon performed the dissection with little effort at critical review. Vesalius respected Galen enormously and recognized that Galen had gotten most of it right. But he did not hesitate to criticize errors when he found them—for example, his inability to find the holes in the wall separating the left and right sides of the heart that Galen had posited. In his more active empirical approach to anatomical dissection, Vesalius initiated a tradition at Padua that culminated in experimental physiology.

By the early 1600s, genuine experimentation was evident in several areas of science. In addition to William Harvey's work on the motion of the blood, William Gilbert applied experimentation to the study of magnetism and static electricity. Galileo used experiment in attempts to verify his law of falling bodies. Recognizing the implications of this work, Francis Bacon (1561–1626) praised experimentation as an essential means to interrogate nature. Bacon vigorously denied the traditional Aristotelian notion that the imposition of artificial or controlled conditions rendered laboratory phenomena "unnatural" and therefore unsuitable for consideration in "natural philosophy." For Bacon, laboratory phenomena were as natural as the growth of plants and animals or the actions of wind and rain.

This Baconian analysis extended to the products and processes of artisans, craftspeople, and industrial technology. They too were no less natural than the vegetative, animal, and mineral substances in nature. Bacon consciously linked experimental method, natural philosophy, and technology. He recognized the potent impact on astronomy of the telescope, which had come out of technological tradition. Soon to follow would be the barometer, the air pump, and the microscope—all derivatives of technological tradition that would deeply affect scientific theory. Bacon predicted as well that scientific theory would benefit technological development. He believed that experiment would yield new knowledge, which in turn would enhance the material conditions of life. Ultimately, he felt this would elevate human morality.

The new ideas and method of science were not welcome in most European universities. Neither was the effort to associate science and technology. Emphases on logical analysis, Aristotelian natural philosophy, and the Latin language in universities discouraged entry of the new physics and astronomy, experimental method, and technological training. Instead, other organizations arose as centers of scientific communication. The short-lived Lincean Academy of Rome (1603) and Florence's Accademia del Cimento (1657–1667) initiated this tendency. More permanent were the Royal Society of London (1660) and the Paris Royal Academy of Sciences (1666). These societies communicated in the vernacular languages, published scientific journals, undertook investigation of industrial and agricultural processes, and encouraged experimental activities among their memberships. While both Protestant and Catholic universities maintained ties with the administrative leadership of their denominations, the new scientific societies affiliated with secular and political authorities. Members of the Paris Academy of Sciences were salaried by the French crown. Their British counterparts obtained a Royal charter but began and remained a private organization financially and administratively independent of the crown.

In the 200 years between 1500 and 1700, novel and traditional threads of European culture interweaved to produce intellectual, methodological, and institutional forms of modern science. In the realm of scientific theory involving astronomy and physics, two levels of discourse merit attention. The philosophical background involved four broad patterns of interpretation that originated in Greek Antiquity. Each had its adherents among leading figures of astronomy and physics. Debate at the level of specific ideas or explanations of phenomena cannot be divorced from this philosophical background.

Firmly established in the universities, the teleological pattern of interpretation advocated by Aristotle portrayed nature as a logically organized stage of objects that moved and changed in order to achieve goals. A heavy body fell, for example, because its inner mover impelled it to its "natural place" at the center of the universe (center of the earth) in order to attain rest. Higher intelligences moved solid transparent spheres bearing the planets in order to manifest a love for God, the "Unmoved Mover." An acorn grew and changed in order to achieve the goal of a mature oak tree.

Belief that natural processes are organized according to exact mathematical relationships had originated with the Pythagoreans. Plato and later St. Augustine regarded mathematics highly, and the Platonic influence on European culture was growing in competition with the Aristotelianism of the universities by the early sixteenth century.

A great revival of magic began when Marsilio Ficino of Florence translated the *Hermetic Corpus* from Greek to Latin in the 1460s and defended the Christian orthodoxy of these writings. In late Antiquity (when the Hermetic works actually originated), the figure of Hermes had been a Greek god also identified with the Roman god Mercury and the Egyptian god Thoth. Ficino believed Hermes to have been an ancient Egyptian priest through whom God revealed magical and alchemical secrets later transmitted selectively from generation to generation. Ficino's magic purported to manipulate the "virtues" or "forces" emanating from stars and planets that gave substances such as metals their characteristics and powers to act. In Ficino's magic and the subsequent magical writings of Giovanni Pico della Mirandola and Cornelius Agrippa, these forces were considered "occult" because they could be neither perceived by human senses nor understood by human intellect. This occult pattern of interpretation emphasized human ability to transform metals, alter behavior (e.g., induce one person to fall in love with another), and perform other operations on things and people. But it imposed limitations on the ability of the human intellect to understand the workings of nature that neither the Aristotelian nor Pythagorean view accepted.

The fourth pattern of interpretation was mechanical. Deriving from the tradition of atomism, this approach emphasized the motion, collision, and aggregation of microscopic particles (atoms) to account for processes in nature. Never a popular philosophy, atomism remained far less influential than the other three patterns of interpretation in the early sixteenth century. But machinery was steadily developing into more sophisticated forms in European technology. In the early fifteenth century, Poggio Bracciolini had recovered the poem *De rerum natura* by the Roman author Lucretius (55 B.C.) that praised atomic philosophy. Each of these developments boded a brighter future for atomism and the mechanical pattern of interpretation.

Copernicus introduced an early modern version of sun-centered cosmology, but his reform of astronomy went only so far. Indeed, the technicalities of his astronomy remained traditionally Ptolemaic. Ptolemy's *Almagest* had been the most influential astronomical text in the European-Mediterranean world for almost 1,500 years. In it, Ptolemy had applied Plato's and Aristotle's belief that the geometry of astronomical phenomena was fundamentally circular. Ptolemy's aim was to devise a model for a planet that combined simple circular motions to generate a complex, irregular resultant motion that replicated the planet's observed movement. Although Ptolemy and his successors achieved fair accuracy in their predictions of planetary motions, an exact match between their models of calculation and actual planetary movements eluded them. Copernicus continued to follow a strategy of combining simple circular motions in his technical astronomy (as would all sixteenth-century astronomers including Tycho Brahe). Neither did Copernicus issue serious challenges to Aristotelian physics. He said virtually nothing about the causes of planetary motions.

Copernicus' Pythagorean quest to discover exact mathematical relationships in astronomy was achieved by Johannes Kepler in the first decade of the seventeenth century. Kepler's astronomy of the elliptical orbit and the area law constituted a technical revolution in astronomy. These innovations also demanded an explanation for planetary movements that Kepler eagerly sought. Kepler believed that God had ordered nature in mathematical terms and that occult forces maintained this order. Two forces acted on the planets. One force issued from the sun and moved the planet along its orbit. The other was a pseudomagnetic force that alternately induced attractions and repulsions between the planet and the sun. If the solar force acted alone, it would spawn a uniform circular motion of the planet about the sun at the geometric center of the circle. The pseudomagnetic force was responsible for the ellipticity of the orbit. Thus, however revolutionary Kepler's astronomy was, it embodied a circular motion as a component of the elliptical orbit and therefore preserved a link with ancient and medieval traditions of astronomy and physics.

Kepler's contemporary Galileo had a much different view of natural philosophy. He had little place for occult forces in his science. In his *Dialogue*, he disparaged magicians and alchemists and criticized Kepler's view that the moon exerts its influence on the tides via an occult force. For Galileo, the desirable framework of science was mechanical causes maintaining exact mathematical relationships.

But Galileo was no Descartes. Aristotelian teleology remained an essential aspect of his terrestrial physics to the end of his life. Moreover, the circle continued to dominate his discussions of planetary movements. Galileo does not seem to have decided whether his perpetual motion at constant speed was linear or circular. At places in his writings he envisioned a horizontally projected cannonball moving without resistance and free of gravitational effect that continued at constant speed in that line. More frequently his reference was a ball rolling along a perfectly smooth, resistanceless surface of the earth at uniform speed. He described this as a third type of motion, neither natural nor forced. Natural motion for him remained a spontaneous movement toward a natural place propelled by an inner mover. Forced motion was movement away from the natural place propelled by an external mover. Since a uniform circular motion about the center toward which the body tended neither approached nor receded from the center, Galileo imagined that the body could continue in that motion indefinitely. But the entire framework was medieval, based on traditional concepts of natural and forced motions.

When Descartes denied the existence of natural place and therefore natural motion, and when he redefined motion itself as a state (in which the body moves in a line at constant speed perpetually without need for causal maintenance), he severed ties to medieval physics that had still bound Galileo. When Isaac Newton defined force as a causal agent inducing change of motion, he cut the final link to medieval mechanics wherein force had been associated with movement in an absolute direction (opposite to that of natural motion). By identifying the force causing a body to fall with the force coercing a body from a state of uniform linear motion into a circular motion, Newton finally removed the pure and privileged status of circular motion in Western physics/astronomy from Plato through Copernicus to Galileo.

On the more general philosophical level, Newton reinforced Descartes' elimination of Aristotle's teleological pattern of interpretation from physical science. He retained Descartes' belief that mathematical relations and mechanical causes were legitimate modes of scientific analysis. But he reintroduced the occult pattern of interpretation by positing attractive and repulsive forces in his explanations of astronomical, chemical, optical, electrical, and magnetic phenomena.

While Newton's concept of force culminated a revolution, it also established critical agendas for physical science of the following two centuries. His use of it in his *Principia mathematica* compelled most educated Europeans to accept the Copernican planetary arrangement. Not until later would empirical support clinch the Copernican victory.

Moreover, Newton's spectacularly successful use of force in mechanics and astronomy encouraged efforts to apply his concept of force to other areas of science. Chemists envisioned Newtonian attractive forces as agents of chemical reactions among microscopic atoms or atomic conglomerates. In magnetic and electrical theories, Newtonian force became prominent. Ultimately, the concept of force was not to prove as successful for understanding chemical, optical, thermal, electrical, and magnetic phenomena as the new nineteenth-century concept of energy. But Newton's force remained useful in these areas and vital in astronomy and mechanics.

Instances of experimentation in the ancient and medieval periods are evident in the literature that survives. Galen, for example, performed experiments designed to uphold his opinion that the arteries convey blood. In alchemical laboratories, metallurgical workshops, and apothecary shops, some experimentation seems to have occurred. Yet experimentation lingered at the periphery of ancient and medieval Western science for several reasons. Both Plato and Aristotle had disparaged it. For Plato, sense experience was at best an imperfect knowledge, and he focused his philosophy on the activity of pure thought or intellect. Aristotle believed that understanding of objects and processes in nature could not result from imposing artificial conditions. When universities arose in the West at the beginning of the thirteenth century, Aristotelian emphases on logic and natural philosophy discouraged entry of laboratory or technological activities into that culture.

Several contributing factors seem to have led to recognition of experimentation as an essential means of attaining scientific knowledge by the opening of the 1600s. The transitional roles of Paracelsus and Vesalius in medicine and anatomy were surely significant. In addition, ancient intellectual authorities seemed more vulnerable to western Europeans who seemed increasingly eager to critique received knowledge. Classical humanists sought to recover manuscripts from ancient Greece and Rome. Related to this was an effort to broaden European intellectual life from the Aristotelian predominance of logic and the literary form of the treatise in universities. By the 1500s, humanist translating activity extended to scientific writings. Previously untranslated works of Galen, Archimedes, and the *Geography* of Ptolemy were translated into Latin. Most humanists were not interested in science itself as much as the recovery of classical writings, but their work exposed ideas of ancient authorities that proved misconceived and occasionally false. For example, maps in Ptolemy's *Geography* did not stand up well against the increasingly sophisticated cartography resulting from sixteenth-century explorations. This and similar instances encouraged criticism and alternative explanations that could meet the tests of experience. When Francis Bacon praised experimental method in the 1620s, he was less a prophet than a witness. Many of Europe's leading scientists and natural philosophers were using and publicly touting experimentation. By the mid- to late 1600s, its acceptance among active scientific investigators was so widespread that its centrality in discussions and activities of the new scientific societies was unquestioned.

Bacon's vision of a mutual relationship between science and technology merits our attention. A considerable gap long had endured between the Latin textual tradition of university intellectual life and the largely oral vernacular communication among artisans and craftspeople. Exceptions to this generalization occurred infrequently. Not until the sixteenth century did science and technology interact consistently, stimulated by richer interactions among university-trained intellectuals and a range of people who operated on materials (alchemists, artisans, apothecaries, skilled craftspeople).

By the time of Bacon's writing in the 1620s, the scientific impact of instruments originating in the technological tradition was evident. But was the relation between science and technology actually mutual as he asserted? Did evolving scientific theory affect technological development as profoundly as technological tradition was now influencing science? Clearly the answer is no. Up to the nineteenth century, major areas of technological development including armaments, agriculture, and cloth making benefited only minimally from scientific ideas and scientifically trained individuals. Inventors with hands-on experience furthered these technologies, not scientists. Not until the late nineteenth century in the areas of electrical technology and synthetic dye manufacture would branches of technology emerge that required the sustained and essential efforts of scientifically trained people in a setting we know as the industrial research laboratory. The nineteenth-century sciences of current electricity and organic chemistry became the first major sources of science-based technological change. Two and a half centuries after Bacon died, his notion of a mutual science-technology relationship reached complete fulfillment.

Medieval universities were affiliated with the ecclesiastical structure of Western Christendom, and all received formal recognition through issuance of a Papal Bull (charter). But at Paris, Oxford, Padua, and Bologna, faculties of Philosophy, Medicine, and Law proceeded largely independent of ecclesiastical influence. Indeed, the recently translated pagan works of Aristotle, Ptolemy, and Galen were predominant influences on teaching, writing, and debate. Latin translations of Islamic philosophers and scientists such as Alhazen, Avicenna, and Averroes were also prominent. In all faculties, logical analysis and the formal style of the treatise were vehicles of instruction and debate. Natural philosophy, mathematics, and the range of theoretical issues covered in Aristotle's writings profoundly affected Philosophy faculties. Yet the link with Rome remained significant, because teachers and students alike maintained clerical status, meaning that they were presumed under the protection of the Church and bound to its basic tenets.

Humanist scholarly activities that came to challenge the substance and style of university learning by the sixteenth century obtained support from a different patronage of secular wealth and court culture. For example, Marsilio Ficino's translations of Plato's writings and the *Corpus Hermeticum* occurred in a house and with funding provided by the merchant prince of Florence, Cosimo de Medici, and his Platonic Academy of Florence was an early instance of a secularly supported organization for pursuing scholarly and aesthetic enterprises. The London Royal Society (1660) and the Paris Academy of Sciences (1666) began with and retained court recognition. Initially the Academy of Sciences might seem to have been one more addition to the various cultural activities patronized by King Louis XIV. However, by the 1700s it was the most prestigious assemblage of scientific talent in the world during the period when France (Paris) became the most dynamic scientific center in Europe. In fact, in microcosm the Paris Academy reflected the French national tradition of scientific organization and patronage into the twentieth century: small assemblies of talented scientists in institutions tied administratively and financially to the central government in Paris.

Quite a different circumstance developed across the English Channel. In Britain, the Royal Society included a large, primarily amateur membership through the eighteenth century, although virtually all leading English scientists were members as well. The Royal Society remained administratively and financially independent of the British government. Other British scientific organizations of the eighteenth and nineteenth centuries followed its example as privately funded activities established primarily for communication among people in the various areas of science. In Great Britain, with few exceptions the government neither administered nor financed scientific institutions up to the twentieth century.

In neither France nor Great Britain did universities train or cultivate scientists. Universities opposed the content and spirit of the new experimental sciences during and following the Scientific Revolution. Although individuals who taught in universities might participate and excel in the development of eighteenth-century science, very few people conceived the university as an appropriate setting for the pursuit of experimental science. Not until the second quarter of the nineteenth century—and then in the German states—did the university take on this role. Thus, the institutional framework of modern science arose in two primary stages: the scientific societies of the Scientific Revolution and the research-minded university that appeared first in Germany and then in virtually every Western nation by the opening of the twentieth century.

Notwithstanding novel ideas, method, and institutional forms, Western science stayed rigidly traditional in a crucial way. It remained an almost exclusively male preserve. Exclusion of women from positions of status and influence was not unique to western European Christian civilization. In Jewish, Islamic, Chinese, and many other cultures, bias against women endured without challenge. Universities were closed to women and would remain so until the latter nineteenth century. With the added elements of witch-hunting mania and clerical efforts to root out heretical women, a feminine presence in institutional science seemed farther away than ever at the turn of the seventeenth century. Indeed, the new scientific societies would retain strict closure to women. The Lincean Academy of Rome demanded chastity of its membership. Both the Royal Society and the Paris Academy of Sciences began and remained uncompromisingly male. Not until 1979 was a woman elected to full membership in the successor to the Paris Academy. (Marie Curie's Nobel Prize–winning scientific achievements had not been sufficient to gain her membership in the early twentieth century.) Not until 1945 was a woman elected to full membership in the Royal Society. From the perspective of women's history, the Scientific Revolution produced no revolution at all!

SELECTED BIBLIOGRAPHY

Ackerman, James. "The Involvement of Artists in Renaissance Science." In *Science and the Arts in the Renaissance*, pp. 94–129. Edited by John W. Shirley and David Hoeniger. Washington, DC: Folger Shakespeare Library, 1985. An analysis of the contributions of artists to Renaissance science.

Debus, Allen G. *Man and Nature in the Renaissance*. Cambridge, U.K.: Cambridge University Press, 1978. A survey of science and medicine between the fifteenth and seventeenth centuries emphasizing the impact of humanism and magic.

Drake, Stillman. *Galileo at Work: His Scientific Biography*. Chicago: University of Chicago Press, 1978. Narrative chronology of Galileo's activities that focuses on the substance of his science and largely ignores his personal history, the social context, and the philosophical background.

Frank, Robert G., Jr. *Harvey and the Oxford Physiologists: Scientific Ideas and Social Interaction*. Berkeley: University of California Press, 1980. Study of the early scientific community and the transformation of physiology by Oxford-trained natural philosophers in the two generations following the discovery of the circulation of blood.

Huff, Toby. *The Rise of Early Modern Science: Islam, China, and the West*. Cambridge, U.K.: Cambridge University Press, 1993. An attempt to explain why the Scientific Revolution occurred in western Europe rather than in non-Western cultures.

Hunter, Michael. *Establishing the New Science: The Experience of the Early Royal Society*. Woodbridge, U.K.: Boydell, 1989. Discussion of the early years of the Royal Society, including the relationship of science to technology, the history of museums, and Robert Boyle.

Koyre, Alexandre. *From the Closed World to the Infinite Universe*. Baltimore, MD: Johns Hopkins University Press, 1979. An important intellectual history detailing the changing cosmological concepts of the Scientific Revolution from Nicolaus of Cusa to Isaac Newton.

Lindberg, David C., and Robert S. Westman, eds. *Reappraisals of the Scientific Revolution*. Cambridge, U.K.: Cambridge University Press, 1990. An important collection of revisionist historiographical essays on the Scientific Revolution.

Orenstein [Bronfenbrenner], Martha. *The Role of Scientific Societies in the Seventeenth Century*. New York: Arno, 1975. Pioneering work that remains fundamental for understanding the seventeenth century's new forms of scientific organization.

Perez-Ramos, Antonio. *Francis Bacon's Idea of Science and the Maker's Knowledge Tradition*. Oxford, U.K.: Clarendon, 1988. Study of Bacon's empirical philosophy.

Shapin, Steven. *A Social History of Truth*. Chicago: University of Chicago Press, 1994. A treatment of scientific theory and method as a social construction.

Shea, William R. *The Magic of Numbers and Motion: The Scientific Career of René Descartes*. Canton, MA: Science History, 1991. Survey of Descartes' natural philosophy, emphasizing his mathematical approach.

Stroup, Alice. *A Company of Scientists: Botany, Patronage, and Community at the Seventeenth-Century Paris Royal Academy of Sciences*. Berkeley: University of California Press, 1990. Stroup examines the early years of the academy, viewing it as both a mercantilist company trading in knowledge for the crown and a key stage in the development of scientific professionalism.

Swerdlow, N. M., and Otto Neugebauer. *Mathematical Astronomy in Copernicus' "De Revolutionibus."* 2 vols. New York: Springer-Verlag, 1984. Technical exposition of Copernicus' work including masterful summary of links between Copernicus and his Latin and Arabic predecessors.

Taton, René, and Curtis Wilson, eds. *Planetary Astronomy from the Renaissance to the Rise of Astrophysics. Part A: Tycho Brahe to Newton*. Cambridge, U.K.: Cambridge University Press, 1989. Detailed collection of topical articles surveying the history of early modern astronomy.

Van Helden, Albert. "The Telescope in the Seventeenth Century." *ISIS* 65 (1974): 38–58. An essay on the development and impact of the telescope on seventeenth-century science.

Wertheim, Margaret. *Pythagoras' Trousers: God, Physics, and the Gender Wars*. New York: W. W. Norton, 1997. Survey of the role of women in the histories of mathematics and physics, with extensive references to the general scientific environment of the sixteenth and seventeenth centuries.

Westfall, Richard S. *The Construction of Modern Science: Mechanisms and Mechanics*. Cambridge, U.K.: Cambridge University Press, 1977. Survey of mid- to late-seventeenth-century science, emphasizing the revolution of ideas against the background of Pythagorean mathematical and Democritean mechanical philosophies.

———. *Never at Rest: A Biography of Isaac Newton*. Cambridge, U.K.: Cambridge University Press, 1986. Outstanding biography of the Scientific Revolution's culminating figure.

Yates, Frances A. *Giordano Bruno and the Hermetic Tradition*. Chicago: University of Chicago Press, 1991. A classical work that describes the influence on Renaissance culture of ancient magical writings attributed to Hermes Trismegistus.

8

The Golden Age of Mogul Power, c. 1650

INTRODUCTION

India, the massive Asian subcontinent, had been divided for hundreds of years. When the Mauryan dynasty that had unified India and had produced the memorable Ashoka, one of the ancient world's great rulers, disintegrated in the second century B.C., India broke into countless pieces. An array of local dignitaries exercised varying degrees of control over small- to medium-sized principalities. From time to time, ambitious leaders would consolidate territories and build a large, strong state; but their efforts always ended in failure. The best example of this was the Gupta Empire, which prospered in the fourth and fifth centuries before collapsing.

Islam, a new force in Indian history, appeared in the eleventh century. Based on the seventh-century teachings of Muhammad, Islam had arrived in India as early as the eighth century when Arabs conquered the western province of Sind. However, Islam encroached no further in India until Islamic raiders from central Asia seized the Punjab region of northwestern India early in the eleventh century. By the end of the twelfth century, the central Asians, or Turkic peoples, had extended their rule throughout the valley of the Ganges River and in 1206 established a sultanate at Delhi. Their rule was quite liberal; many native Hindu po-

The Taj Mahal, built to memorialize Mumtaz Mahal, the favorite wife of Mogul ruler Shah Jahan, is one of the world's most famous structures. (Reproduced from the Collections of the Library of Congress)

tentates continued to command their principalities as long as they recognized the sultanate's authority. Moreover, the Turkic conquerors
lacked the manpower to rule effectively. This led them to integrate native
Indians into their administration and military despite religious differences. Gradually the Turkic empire spread outward from the Ganges
valley to include the Bengal region at the delta of the Ganges and some
of the subcontinent's western coast and southern regions, although the
latter were never brought fully into the empire. However, at the end of
the fourteenth century a marauding army under Timur Lang (Tamerlane), another central Asian conqueror, made its way down the Ganges
valley, destroying all in its path. Timur Lang's Mongols captured Delhi
in 1398, and the Turkic empire collapsed. Eventually the Mongols withdrew to rape, loot, and pillage elsewhere and the sultanate was restored,
but it proved to be a mere shadow of its former self.

India's decline continued until the appearance of Babur, known as
"The Tiger," early in the sixteenth century. Born in 1483 in central Asia,
Babur claimed an impressive pedigree. On his father's side he was de-
scended from Timur Lang; on his mother's side, from the Mongol con-
queror Chinggis Khan. He is credited with establishing the Mogul (the
Persian word for Mongol) dynasty in India.

Early in his career Babur hoped to build an empire in central Asia.
When his plans failed, he took the Afghan city of Kabul in 1504 and
turned his attention to India, where dissident Afghan princelings resid-
ing there appealed to him for aid in their seemingly endless struggle
against the sultan. Babur easily overran the Punjab and then moved into
the Ganges valley. In 1526 he defeated the sultan's numerically superior
forces at the Battle of Panipat, after which he occupied the twin capitals,
Delhi and Agra. Babur then pacified the Afghan chieftains who had invited him to India in the first place and defeated several Hindu princes
who had seized upon the sultanate's downfall to proclaim their own
independence. By the time of his death in 1530, Babur's empire stretched
from Kabul eastward to Bihar, not far from the Ganges delta. Much of
what is known about Babur comes from his *Memoirs*, an autobiographical
account constructed from notes he made over his lifetime that reveals
him to be a highly cultured, literate man as well as an important and
successful warrior.

Although the Mogul Empire emerged under Babur, he died before he
could consolidate his gains. Consequently, the empire's foundations remained shaky, and Babur's son and heir Humayun did little to lessen
this danger. A gifted warrior and personally quite attractive, Humayun

was also dissolute and indecisive. His weakness inspired the local nobility—both Islamic and Hindu—as well as his own brothers to challenge
him. Defeated at every turn but not vanquished, Humayun fled to Sind,
where his son Akbar was born in 1542. Only at the end of his life did
Humayun return to India, and only then because his rivals, who contin-
ually fought among themselves, had severely weakened each other.

When Humayun died in 1556, Akbar ascended the throne and began
to build a magnificent empire upon the foundations laid by Babur. Akbar
was a complex man. He was strong, daring, and courageous, qualities
that endeared him to the warriors who dominated Indian society. He
also possessed exceptional leadership qualities that sparked intense personal loyalty. He was highly intelligent and revered learning; during the
latter part of his reign his court became a gathering place for intellectuals
of all stripes. Although Akbar loved learning and held books in high
esteem, curiously enough he alone among the Mogul rulers was illiterate.
Nevertheless, he collected a large library and proved a great patron of
the arts. At the time of his death in 1605, Akbar's success had earned
him the title the "Great Mogul."

One of Akbar's first tasks was to restore the Mogul Empire to the
boundaries it enjoyed under Babur. By the middle of the 1560s, this goal
had been accomplished. Akbar then began to expand his empire. In 1573
he secured Gujarat, the wealthy province bordering the Arabian Sea, and
in 1576 he took Bengal, the even wealthier province in the Ganges delta.
After a pause, Akbar added Kashmir, Sind, and Baluchistan. He then
turned to the Deccan region of southern India, where he made significant
but less permanent gains.

Perhaps Akbar's greatest accomplishment was not his conquests but
rather his style of governing. Following Babur's advice, Akbar ruled by
conciliation rather than force. He consciously made allies of his enemies
and worked to break down the barriers separating the Muslim rulers
from the vast horde of Hindus.

To achieve his objectives, Akbar undertook several initiatives. His
harem, which reputedly numbered more than 500, included wives from
many different nationalities. Prominent among them were Hindu prin-
cesses, drawn from the empire's leading Hindu, or Rajput, families. Akbar's favorite wife and the mother of his successor was a Rajput princess.
In 1564 Akbar lifted the poll tax that all non-Muslims had to pay. Subsequently, he rescinded several other humiliating taxes levied solely on
non-Muslims. Akbar also staffed the empire's administration with Hindus, especially Rajputs, including the vital post of finance minister. Fi-

nally, much to the disgust of the ulema, or Muslim scholars who directed Islam, Akbar forbade any attempts to win conversion to Islam by coercion and, instead, practiced a form of religious toleration.

Akbar's administrative innovations also benefited the empire. He established a modern chain of command, with himself—of course—at the top. Appointment to his administration tended to be based on merit, and he borrowed from the Persians, whom he knew well, the concept of paid officials called *mansabdars*. Under Akbar, there were thirty-three grades of *mansabdar*, ranging from commander of ten horses to commander of 5,000. To ensure fiscal resources for his empire, Akbar introduced a uniform land tax. While this tax was steep—one-third of the annual crop—it was administered uniformly and honestly. During Akbar's reign, India prospered, but the wealth was distributed very unevenly.

Relying on the momentum achieved under Akbar, his successors spread their influence even further throughout India, and the Mogul Empire entered its "Golden Age." At the same time, however, internal contradictions weakened the empire's superstructure and cleared the way for its downfall.

Akbar's immediate successor was Jahangir, a cruel and dissolute alcoholic who was also highly cultured and a renowned patron of the arts, especially painting. Without too much thought about the subject, Jahangir continued his father's basic policies, including the expansion of the empire. He conquered the fortresses of Mewar (1614) and Kangra (1620), and seized half of the Deccan kingdom of Ahmadnagar (1616).

Jahangir's son and successor, Shah Jahan, continued to annex the Deccan principalities; however, he also took the first small steps that wrecked the empire's religious balance. Unlike Akbar, Shah Jahan's commitment to religious toleration was not heartfelt. Nevertheless, he maintained toleration as official policy and continued to fill his administrative ranks with Muslims and Hindus alike. However, he allowed the influence of Muslim clerics, who had bitterly opposed Akbar, to increase. Shah Jahan also spent lavishly on palaces and court life. He is perhaps best known for constructing the Taj Mahal, a magnificent tomb for his favorite wife that required the labor of 20,000 workmen for twenty years.

Even before his death in 1666, Shah Jahan had been superseded by his son, Aurangzeb, the last of the great Mogul rulers. In order to seize power, Aurangzeb defeated and killed his brothers—a not-unheard-of practice at the time—and imprisoned his dying father. Perhaps the most cunning, despotic, and ruthless of India's rulers, the highly intelligent but puritanical Aurangzeb was also a true son of Islam. His policies aimed at both elevating an orthodox Islam over all other forms of Islam and establishing this Islam as the empire's official religion at the expense of all other religions. His abandonment of the traditional Mogul policy of toleration proved harmful to the interests of the Mogul Empire. Despite their importance, Aurangzeb stunned the empire's Hindus when he reimposed the head tax on non-Muslims and destroyed Hindu temples and schools.

In some instances, Aurangzeb's policies led to outright rebellion. For example, in the empire's Punjab heartland, the already suspicious and unfriendly Sikhs rejected Aurangzeb's choice as guru, or spiritual leader. Disturbances followed, and when Aurangzeb seized and executed the Sikh's preferred candidate for guru who refused to convert to Islam, he precipitated a Sikh rebellion of massive proportions.

Meanwhile, an even more serious rebellion broke out in the Deccan, where the Marathas, a Deccan hill people, challenged the empire. Under the leadership of their prince, Shivaji, and his son, Sambhaji, the Marathas formed a Hindu confederation and waged a seemingly interminable guerrilla war. Although they lost a number of battles, the Marathas were never defeated, and their rebellion remained an open sore for the Moguls.

By the time of Aurangzeb's death in 1707 at the age of eighty-eight, the Mogul Empire's golden years were fading, and a new force—the Europeans in general and the British, who had founded their first permanent settlement on the subcontinent in 1639, in particular—was gathering the necessary strength to replace the Moguls as masters of India.

INTERPRETIVE ESSAY
John McLeod

On June 17, 1631, a thirty-nine-year-old woman died in childbirth at Burhanpur in central India. The woman was named Mumtaz Mahal, and she was the favorite wife of Shah Jahan, the fourth Mogul ruler of India. The grieving emperor commemorated his beloved with the Taj Mahal, perhaps the most famous building in the world, which for 350 years has stood as a monument to the Golden Age of Mogul power. But the death of Mumtaz Mahal also foreshadowed the end of that power. The imperial couple had taken up residence in Burhanpur because Shah Jahan was campaigning in the great peninsula of south India, and the dream of southern conquest brought death to Mumtaz Mahal hundreds of miles from the luxurious palaces at Agra and Lahore in the north. In the end, it also paved the way for the destruction of the Mogul Empire. Nor is Mumtaz Mahal the only link between the grandeur and the decline of seventeenth-century India, for imperial policy contributed much to both Mogul greatness under the emperors Jahangir (r. 1605–1627) and Shah Jahan (r. 1628–1658) and collapse after Aurangzeb (r. 1658–1707) and Bahadur Shah (r. 1707–1712).

In 1605, the emperor Akbar bequeathed to his son Jahangir one of the great powers of the Muslim world, extending from Afghanistan in the west to Bengal in the east, and from the Himalaya Mountains in the north to the Godavari River in the south. Akbar's predecessors had ruled a loose confederation of fellow immigrant Muslim warrior nobles, mostly Afghans and Central Asian Turks, who had a tendency to turn on their king whenever he seemed weak enough to make possible a successful rebellion. Akbar had realized that this was not the sort of base on which to build an empire, and he therefore made two changes to the state. First, he broadened his power base beyond Afghans and Turks. Into the top ranks of his court, administration, and army, he brought Persian, African, and Indian Muslims and—in a break with tradition—Hindus. Previous Muslim kings in India had usually restricted administrative and military power to followers of their own religion; Hindus, while playing vital roles in running the state, had remained subordinate. Akbar's most important Hindu recruits came from a community called the Rajputs, the principal regional chiefs of north India. Akbar married a Rajput princess, who became the mother of his heir Jahangir. He also ended official religious discrimination, most notably in 1564 when he abolished the *jizya* (a poll tax paid by non-Muslims in return for the right to practice their religions).

Akbar's second innovation was to create a bureaucracy so that he could rule through loyal officials rather than depending on unreliable nobles. Akbar's civil administrators and military officers were all *mansabdars*, literally cavalry commanders, but here a corps of aristocratic state servants. The emperor personally selected and promoted all his *mansabdars*, thereby ensuring that his subordinates were men of unquestionable loyalty; and he assigned them new duties every few years, so that no *mansabdar* could build a power base from his position in the administration. *Mansabdars* were expected to supply horsemen for the imperial army, but generous salaries allowed them in addition to support a lavish lifestyle. This reinforced their dependence on the emperor, since disloyalty would cut off the income. Akbar usually paid *mansabdars* with cash, but Jahangir and his successors preferred to pay in *jagirs*. A *jagir* was the right to collect taxes, and each *mansabdar* was given this privilege in a region where the estimated yield of revenue equaled his salary. The emperor maintained control by regularly confiscating *jagirs* from one *mansabdar* and regranting them to another. Both the bulk of the money in the imperial treasury and the *mansabdars' jagir* salaries came from the land revenue, or tax on agricultural produce. In Akbar's day, the peasant paid one-third of his crop as land revenue, which was the principal tax in Mogul India. This was natural, as about 85 percent of the people of the empire made their living from agriculture. The land revenue channeled agricultural wealth into the urban economy. The emperor and his *mansabdars* spent their large incomes on servants, artists, and entertainers, who in turn supported the merchants and craftsmen of the imperial and provincial capitals. The result was that in the seventeenth century India had a huge urban population; Agra, one of the Mogul capitals, had half a million inhabitants and ranked among the largest cities of the Muslim world.

One reason that Muslim dynasties in India were often short-lived was that their rulers had no claim on the loyalty of their subjects, who did not care if one king were overthrown by another. To overcome this, Akbar sought to create a kind of imperial cult, in which the emperor stood so far above other men that his people regarded him as the beneficiary of God's favor and therefore as their divinely chosen monarch. This is suggested in official paintings of Akbar and his successors, who are usually depicted wearing haloes (a borrowing from European art). But Akbar also demonstrated his greatness by spending on a scale that no other man in India could afford. He recognized the value of building in projecting imperial glory and personally recruited talented architects of all nationalities. The result was the emergence of a new style of architecture, fusing central Asian, Indian, Persian, and European elements. This was a natural development in Indian Muslim building, which for centuries had shown the influence of Muslim design and Hindu workmanship, but Akbar made synthesis a matter of policy. He also fostered another royal monument, poetry. Although his mother tongue was the Moguls' Turkish dialect, he made Persian the official language of his empire. Persian was the traditional medium of culture in Muslim India and therefore appropriate for use at the court of a great ruler. Akbar gave generous support to Persian men of letters, who made India a center of Persian poetry. At the same time, he encouraged poetry in Hindi, the main language of the Hindus of northern India. Akbar also financed painters, musicians, and dancers. By the end of his reign, imperial sponsorship had begun to create a unique Mogul culture, which symbolized his unification of a diverse population.

Nevertheless, the strengths of the empire concealed weaknesses. Cultural patronage was costly and did not generate wealth. Even in a land as vast as India, there were limits to the money that could be raised from a tax on agriculture. And religious toleration might yield to political necessity, as became clear soon after Jahangir's accession. In 1606, the new emperor put down a rebellion by his own son Khusrau. The defeated prince's supporters included Arjan, the leader or guru of the Sikh sect, which had flourished in the Punjab region since its foundation almost a century earlier. Jahangir executed Arjan for his treason, inaugurating a hundred years of hostility between the Mogul emperors and the Sikh gurus. Khusrau's rebellion points to another Mogul weakness. The dynasty produced more than its share of capable men. This meant that all of the seventeenth-century emperors were talented rulers, but it also gave them able sons who were eager to ascend the throne. Jahangir himself had rebelled against Akbar in 1601, and Khusrau's rebellion followed this example set by his father. It has been suggested that such uprisings ensured that the throne was always held by the strongest member of the dynasty, but they also cost money and diverted the emperor's attention from ruling.

Besides cultural expenditure, the Mogul emperor could use war to demonstrate his power. The unification of northern India had shown Akbar's subjects that he was the greatest general in the subcontinent and set a model of military success for his descendants. This, however, was another source of danger, as imperial dreams of expansion could lead to expensive and unwinnable campaigns. Mogul India was particularly susceptible to such dreams. To the west lay Persia, a cultural inspiration and the only power with which the Moguls maintained regular diplomatic relations. But the frontier between India and Persia, running through modern Afghanistan, was shifting and uncertain. Far to the northwest in modern Uzbekistan was Samarkand, home of Babur's ancestor the great conqueror Timur, which every Mogul wished to regain for the dynasty. And in the south, the Muslim-ruled kingdoms of Ahmadnagar, Golconda, and Bijapur seemed to invite conquest, both to round out Mogul control over India and to enrich the imperial coffers (the diamond mines of Bijapur and Golconda were famous around the world).

The weaknesses of the Mogul Empire remained latent throughout the reign of Jahangir, who consolidated his hold on northern India and seized territory from Ahmadnagar in the south. On the whole, he ruled during a time of peace and, like his father, promoted religious coexistence. Perhaps in deference to the heritage of his Rajput mother, he celebrated the major Hindu festivals. In his cultural policy, he was influenced by his Persian wife Nur Jahan, whom he married in 1611 and who by the early 1620s was the real ruler of the empire. Nur Jahan patronized Persian philosophers, and Jahangir himself was a skilled writer of Persian prose and poetry. At the same time, Jahangir was half Indian, and his reign saw the continued absorption of Indian influences into Mogul culture. He took a personal interest in designing palaces and gardens, but Jahangir and Nur Jahan are best remembered for their support of painting. Orthodox Muslims frown on painting as a blasphemous attempt to imitate the creativity that belongs only to God. Despite this, Persian monarchs had long patronized artists, and Akbar's court had included Persian and Indian painters. Jahangir and Nur Jahan encouraged artists to experiment, and the result was the birth of the Mogul style of painting. Like Mogul culture in general, this united different traditions, including the naturalism of Hindu art and European techniques of shading. Mogul painting is one of the great classical schools of art and set models that were followed in India through the nineteenth century.

Then, in 1622, Persia seized the border city of Kandahar. Jahangir never recovered from the shock, which was followed by a three-year rebellion of his son Shah Jahan and struggles for power between Nur Jahan and powerful courtiers. The confusion was exacerbated by the emperor's death in 1627. Order was restored by Shah Jahan, who in 1628 ascended the throne. Shah Jahan and his beautiful wife Mumtaz Mahal (the niece of Nur Jahan) presided over the Golden Age of Mogul India, yet at the same time the empire's weaknesses began to reveal themselves. Shah Jahan was fortunate to rule in prosperous times. By and large, despite local famines, the agricultural base of the Indian economy flourished. Tobacco, maize, and other new crops supplemented such traditional ones as rice, wheat, and cotton. Industry and commerce also thrived. Next to agriculture, textile production was probably the largest employer in India. Craftsmen and artisans prepared cloth and other products, usually in their own homes but often in workshops maintained by the emperor or his nobles. Akbar and Jahangir had encouraged commerce by abolishing many taxes on internal trade, and under Shah Jahan a network of roads and rivers carried raw materials and manufactured goods across the empire.

Indian products were sold abroad as well as locally, and foreign trade made Shah Jahan's India one of the world's great commercial centers. Caravans transported goods to the Middle East, but this land trade was dwarfed by seaborne commerce, much of which was in the hands of Europeans. Akbar had taken the Mogul Empire to the Indian Ocean, both at the port of Surat on the Arabian Sea in the west and on the Bay of Bengal in the east. Throughout the sixteenth century, the Portuguese had monopolized shipping in the Indian Ocean, ensuring that all vessels either belonged to, or had bought licenses from, them. Under Jahangir, the Portuguese were displaced by competitors from England and the Netherlands. Merchants of the English and Dutch East India Companies built "factories," or trading posts, across India, where they bought wares from local producers and middlemen. Company ships then carried the goods for resale in America, Europe, and Japan. For hundreds of years, India's main export had been cotton cloth, but the English and Dutch also bought commodities such as silk, indigo, and sugar. (South India produced spices, but until the end of the seventeenth century, it lay outside Mogul control.) In return, wealthy Indians purchased wine and the occasional novelty, but the principal European exports to India were gold and silver, much of it mined in Spanish America. Nevertheless, European trade directly affected few Indians beyond the merchants, artisans, and agriculturalists who were involved in it. Except as a source of silver for minting coins, it was of little concern to the imperial government, which earned far more from the land revenue than from customs duties. Mogul India was an integral part of the world trade of the seventeenth century, but commerce ranked low in the empire's list of priorities.

Like his father and grandfather, Shah Jahan furthered his glory with lavish spending. He patronized philosophers, poets, painters, musicians, and dancers, but his greatest love was architecture. He worked with court architects to design new buildings, and some critics say his reign saw the high point of Muslim building anywhere in the world. Shah Jahan's style affected the whole subsequent history of Indian architecture. Like Jahangir, Shah Jahan had a Rajput mother (not his father's favorite wife Nur Jahan), which made him three-quarters Indian. It was therefore fitting that he presided over the final integration of Islamic and

Indian architecture, but his projects drew on many other influences to create a spectacular blend. In 1628, the dowager empress Nur Jahan completed a tomb for her father at Agra, which introduced to India the mosaics known as *pietra dura*. Meanwhile, Shah Jahan was renovating the old fort-palace at Agra, where for the first time he built in white marble. The Taj Mahal is the sequel to these two projects, with marble decorated in *pietra dura*. It also shows the eclecticism of Mogul architecture, for this greatest of Shah Jahan's monuments was designed by two Persian architects, built by Indian laborers, and decorated by the Italian Geronimo Verroneo and other foreign artists. Like many Mogul buildings, the Taj Mahal is set in a garden. Shah Jahan established new standards for gardening, and in 1637 he built the famous gardens of Shalimar at Lahore. Two years later, he embarked on his greatest architectural project, a new capital. Near the medieval town of Delhi, he built a palace called the Red Fort and the Jami Masjid, the largest mosque in India. He engaged talent from around the world, and the palace throne room was decorated by Frenchman Austin of Bordeaux. Shah Jahan encouraged princes and nobles to establish their residences near the imperial buildings, and service industries and commerce quickly followed. The result was a dynamic city, now called Old Delhi, which remained the Mogul capital until the end of the dynasty.

Shah Jahan was as keen a general as he was a builder. He regained Kandahar in 1638 but lost it again in 1649, and 5,000 of his men died in a vain attempt to seize Samarkand. He was victorious only in the south, where he first went in pursuit of a general who, under suspicion of treason, fled to the kingdom of Ahmadnagar in 1629. Shah Jahan directed operations from Burhanpur (where Mumtaz Mahal died), and in 1633 he defeated and annexed Ahmadnagar. This triumph, however, set in motion forces that would help destroy the Mogul Empire. The conquest of Ahmadnagar brought Shah Jahan's border to Bijapur and Golconda, the other two Muslim kingdoms of the south. For fifty years, relations between the Moguls and their new neighbors alternated between war and uncertain peace. Much of the population of Ahmadnagar and Bijapur belonged to a Hindu community called the Marathas, who served their Muslim kings as administrators and soldiers. When a fresh round of hostilities broke out between the Moguls and Bijapur in 1656, Maratha chieftain Shivaji Bhonsle took advantage of the confusion to seize some forts in northern Bijapur. On this base, Shivaji built a Maratha military machine that was to sap the strength of Mogul India.

Shah Jahan's pursuit of glory was expensive, and the land revenue rose from one-third of the crop to one-half. In 1657 the emperor fell seriously ill, and his four sons began quarreling over the succession to the throne. Shah Jahan's eldest son Dara Shikoh was his favorite; but the third son, Aurangzeb, was the most able of the princes, and he and Dara Shikoh particularly hated each other. Apparently, the heir apparent Dara Shikoh blocked the ambitious Aurangzeb from the throne, but the two men were also separated by temperament and religion: The indolent Dara Shikoh was a mystic who—like his great-grandfather Akbar—believed that both Islam and Hinduism contained a core of truth, whereas the hardworking Aurangzeb was a devout Muslim. Shah Jahan unexpectedly recovered his health, but by then the conflict among his sons had reached the point of no return, and the emperor could not prevent a familial war. In 1658 Aurangzeb triumphed and deposed his father, who had sided with Dara Shikoh, and imprisoned him in the fort at Agra. The following year, Aurangzeb executed Dara Shikoh for deviation from the Muslim faith. Shah Jahan lingered on until 1666, when he was buried beside his long-dead empress in the Taj Mahal.

Aurangzeb is remembered as the man whose intolerance toward non-Muslims provoked revolts that destroyed the Mogul Empire. He was a Muslim in a way that none of his predecessors had been, and he sought to end un-Islamic behavior that had hitherto been permitted or even encouraged. To Aurangzeb, to try to raise the emperor above other men was the sinful deification of a human being. As a result, he ceased to sponsor secular cultural projects that promoted imperial glory, which in any case violated the austerity expected of a good Muslim. Painters, musicians, and poets were banished from the court. While nobles and members of the imperial family continued to support the arts, the withdrawal of the emperor's generous patronage ended the Golden Age of Mogul culture. Changes in artistic policy were of little concern to the majority of Aurangzeb's subjects, but they were affected by other manifestations of the emperor's desire to be a true Muslim. He implemented Koranic injunctions that relegated non-Muslims to an inferior position in an Islamic state: He taxed Hindu merchants at a higher rate than Muslim ones; he first forbade the construction of new Hindu temples and then ordered the demolition of Hindu temples and centers of learning; and most dramatically of all, in 1679 he reimposed the *jizya* tax on non-Muslims.

But the picture of Aurangzeb's reign as an era of philistinism and religious bigotry is incomplete. Aurangzeb stopped building palaces, but he did oversee several major projects of religious construction, notably the Pearl Mosque at Delhi and the Imperial Mosque at Lahore. He patronized intellectuals if their work did not challenge Islam; one of his closest friends was Danishmand Khan, who studied Hindu philosophy and the writings of René Descartes and William Harvey. Nor did he appoint or promote officials simply because they were Muslims, and throughout his reign, there were Hindu *mansabdars* at the highest levels of the court, administration, and army. Aurangzeb's war against Dara Shikoh is often cited as proof of his religious intolerance, but the quarrel between the two brothers was political in nature. Dara Shikoh's heretical views provided an excuse for executing him, but he would probably not have been put to death had he not stood between Aurangzeb and the throne. Historians still debate the practical effects of Aurangzeb's discriminatory laws. Hindu merchants evaded the higher duties by having Muslims carry their goods, and it has been suggested that Hindu temples were only selectively demolished.

Aurangzeb was an experienced soldier before he seized the throne, and as emperor he sought glory in conquest. This was permissible to a strict Muslim where artistic patronage and the imperial cult were not. He abandoned the impractical dreams of recapturing Kandahar and Samarkand and instead concentrated on India. By the time of his death in 1707, he had unified India for the first time in 2,000 years. At the same time, however, he was confronted by rebellions across his vast realm. Most of the rebels were non-Muslims, which suggests that the uprisings were caused by the emperor's Islamic policy. Actually, nonreligious concerns underlay all the major revolts, and the preponderance of non-Muslims among the rebels is explained by their strength in the population of India. The two most famous rebellions were those of the Sikhs in the Punjab and of the Marathas in the south. The Sikhs had generally been hostile to the Moguls since Jahangir's execution of their guru Arjan, but the roots of the great Sikh rising lie not in religious persecution but in Aurangzeb's friendship with one Sikh. This was Ram Ray, son of one guru and brother of another, whom the emperor recognized as guru in 1664. The Sikh religious leaders, however, rejected Aurangzeb's nominee and chose Ram Ray's kinsman Tegh Bahadur instead. A decade of hostility between Aurangzeb and Tegh Bahadur ensued, until in 1675 the guru was executed. He was succeeded by his son Gobind Singh, who reformed the Sikhs into a military brotherhood that sought revenge in a revolt against Mogul rule.

More than anything else, the Maratha rising launched by Shivaji Bhonsle undermined Aurangzeb's empire. To win the support of his fellow

Marathas, Shivaji depicted the revolt as a Hindu war of liberation against Muslim oppression. This image was adopted by nineteenth-century Indian nationalists in search of inspiration for struggles against their British rulers, whom they saw as modern counterparts of the Mogul conquerors. But Shivaji's rebellion actually originated in his desire to raise himself from chieftain to monarch. In the late 1650s and early 1660s, he waged a guerrilla war to seize territory from Bijapur, and in 1664, he raided the Mogul port of Surat. An imperial army thereupon defeated Shivaji, whom the generous emperor appointed as a *mansabdar*, and in 1666, the Maratha joined the imperial court at Agra. Not long afterward, however, Shivaji fled in a rage and recaptured his forts. There were several reasons for his anger, but Aurangzeb's religious policy was not among them; the principal one was that his fellow Hindus among the Rajput courtiers treated him as a low-caste upstart rather than a king. By this time Bijapur was in decay after years of conflict with the Moguls, and Aurangzeb was away in the northwest quelling an Afghan revolt. This allowed Shivaji to make himself master of much of the Maratha country, and in 1674, he crowned himself king. After his death in 1680, his son Sambhaji continued the rebellion.

Soon after this, Aurangzeb decided to bring Bijapur and Golconda under Mogul rule. Forty-five years earlier, Shah Jahan had sent him to the south as its viceroy, and ever since then, Aurangzeb had dreamed of uniting India. He was not, however, motivated merely by expansionism. The fabled wealth of Bijapur and Golconda would replenish the imperial treasury, but more important, Aurangzeb anticipated that the conquest of the two southern kingdoms would enable him to defeat the Marathas. For twenty-five years, Shivaji and Sambhaji had harried the borderlands of the empire, moving back and forth into what was nominally Bijapuri territory. Bringing the south under imperial rule would make it possible to surround and crush the Marathas. Sambhaji had recently given Aurangzeb particular cause for anger by giving refuge to the emperor's son Akbar after the latter had mounted an unsuccessful rebellion. And so in 1681 Aurangzeb, now over sixty years old, left north India to take up personal command of the army in the south. The campaign began well: Bijapur fell in 1686 and Golconda in 1687, and in 1689 Aurangzeb's men captured and executed Sambhaji. The army swept southward until the emperor ruled all of the subcontinent, save the southernmost tip. By uniting India, Aurangzeb had made real the old Mogul dream. It has, however, been suggested that that dream had united the emperor, his nobles, and his subjects in pursuit of a shared goal; and with the goal attained, unity began to evaporate. Outbreaks against imperial rule became frequent, and the conquest of Bijapur and Golconda freed the Marathas to focus all of their energies on the Moguls. Worse, the execution of Sambhaji meant that Aurangzeb was confronted by several Maratha chiefs rather than a single king; he might defeat one chief and secure his submission, but this would be renounced as soon as the Mogul army moved on against the next band of warriors. The Marathas were emboldened by Aurangzeb's failure to crush them and exploited the opportunities for plunder that were opened by the emperor's absorption in his southern campaign: In 1699, they crossed the Narmada River into northern India, in 1702 they reached the ancient city of Ujjain, and in 1706 they looted the wealthy province of Gujarat.

The strains of the war against the Marathas now brought out the latent weaknesses of Mogul India. Aurangzeb's huge army was expensive, and by the late seventeenth century, it absorbed half of the empire's income from taxes. The land revenue, the principal tax, was becoming a serious burden for the peasant. At the same time, the bureaucracy was growing increasingly oppressive. The Mogul emperors had always appointed many of their *mansabdars* for political reasons rather than administrative ability, buying the allegiance of potential enemies with high ranks and lucrative *jagirs*. Aurangzeb found this to be a good way of winning over the nobles of the southern kingdoms or obtaining the submission of Maratha adventurers and other rebels. Unfortunately, even with the new conquests in the south, the empire was running out of *jagirs*. Fearful for their incomes, many *mansabdars* accordingly ceased to concentrate on their administrative and military duties and instead intrigued against one another, trying to win the emperor's favor and consequently additional *jagirs*. This increased the tendency of each *mansabdar* to maximize the revenues from his *jagir*, with no regard for the well-being of its peasants after it passed from his control. All this was compounded by the emperor's absence on campaign, which ended the imperial vigilance that had checked the oppressiveness of the *mansabdars*. Desperate *zamindars*, the local notables who remitted the land revenue, countered by leading their peasants in revolt. Now, by eroding the loyalty to the emperor that many non-Muslims had felt during the previous century, Aurangzeb's religious policy may have begun to bear fruit. This destroyed what had been a major psychological barrier to rebellion, even under great provocation.

The eighty-eight-year-old Aurangzeb died in 1707 and was succeeded by his eldest surviving son Bahadur Shah. Despite the Maratha war and the local rebellions, the Mogul Empire remained powerful, and the new emperor tried to restore order. Aurangzeb had enrolled Sambhaji's son Shahu as a *mansabdar* and brought up the Maratha prince as a loyal Mogul noble; and Bahadur Shah now sought to bring the Marathas to heel by allowing Shahu to return to his homeland and take up his father's throne. He also made peace with the Sikhs, whose guru Gobind Singh entered the imperial court. But Bahadur Shah was already sixty-three years old when he came to the throne, and he did not have the strength or the time to rejuvenate the empire. The Sikhs rebelled again after Gobind Singh was assassinated by a servant; and Bahadur Shah's death in 1712 touched off power struggles among princes and courtiers and a new Maratha rising under Shahu's prime minister. All this combined to destroy the empire that had been weakened by the war in the south. By 1750, Mogul power was a thing of the past. A member of the imperial dynasty still lived in Delhi, but India was divided among rival *mansabdars* who had established themselves as virtually independent regional rulers, Maratha insurgents, and Afghan invaders. The merchants of the English East India Company were about to take advantage of this political realignment, by launching a process of expansion that ended a century later with the entire subcontinent under British control.

Ultimately, the Mogul emperors' quest for glory helped to destroy them. But it also gave the world some of its most beautiful buildings and paintings, fine prose and poetry in Persian and Hindi, and the bases of Indian classical music and dance. The military victories of Akbar, Shah Jahan, and Aurangzeb made the Mogul Empire one of the great powers of Asia in the seventeenth century. This in turn made India stable and wealthy. Its flourishing export trade attracted the foreign merchants who first clothed much of Europe with Indian textiles and then replaced the Moguls as the rulers of India. It has been suggested that the unification of India under the Moguls prepared its people for a modern subcontinental administration transcending local differences. Be that as it may, when the British left in 1947, Jawaharlal Nehru, the first leader of the new India and descendant of a family of Hindu *mansabdars*, sought strength by reviving the sort of communal integration and national culture that had underlain the achievements of the Golden Age of Mogul power and drew on the best traditions of both India and the rest of the world to win back his country's greatness.

SELECTED BIBLIOGRAPHY

Ali, M. Athar. *The Apparatus of Empire: Awards of Ranks, Offices, and Titles to the Mughal Nobility (1574–1658)*. Delhi, India: Oxford University Press, 1985.

A complete list of Mogul *mansabdars* from the reign of Akbar to the accession of Aurangzeb, categorized by ethnic origin and religious affiliation.

Araly, Abraham. *The Last Spring: The Lives and Times of the Great Mughals*. New Delhi, India: Penguin Books, 1997. A new popular history of the Moguls.

Asher, Catherine B. *Architecture of Mughal India*. Cambridge, U.K.: Cambridge University Press, 1992. An illustrated history, showing the relationship of architecture to the cultural and political history of the Mogul Empire.

Beach, Milo Cleveland. *Mughal and Rajput Painting*. Cambridge, U.K.: Cambridge University Press, 1992. A good synthesis of recent scholarship on Mogul painting and the painting sponsored by Rajput princes in India; marred by poorly reproduced photographs.

Blake, Stephen P. *Shahjahanabad: The Sovereign City in Mughal India, 1639–1739*. Cambridge, U.K.: Cambridge University Press, 1991. A study of Shah Jahan's Old Delhi, emphasizing the role of the imperial palace and noble households in the development of the city.

Crowe, Sylvia, Sheila Haywood, Susan Jellicoe, and Gordon Patterson. *The Gardens of Mughul India: A History and a Guide*. London: Thames and Hudson, 1972. An illustrated history of the great imperial gardens of Mogul India.

Day, U. N. *The Mughal Government, A.D. 1556–1707*. New Delhi, India: Munshiram Manoharlal, 1970. A descriptive account of the political institutions of the Mogul Empire.

Elliot, Sir H. M., and John Dowson. *The History of India as Told by Its Own Historians: The Muhammadan Period*. 8 vols. Originally published 1867–1877; frequently reprinted since then, for example, Delhi, India: Low Price Publications, 1990. Translated excerpts from the major Persian-language histories of India; still a useful reference tool, despite flaws.

Findly, Ellison Banks. *Nur Jahan, Empress of Mughal India*. New York: Oxford University Press, 1993. A thoroughly researched biography of Jahangir's empress, the most powerful woman of the Mogul dynasty.

Gascoigne, Bamber. *The Great Moghuls*. New York: Harper & Row, 1971. A popular history full of outstanding photographs.

Gordon, Stewart. *The Marathas, 1600–1818*. Cambridge, U.K.: Cambridge University Press, 1993. The most recent history of the Marathas, with particular focus on the structure of the Maratha state under Shivaji and his successors.

Grewal, J. S. *The Sikhs of the Punjab*. Cambridge, U.K.: Cambridge University Press, 1990. A history of the Sikhs since the birth of the religion, with a useful account of their relationship with the Moguls.

Gupta, Ashin Das, and M. N. Pearson. *India and the Indian Ocean, 1500–1800*. Calcutta, India: Oxford University Press, 1987. A collection of essays on trade and traffic in the Indian Ocean and their effects on the population of coastal India.

Hansen, Waldemar. *The Peacock Throne: The Drama of Mogul India*. New York: Holt, Rinehart & Winston, 1972. A readable popular history of the Mogul dynasty.

Koch, Ebba. *Mughal Architecture: An Outline of Its History and Development (1526–*

1858). Munich: Prestel-Verlag, 1991. An informative summary that links architectural developments with individual emperors.

Moosvi, Shireen. *The Economy of the Mughal Empire: A Statistical Study*. Delhi, India: Oxford University Press, 1987. An examination grounded in detailed research.

Raychaudhuri, Tapan, and Irfan Habib, eds. *The Cambridge Economic History of India*. Vol. 1: *c. 1200–c. 1750*. Cambridge, U.K.: Cambridge University Press, 1982. The bulk of this collection deals with the Mogul age; it includes treatments of the land revenue system and internal and foreign trade.

Richards, John F. *The Mughal Empire*. Cambridge, U.K.: Cambridge University Press, 1993. Largely a political history of the empire.

————. *Power, Administration and Finance in Mughal India*. Aldershot, U.K.: Variorum, Ashgate Publishing, 1993. A collection of essays by one of the doyens of Mogul history, dealing with the creation of the Mogul state and its decline.

Rizvi, S. A. *The Wonder That Was India*. Vol. 2: *A Survey of the History and Culture of the Indian Sub-Continent from the Coming of the Moslems to the British Conquest 1200–1700*. London: Sigwick & Jackson Ltd., 1987. A useful reference book summarizing the dynastic history of Muslim India and outlining developments in political theory, society and economy, religion, and the arts.

The "Pestsäule," or "Pest-column," erected rather prematurely in 1679 in Vienna as an offering to the Holy Trinity for saving Vienna from the pestilence of the Turkish Wars. (Reproduced from the Collections of the Library of Congress)

9

The Siege of Vienna, 1683

INTRODUCTION

For several hundred years prior to the appearance of the Turks at the gates of Vienna in 1683, the cry ''The Turks are coming!'' had struck fear in the hearts of Europeans, especially those who lived in the Balkans and the valley of the Danube River. Because of their well-deserved reputation for aggressiveness and brutality, and because they were Muslims rather than Christians, the Turks terrified most Europeans.

The Turks originated in central Asia, but by the eleventh century they had drifted into western Asia Minor, where they settled. However, the Turks were not unified; rather, there were several different branches of Turks. In the eleventh century the most important Turks were the Seljuk Turks; but the Ottoman Turks, named after Osman or Othman who founded a dynasty early in the fourteenth century, soon eclipsed the Seljuk Turks in importance.

From their base in Anatolia the Turks eyed their western neighbor, the Byzantine Empire, with its rich and sophisticated capital at Constantinople. The Byzantine Empire had been in decline for centuries, a dangerous state of affairs made worse when the Seljuk Turks smashed the Byzantines at the Battle of Manzikert in 1071 and when Roman Catholic knights of the Fourth Crusade ignored their stated objectives in the Holy Land to sack Orthodox Christian Constantinople in 1204.

As Byzantium decayed, the Ottoman Turks expanded. In 1354 they crossed the Dardanelles and seized Gallipoli, thereby gaining a foothold in Europe. Later in the century the Turks subjugated the Serbs and the Bulgarians, both of whom had taken advantage of Byzantium's weakness to declare their independence. What was left of Byzantium now found itself surrounded by the Ottomans and virtually abandoned by western Christianity.

In the early fifteenth century Timur Lang (Tamerlane) swept out of central Asia with the intention of reestablishing the sprawling empire of Chinggis Khan. Tamerlane's threat to the rising power of the Ottoman Turks was very real, and they escaped destruction only narrowly. This diversion prevented the Turks from destroying Byzantium for about a half century; however, in 1453 the Ottomans under Sultan Mehmed II took Constantinople, which they renamed Istanbul and made their capital.

After annihilating Byzantium, the warlike Turks continued their conquests unabated. That part of Serbia that had retained its independence was taken in 1458–1459, and the Morea fell at about the same time. A few years later, Albania, Bosnia, and part of Herzegovina passed under Turkish control.

But the Turks did not confine their empire building to Europe alone. The Black Sea was turned into a Turkish lake, and the Arab lands stretching from Damascus in the north to the Islamic holy cities of Medina and Mecca in the south were conquered. So too was Egypt. At the same time that the Ottomans moved overland, they also pursued an expansionistic policy on the waters. Determined to control the eastern Mediterranean Sea, the Turks initiated a conflict with Venice, the dominant maritime power of the era, that lasted for generations and resulted in the Ottomans absorbing much of Venice's eastern Mediterranean empire.

Turkey enjoyed its most glorious years under Sultan Süleyman I the Magnificent, who reigned from 1520 until 1566. In 1521 Süleyman seized Belgrade, thereby opening the middle Danube valley and the Hungarian plain beyond to his armies. At the Battle of Mohacs in 1526, Ottoman troops crushed the Hungarians, who had been seen as a strong bulwark against Turkish expansion. With this resounding victory, the Turks occupied most of Hungary, including the capital Buda located on the western heights above the Danube and commanding the fertile plain to the east.

The Hungarian defeat at Mohacs brought the Turks to the border of the Habsburg Empire, ruled by Charles V, Europe's most important monarch. Caught up in the fate of Hungary, the Habsburgs soon found themselves at war with the Turks. In 1529 Süleyman besieged Vienna, the Habsburg capital, but he failed to bring the Habsburgs to their knees and subsequently lifted the siege. Nevertheless, the Turkish position in Hungary was well established. Much of that country was absorbed directly into the Ottoman Empire in 1541, while a Turkish puppet ruled over the important Hungarian province of Transylvania. Only a small sliver of Hungary, called Royal Hungary, passed to the Habsburgs.

After Süleyman the Magnificent's death, the Ottoman Empire entered a long period of slow decline. Causes for its stagnation included the empire's sprawling nature, which led to an overextension that strained both the country's human and financial resources, a general decline in the competency of the sultans, extensive corruption within the bureaucracy, the shift of trade routes from the eastern Mediterranean to the Atlantic Ocean, chronic unrest among the Janissary corps (the heart of the sultan's army), and a failure—especially within the military—to keep pace with advancing Western technology. Nevertheless, despite these shortcomings the Ottomans remained the preeminent power in the eastern Mediterranean and southeastern Europe.

By the middle of the seventeenth century, the decades-long failure to address the serious problems confronting the Ottoman state had become intolerable. During the preceding 100 years, the sultans had spent more and more time in the harem, ignoring their princely duties but especially their warrior role as head of the Ottoman army. As the sultans absented themselves from the daily affairs of state, the grand vezir, an office akin to that of prime minister in the West, filled the void. In 1656, at the advanced age of seventy, Mehmed Köprülü became grand vezir. The ironhanded Köprülü proved to be the architect of Ottoman revitalization.

Prior to accepting the post of grand vezir, Mehmed Köprülü, who understood that grand vezirs rose and fell with alarming frequency in the morass of Ottoman court politics, negotiated an agreement that gave him a free hand to impose his will. He is perhaps best remembered for applying Draconian measures to reduce the staggering level of corruption. Estimates of the number of corrupt officeholders executed during his five years as grand vezir range from 30,000 to 60,000. Furthermore, Mehmed Köprülü understood that the Ottoman state's stability rested on its military character. He concluded that trouble would surely ensue if the Ottoman armies were not constantly moving forward, giving the soldiers who were the regime's backbone the opportunity for conquest and the booty that went with it. This renewed emphasis on Ottoman military activity ultimately led to the siege of Vienna in 1683.

The Habsburg family was the most important one in sixteenth-century

Europe. When the powerful Charles V abdicated in 1555, he split his immense holdings between his son, Philip II, who received the Spanish crown, and his brother, Ferdinand I, who received the Austrian patrimony and became Holy Roman Emperor, a position that gave him a preponderant but not absolute role in the German-speaking world.

The ambitious Austrian Habsburgs laid claim not only to leadership of the German-speaking world but also to outright ownership of many of central Europe's small kingdoms and principalities. Interestingly, Turkish success in the early sixteenth century paid huge but unexpected dividends for the Habsburgs. Süleyman the Magnificent's victory at Mohacs so alarmed both the Bohemian (Czech) and Hungarian nobility that they offered their respective crowns to the Habsburg Ferdinand, who readily accepted. While the Habsburgs added Bohemia to their domains, Hungary was divided between the Habsburgs and the Turks, with the latter receiving the lion's share. In any event, Turkey in Europe now abutted upon a strong and wealthy Christian Habsburg state.

From the time of Süleyman through the middle of the seventeenth century, the Habsburgs and Ottomans were either at war or bound by uneasy truces that foreshadowed the resumption of hostilities. War between the two once again broke out in the early 1660s, owing to the confused and tangled nature of Hungarian affairs. George Rakoczi, a Hungarian nobleman who served as the Ottoman Empire's vassal prince of Transylvania, an autonomous Hungarian province, began to break away from Turkish authority. The Turks responded by attacking Rakoczi, killing him in battle, and nominating a different Hungarian nobleman, Michael Apafi, to succeed him.

The victorious Ottoman armies now turned westward. In 1663 they clashed with the Habsburgs, who were also intently interested in Hungarian affairs and who had sent an ineffective force to aid Rakoczi. Threatened by the Turks, the Habsburgs appealed to Christian Europe for help. The response was a tepid one; most European states were so consumed with their interminable rivalries in central and western Europe—rivalries that often involved Habsburg ambitions—that they balked at sending aid to a competitor even in the face of the Islamic threat that the Turks posed. Nevertheless, men and money from western Europe did arrive, albeit grudgingly, and these forces proved superior to those of the Turks. The Ottomans suffered a crushing defeat at the Battle of St. Gotthard in 1664. However, instead of capitalizing on their victory, the Habsburgs, who fixated on the growing influence of France's Louis XIV in Germany, hastened to conclude the Truce of Vasvar, which rewarded the Turks despite their military defeat. Vasvar confirmed Apafi as prince of Transylvania, allowed the Turks to keep several Hungarian fortresses they had seized, and even required the Habsburgs to pay an indemnity. Vasvar also provided for a truce between the Habsburgs and the Ottomans to expire in 1682.

Buoyed by their good luck in Hungary and a major victory over Venice that brought the island of Crete under their rule, the Ottomans invaded Poland in 1672 and added the western part of the Ukraine and the Polish province of Podolia to their holdings, although it should be noted that the Ukraine was soon lost to Russia.

A climax to this period of Ottoman expansion and regeneration occurred in 1683 when a huge Ottoman army, estimated at perhaps 275,000 including camp followers, besieged Vienna for months. The moving force behind the Ottoman invasion, code-named "Red Apple," was the grand vezir, Kara Mustapha, a member of the Köprülü family and a man determined to make a name for himself. Sweeping up the Danube valley in the spring of 1683, Kara Mustapha invested Vienna in July.

The Habsburgs fled before the Turks, leaving their capital's defense to an 11,000 man force commanded by Count Ernst Rüdiger von Starhemberg. Relying on stout defensive fortifications and greatly benefiting from the military incompetency of Kara Mustapha, who failed to make a concerted attack on the city, Vienna held out. With some difficulty, the Habsburgs gathered forces from Germany and Poland to bolster their own army, and on September 11 a relief column led by Charles, duke of Lorraine, and the Polish king Jan Sobieski arrived at Vienna's outskirts. On the following morning, the imperial forces routed the Turks. The remnants of the Turkish army fled in disarray, and Kara Mustapha was executed by order of the sultan.

The Habsburgs pursued the Turks, and during the next decade and a half the Ottomans suffered several telling defeats, including a setback at the second Battle of Mohacs (1687), which reversed the outcome of the first battle, and the loss of Buda, which they had held for 145 years. When the Habsburg general Prince Eugene of Savoy smashed the Turks at the Battle of Zenta in 1697, the Ottomans sued for peace. The result was the Treaty of Karlowitz (1699), which awarded almost all of Hungary to the Habsburgs and gave the Dalmatian coast to Turkey's other European rival, Venice.

INTERPRETIVE ESSAY
David Stefancic

The sound of bells spread across central Europe in the summer of 1683. The bells did not herald a happy event; rather, they told of great danger. The bells being rung were known as Turk Bells, and they sounded the warning that the Ottoman army was again on the march. This time Vienna appeared to be its target.

The news of a new Ottoman onslaught came as a shock. Everyone thought the weakened Ottoman Empire incapable of threatening Europe as it once had. The last major threat to central Europe and Vienna had come under the leadership of Süleyman the Magnificent in 1529, over a century earlier. Since then, a number of ineffective sultans such as Selim the Sot had run the empire. In the absence of strong leadership, the empire had declined. Both the Janissaries and Sipahis (the Ottoman army's elite infantry and cavalry, respectively) repeatedly staged revolts within the army. This almost constant distraction allowed various national groups within the empire to push for greater autonomy or even independence. A national revolt of this type broke out in the territory of modern-day Romania. Moreover, the local governors took advantage of the growing chaos to carve out their own little kingdoms. All this greatly diminished the tax revenues flowing to Istanbul. Insufficient revenue undermined the general economy, and the state's infrastructure began to collapse. Without bridges and roads in good repair, trade declined. Revolution and corruption brought a once powerful empire to near destruction.

The Ottoman decline was arrested under the leadership of Mehmed Köprülü, the grand vezir of Mehmed IV. He deserved the credit for a resurgent Ottoman Empire that once again threatened to bring death and destruction to central Europe and Vienna.

When Mehmed IV came to the throne in 1648, he was but a boy of ten and under the regency of his mother. Until 1656 anarchy still reigned over the empire. However, in that year the appointment of a new grand vezir, Mehmed Köprülü, marked the beginning of Ottoman reform. Sir Paul Rycaut, a contemporary writer, described Mehmed IV thusly: "Never was a prince [sultan] so great a nimrod." Mehmed was not the man to renew the empire, so it fell to the regent mother to find the right candidate. Mehmed Köprülü kept being brought to her attention. Köprülü was a capable local governor who ruled his district well by keeping a tight rein on his own officials and rooting out all corruption. He had started out as a stable hand and had risen through the ranks to become governor. He could neither read nor write, but he was a good administrator. He was perhaps seventy years old when he arrived in Istanbul. He agreed to become the grand vezir only if given a free hand to reform the Ottoman system. The regent mother agreed that the sultan would ratify all of his acts. He also sought out and received the support of the empire's religious leaders.

Power now shifted from the sultan's palace to that of the grand vezir. Köprülü aimed to centralize and expand the empire. The former would be the prerequisite for the latter. Köprülü chose Sultan Murad II, a great reformer, as his model, and he declared war against all corruption.

Mehmed Köprülü understood how the army's behavior had destabilized the empire over the last century, so military reform became his first priority. To regain control over the army, he ordered the execution of all mutinous officers. He then organized new recruits from Albania and Bulgaria to fill the openings. Köprülü kept the army busy reestablishing border fortifications and building new military bases throughout the empire. He also revived the Ottoman navy, which had never been rebuilt after its last defeat by the Venetians. The military reforms had the desired effect: Istanbul regained control over the army, and a sense of pride and mission as defenders of Islam and the sultan now infused the military.

Köprülü also rooted out corrupt officials and judges. Arrests and executions came without warning or appeal. Tens of thousands were put to death over a five-year period. The palace executioner claimed to have strangled 4,000 victims himself. The very real threat of death, however, did much to wipe out corruption in the empire.

Köprülü also suppressed the rebellious minorities in the Romanian territories. In crushing the Romanian revolt, Köprülü used great cruelty as a warning to any future rebels. The result was to check temporarily nationalistic rebellion within the empire.

By the time of his death in 1661, Mehmed Köprülü had restored the strength and stability of the empire. His iron-fisted rule now passed to his son, Ahmed Köprülü, who became the new grand vezir. Before he died, Mehmed left his son two bits of advice: Never heed the words of a woman, and always keep the army in constant action. He took these words to heart. Ahmed received the same support from the sultan and the mufti, or religious leaders, that his father had, and he continued to execute corrupt officials for three more years before dismantling the terror apparatus slowly and quietly.

Ahmed launched an aggressive foreign policy to keep his soldiers occupied and to expand the borders of Islam. The opening volley was heard in 1663 as an army of 120,000 led by Ahmed attacked the Austrian fortress at Neuhäusel. After a five-week siege, the fortress fell. At the same time, Ahmed's allies, the Crimean Tartars, carried out a secondary assault into Moravia. The following year, Ahmed led his troops toward the St. Gotthard Pass.

The Austrians quickly rallied an army when news of the defeat at Neuhäusel reached Vienna. Other countries sent men to bolster the Austrian defense at St. Gotthard. Prince Charles of Lorraine was named to lead the allied army. When the two armies met on August 1, 1664, Ahmed found out how far the Ottoman army had fallen behind its European adversaries. French troops armed with the latest firearms stopped the initial Ottoman assault. While the Ottomans tried to rally, Prince Charles smashed into their forces with his heavy cavalry. Ahmed's army broke, leaving behind its supplies including fifteen cannons. Ahmed, despite losing 10,000 men, managed to regain control of his troops and maintain a disciplined retreat. The Austrians had won a major victory, but they failed to follow it up. Instead of pressing their advantage, the Austrians decided to open negotiations. Remarkably, after ten days of talks, Ahmed emerged victorious. Vienna agreed to the Ottoman retention of Transylvania and the fortress of Neuhäusel plus the surrounding territory. What Ahmed Köprülü almost lost in war, he regained through diplomacy. Upon his return to Istanbul, he was hailed as a great hero of Islam.

After a five-year hiatus, Ahmed struck again. In 1669, he seized Crete from the Venetians, thereby securing a prize that had eluded the Ottomans for twenty-five years. Ahmed was again hailed as a hero. After defeating two of the Ottoman's traditional enemies, one by war and one by diplomacy, Ahmed now turned toward a third: Poland. In 1673 Ahmed organized an army of 6,000, with a support force of Crimean Tartars, to take Podolia from the Polish-Lithuanian Commonwealth. Surprising the Poles, the Turks quickly took the capital of Podolia, Kamieniec. The Polish king tried to open negotiations, but the Polish field commander, Grand Hetman Jan Sobieski, organized counteroffensives at Chocim and Lwów in 1673 and 1675. The Turks were fortunate in that the Polish state had only a small standing army. For the bulk of its force,

Poland relied on the Polish magnates, landed aristocrats, who had private armies that they loaned to the Polish king. The Polish magnates by 1675 had grown tired of war and had decided to return to their homes with their armies. At this time Ahmed counterattacked. He retook Podolia and forced Sobieski into negotiations. The Poles recognized the cession of Podolia to Istanbul at the Treaty of Zurawa (1676).

Ahmed Köprülü did not live to enjoy his victory, dying within days of signing the peace treaty with Poland. It was assumed that Mustapha Köprülü, Ahmed's brother, would succeed him, but instead Mehmed IV named his hunting companion and Ahmed's foster brother Kara Mustapha as the new grand vezir. Kara Mustapha, pompous and ambitious, dreamed of great wealth and power; he envisioned himself as greater than Süleyman the Magnificent. Under Kara Mustapha, corruption and bribery returned to the empire. The grand vezir himself lined his own pockets.

Kara Mustapha also maintained an aggressive foreign policy. Between 1678 and 1681, he fought an inconclusive war along the Ottoman's northern border against the Poles and the Russians that cost the Ottoman treasury dearly. But Kara Mustapha was lucky when a revolt in Hungary offered him a new source of wealth. The Hungarian count Imre Thököly, outraged when Emperor Leopold I tried to introduce the Catholic Counter Reformation into Hungary, organized a revolt against Vienna. Leading Hungary's numerous Protestants, Thököly issued an appeal for help that Kara Mustapha answered. Although Kara Mustapha was openly anti-Christian—he once boasted that he would one day house his horses in St. Peter's Basilica—he now decided to aid Hungarian Protestant rebels and lead a Holy War against Vienna. Kara Mustapha convinced Mehmed IV to recognize Count Thököly as the king of western Hungary and put him under Ottoman protection. In return for this support, Thököly was to pay Istanbul a yearly tribute. The count also received monetary support from the French monarch Louis XIV, who encouraged the Hungarians and Turks in order to distract Vienna from his own attempts to expand France at Habsburg expense. The first Turkish troops were sent to Thököly in 1681, with support coming from Bosnia and Serbia in 1682. These troops played more of an advisory role, with the bulk of the Ottoman troops set to arrive in 1683.

The Ottomans assembled an army of 275,000 men that Sultan Mehmed IV led to Belgrade, where he handed it over to Kara Mustapha along with the banner of the prophet Muhammad. The Turkish army marched into Hungary and linked up with Count Thököly's troops, who marched under the banner "For God and Country." Thököly's troops, calling themselves "men of the cross," were now allies of the soldiers of Allah.

The Ottoman army met little resistance as it marched through the Hungarian countryside in the direction of Vienna. Although Kara Mustapha's advisers encouraged him to occupy a string of Austrian fortresses along the route, he decided to go around them in order to deliver a lightning blow against Vienna. The capture of Vienna would demoralize the countryside as well as the fortresses. The weak defense put up by the Austrian army hinted that Vienna was ripe for the taking. "On to Vienna" became the Ottoman battle cry.

Kara Mustapha was right; Vienna was not prepared for war. Austria felt trapped between two enemies—France and Louis XIV in the west and the Turks in the east. Austria's dilemma was reflected in a contemporary saying, "The Crescent Moon climbs up the night sky and the Gallic cock sleeps not." Nevertheless, Vienna regarded France as the greater threat and assumed that it could placate the Turks through negotiations. The desire to negotiate explains why Austrian resistance was so weak until the Turks arrived at the gates of Vienna.

Emperor Leopold I, described as indecisive, obstinate, and fatalistic, was not the best man to lead a defense against an army of almost 300,000. The emperor named Charles of Lorraine as the principal military commander but then hobbled him by putting him under the control of an Imperial War Council led by Prince Herman of Baden, who detested Charles. Although the Imperial War Council gave Charles an army of 35,000, only 11,000 were designated for the defense of Vienna. With the support of Pope Innocent XI, the emperor sent out an appeal for help to all Christian princes. The German princes responded tepidly. The most important response came from Poland, where Jan Sobieski, now king, agreed to send support. The imperial ambassador, Count Waldstein, agreed that Poland would be reimbursed 1.2 million ducats for its efforts and that Sobieski would be named commander in chief of the allied forces. The Poles had the largest contingent in the allied army and were the most experienced at fighting the Turks. A relief force was on the way, but no one knew how long it would take to get to Vienna.

On July 13, 1683, terror spread through Vienna as the first contingent of the Ottoman army appeared before the city. The emperor and the royal family had left a few days earlier for Passau in Bavaria. This abandonment did not please the people of Vienna. As was custom, Kara Mustapha sent a message to the city: "Accept Islam and live in peace under the Sultan! Or deliver the city and live in peace as Christians under the Sultan. If any man prefer, let him depart peaceably, taking his goods with him." Kara Mustapha wanted the city to surrender to him so that its wealth would fall solely to him. If the city had to be taken by assault, Kara Mustapha would have to share the wealth of Vienna with his soldiers. Count Ernst Starhemberg, the city commander, rejected Kara Mustapha's offer and decided to risk a siege in the hopes that a relief force would arrive in time. He was fortunate that the Turks did not bring any siege guns with them. They had only light and medium cannons, which were effective against infantry but of little use against fortified walls. In order to weaken the walls, mines had to be laid underneath them. This required that tunnels be dug from the Turkish lines to the city walls. This was a slow and tedious process, but Kara Mustapha was patient.

The two-month siege of Vienna began with the firing of cannons on July 15, 1683. All Count Starhemberg could do was hold fast and wait until the relief army arrived. The city had ample supplies of food and ammunition. Kara Mustapha also prepared for a long siege. He placed his main camp to the west of the city in the shape of a crescent. The camp was a city unto itself with 25,000 tents and 50,000 baggage carts.

Through July and August, Vienna suffered daily assaults. In the early days, the population was confident that relief was just around the corner. Confidence turned to despair as the garbage, rubble, and dead bodies began to pile up. Fresh water became a precious commodity, and dysentery became a Turkish ally. By the end of August, food supplies were growing short. On September 4, 1683, the Turks opened a major breach in the wall. A bloody fight ensued before the Turks were forced back and the breach weakly reinforced. The Janissaries wanted to mount a major attack while the wall was still weak, but Kara Mustapha refused. He wanted to give the Viennese time to worry about their weakened defenses and reconsider his offer of surrender.

Kara Mustapha's delay proved costly as the relief force finally arrived. Polish troops, who were familiar with the Ottoman army and its methods, made up the bulk of the army led by King Jan Sobieski. He knew that the Turks would use a conquered Vienna as a springboard into central Europe, threatening central Poland and the German states. He had tried in 1681 and 1682 to organize a preemptive strike against the Turks, but the Austrians had rebuffed him. Sobieski took great pleasure in now organizing the relief of Vienna. The Polish army left Cracow on August 25 with 26,000 men, 29,000 horses, and 8,000 supply wagons.

On August 29 Sobieski linked up with Charles of Lorraine, who

168 Events That Changed the World

brought with him 23,000 Imperial troops and another 28,000 troops from Saxony, Franconia, Bavaria, and Swabia. The allied army now consisted of 77,000 men, as compared to the Turkish army of nearly 300,000. Sobieski reached the heights of the Wienerwald on September 11. From this vantage point, Sobieski could overlook the whole battlefield. He was shocked but pleased to see the sight before him. The Turkish camp was unprotected and spread widely about the field. Sobieski summed up his opponent: "This man is badly encamped. He knows nothing of war; we shall certainly defeat him." Sobieski spent the rest of the day and evening planning the coming battle with Charles and the other military leaders.

Sobieski and his small army failed to impress Kara Mustapha. The Turk was so confident that he neglected to send out pickets or patrols to observe his enemy. Kara Mustapha remained focused on the Vienna prize. The allied attack began on September 12, 1683, with a cannon and rocket barrage followed by a three-pronged attack against the Turks. The battle ebbed back and forth throughout the day. At one point Kara Mustapha panicked and ordered the slaughter of 30,000 Christian hostages. By midafternoon, the battle appeared stalemated when an unexpected gap opened in the Ottoman lines. Sobieski ordered the Polish heavy cavalry, or winged Hussars, to exploit this advantage and seize the tent of the grand vezir. This powerful armored cavalry, distinguished by two rows of feathers that were attached to the rear of each man's armor in such a way that it gave the impression of wings, struck fear in the hearts of the Turks and their Tartar allies. Armed with massive lances, these winged riders astride their huge horses destroyed Turkish resolve. The Tartars were the first to break, followed quickly by the other Turkish allies and finally the Turks themselves. The Janissaries refused to run and died by the hundreds where they stood. The battlefield was strewn with the bodies of 10,000 Turks and Turkish-allied soldiers. Kara Mustapha did not wait to count the bodies but fled the battlefield, barely escaping with the banner of the Prophet. By late afternoon the battle was over and the tent of the grand vezir had a new resident, Jan Sobieski.

Only half of the Turkish army escaped. Kara Mustapha tried to blame others for the disaster, but he eventually paid with his life. When he reached Belgrade, he was strangled on orders of the sultan. Mehmed IV himself did not long survive this catastrophe; in 1687 he was deposed in favor of a new sultan, Süleyman II. With the defeat at Vienna, the decline of Ottoman power resumed. The success of the Köprülüs was completely lost and forgotten, overshadowed by massive defeat.

While Kara Mustapha suffered execution for defeat, the banner of the sultan was paraded throughout the streets of Vienna. The people of Vienna treated Jan Sobieski and Charles of Lorraine as saviors. Emperor Leopold arrived days later to a less than enthusiastic crowd. When the celebration ended, Sobieski said, "I came. I saw. God conquered." The allied army now prepared to press its advantage.

The Ottoman failure at Vienna had great consequences for all those involved. Following their defeat, the Ottomans suffered four consecutive years of setback. One military defeat after another pushed the Ottoman Empire into a steeper decline. The Venetians, the perennial enemies of the Ottomans, sensed weakness and joined the Holy League in 1684. They attacked Turkish forts in the Morea and extended a campaign along the Dalmatian coast. Venice's success there emboldened it to try for an even bigger prize, Athens. The Venetians had dreams of incorporating southern Greece into their commercial empire. The Ottoman army put up a tremendous fight to hold Athens, but one event shifted the battle to the Venetians. The Ottoman army decided to use the ancient Parthenon as a powder magazine, but a stray Venetian artillery shell hit the building, causing its top and sides to blow out. Lacking powder, the Ottoman army temporarily pulled back, allowing the Venetians to hold Athens for awhile.

The Austrians also saw great opportunities after their victory at Vienna. Their army pushed the Ottomans deeper into Hungary, aiming to take the twin cities of Buda and Pest. The war dragged on for four years, reaching a decisive point at the Battle of Mohacs on August 12, 1687. There the Austrian commander Charles of Lorraine decisively defeated the Turks on the same battlefield that had witnessed the monumental triumph of Süleyman the Magnificent in 1526, a victory that had opened Hungary to Ottoman rule. The crown of Hungary now passed to the Habsburgs. Charles of Lorraine prepared to conquer the rest of Hungary, but in 1688 a new war with France forced him to postpone this goal.

The Ottoman military, infuriated by its losses, blamed Mehmed IV and forced him to step down. The new sultan, Süleyman II, proved to be a puppet of the Segbans, a military faction. Other military factions such at the Janissaries and the Sipahis rebelled, and a civil war broke out that resulted in the sacking of Istanbul and other cities by rival Ottoman troops. Süleyman II tried to calm the uprising by naming another member of the Köprülü family as grand vezir. Mustapha Köprülü was forced to pick up where his brother Ahmed had left off. He quickly moved to shore up Ottoman finances and to build a new army that moved to crush the internal revolts and any other potential threats. He was able to retake

Belgrade and Nish from rebels and to stabilize the situation in Istanbul. He attempted to strike back at the Austrians but was killed in 1691 at the Battle of Slankamen. In the meantime, a new sultan, Mustapha II, tried to take up the fight but failed. After the Battle of Zenta in 1697, Hungary and the lands north of Belgrade were lost to Vienna. Mustapha II now named Hüseyin Köprülü as his grand vezir and ordered him to open peace negotiations with all of the Ottoman opponents.

The Poles reentered the picture at the end of 1683. Jan Sobieski had withdrawn the Polish army from the Holy League that opposed the Turks. There were two reasons why Sobieski acted as he did. First, the Polish nobility, who supplied most of the troops for the Polish army, concluded that the Turkish threat had ended and, therefore, saw no reason to continue fighting. Second, the French, who had attempted to keep the Poles out of the war from the start but had failed to overcome Sobieski's Turkophobia, again approached Sobieski—through his wife—and convinced him that continuation of the war would only aid the Habsburgs at the expense of the Poles. Sobieski decided to return to Warsaw. However, Sobieski's successor in 1697, August II, resumed the war against the Turks just in time to enter the peace negotiations.

The Grand Duchy of Muscovy, a new enemy for the Turks, also appeared on the horizon. Muscovy was an up-and-coming state headed by a relatively new ruling family, the Romanovs. Sophia Romanov, who ruled as regent for her two younger brothers, sent her lover, Prince Vasili Golitsin, to take on the Crimean Tartars, Ottoman allies, in two campaigns in 1687 and 1689. This foreshadowed what was to come when Sophia's brother, Peter I, took the throne. Peter's first military campaign as the new tsar was against the Turkish forts on the Sea of Azov. In 1695 Peter met with only minor success, but he returned the following year with an army and navy (the first major naval engagement for the Russian navy). The primary goal was the port of Azov, which was besieged for two months before surrendering to the Russians. Peter used the port of Azov as a center for continued expansion around the sea. The Russians were also brought into the peace negotiations, which ended with the Treaty of Karlowitz.

The principal belligerents of the wars that began in 1683 met at Karlowitz in 1699. The representatives of the greatly weakened Ottoman Empire found themselves in a difficult position. The Austrians demanded and received almost all of Hungary and Transylvania. The Venetians, who had entered the war late, received the Morea and the Dalmatian coast, giving them dominance over the Aegean Sea. The Poles, who had been fighting the longest, regained Podolia and Kamieniec. The European powers gave the Ottomans little room to maneuver. To help soften the European demands, the Ottomans turned to the Greeks to translate and represent them. This tactic did little to stem the Ottoman decline, but it marked the rise to prominence of the Greeks in the Ottoman diplomatic corps.

During the negotiations, the Ottomans resisted Russian claims. The Russian delegation demanded the Sea of Azov and the port of Azov. The Turks tried to ignore the Russian demands because the Russians had little support from the other European powers. Peter I pressed his demands by stepping up his campaign in the Azov region in 1699 and 1700. Negotiations dragged on until 1700, when the Ottoman delegation agreed to transfer control over the sea and the port to Muscovy.

The Treaty of Karlowitz proved to be a short armistice, lasting only twenty-five years and even less in the Russian case as hostilities between Russia and the Ottomans reignited in 1710. The European powers sensed weakness and continued to press the Ottoman Empire for the next two centuries. The Ottoman Empire was no longer viewed as a legitimate military threat, and the Turk Bells, which had once rung to warn Europe of an Ottoman invasion, were now silent.

SELECTED BIBLIOGRAPHY

Barber, Thomas. *Double Eagle and Crescent*. New York: State University of New York, 1967. A detailed description of the siege of Vienna; particularly good at setting the stage for 1683.

Cacavelas, Jeremias. *The Siege of Vienna by the Turks in 1683*. Translated by F. H. Marshall. Cambridge, U.K.: Cambridge University Press, 1925. A readable description of the siege written by a Romanian soldier serving in the Ottoman army.

Coles, Paul. *The Ottoman Impact in Europe*. London: Jarold and Sons, 1968. An overview of the Ottoman Empire in southeastern Europe during the sixteenth and seventeenth centuries.

Davies, Norman. *God's Playground*. 2 vols. New York: Columbia University Press, 1982. A general introduction to Polish history; very good on the reign of John (Jan) III Sobieski.

Evans, R.J.W. *The Making of the Habsburg Monarchy*. Oxford, U.K.: Clarendon Press, 1979. A good work on the origins of the Habsburgs in Austria and their conflict with the Ottoman Empire.

Eversley, Lord George Shaw-Lefevre, and Sir Valentine Chirol. *The Turkish Empire*. New York: Howard Fertig, 1969. A reprint of the classic 1917 study of the Ottoman Empire.

Franaszek, Antoni. *The Relief of Vienna, 1683*. Cracow, Poland: Drukarnia Wydawnicza, 1984. A museum catalog of a Polish exhibit marking the event; a good description of artifacts from the battle.

Kann, Robert A. *A History of the Habsburg Empire*. Berkeley: University of California Press, 1974. An excellent general history of the Habsburg Empire that pays close attention to developments on the empire's southeastern flank.

Kinross, Lord Patrick Balfour. *The Ottoman Centuries*. New York: Morrow Quill, 1977. A standard history of the Ottoman Empire by a recognized British authority.

Macartney, C. A., ed. *The Habsburg and Hohenzollern Dynasties in the Seventeenth and Eighteenth Centuries*. New York: Walter and Company, 1970. A valuable collection of primary documents including the sultan's declaration of war and Sobieski's victory speech.

Parve, Ivan. *Habsburgs and Ottomans: Between Vienna and Belgrade 1683–1739*. Boulder, CO: East European Monographs, 1995. The siege of Vienna as seen through Balkan eyes.

Reddaway, W. F., ed. *The Cambridge History of Poland*. Vol. 1. New York: Cambridge University Press, 1950. A general history of Poland with an excellent chapter on Sobieski and his early attempt to create an anti-Turkish alliance.

Rycaut, Sir Paul. *The Present State of the Ottoman Empire*. New York: Arno Press, 1971. A reprint of the venerable 1668 edition, this work stresses the political and military status of the seventeenth-century Ottoman Empire.

Stoye, John. *The Siege of Vienna*. New York: Holt, Rinehart & Winston, 1964. A lively yet well-balanced account of the battle.

Sugar, Peter F. *Southeastern Europe Under Ottoman Rule 1354–1804*. Seattle: University of Washington Press, 1977. A good overview of the Balkan participation in the battle.

The 300 Anniversary of the Vienna Relief. Warsaw, Poland: Omnipress, 1983. An excellent overview of Polish participation in the events of 1683.

10

The Glorious Revolution, 1688–1689

INTRODUCTION

During the late Middle Ages, England, like most of Europe's nations, developed a quasi-representative body that monarchs tended to consult about important matters. Representing not the nation as a whole but the various interest groups within the nation, these bodies had different names: in Spain, the Cortes; in France, the Estates General; in England, the Parliament.

Perhaps the most important development in England's parliamentary history prior to the seventeenth century occurred in the fourteenth century when King Edward III made concessions to Parliament in order to secure funding for the Hundred Years' War. Most significantly, Parliament gradually acquired considerable power over the levying of taxes and the spending of state revenues. By the end of the century, Parliament virtually controlled the country's finances. It also gained a voice in legislative and administrative matters. Together with the primacy of common law (traditional legal proceedings, judgments, and penalties), Parliament's enhanced importance acted to limit royal prerogative.

During the fifteenth century, England suffered defeat in the Hundred Years' War followed by civil war and anarchy at home. When the Tudor

The execution of Charles I, the king of England; seventeenth-century England experienced considerable political turmoil. (Reproduced from the Collections of the Library of Congress)

family seized the crown in 1485, most Englishmen willingly submitted to its authority in exchange for peace and stability. The Tudors, led by Henry VII (1485–1509), Henry VIII (1509–1547), and Elizabeth I (1558–1603), were absolutists; that is, they subscribed to the theory that God had selected them to rule and had endowed them with absolute power. Under this theory, it was intolerable for any mortal man, group of men, or institution created by men, such as Parliament or the common law, to challenge the monarch. Such a challenge was not only a political crime, but it was also an affront to God.

However, because Parliament and the common law were so entrenched in England, the Tudors had to use great caution in their drive for total control. Nevertheless, over the course of the sixteenth century they established themselves as absolutist monarchs. They worked hard to "manage" Parliament through a mixture of bribery, flattery, threats, and intimidation, and they circumvented common law through the establishment of superior royal courts such as the Court of Star Chamber, which ignored tradition. The Tudors were greatly aided in their quest for absolute power by two unique circumstances: first, the continuing threat to England posed by Spain that encouraged Englishmen to rally behind their sovereign; second, the religious strife associated with the Reformation that, had it not been for a strong royal hand, threatened to engulf the country.

By the time of Elizabeth's death, however, some Englishmen had begun to question the drift toward absolutism. This growing opposition was centered in the Parliament. Consisting of 500 members out of a population of about 5 million, Parliament was divided into a lower and more representative body, the House of Commons, and an upper and more aristocratic chamber, the House of Lords. Parliament had many concerns. It feared for its independence and its relevance; it worried about a large national debt and the exploding cost of maintaining a modern government; it disliked the system of royal courts imposed by the Tudors; and it resented having to pay the bills without having a say in determining national policy.

Furthermore, the religious question in England was heating up. The established church, the Anglican Church (or Church of England) was unpopular in many circles because of its perceived worldliness and corruption. A growing number of Englishmen, especially merchants and small- and medium-sized landowners or gentry, embraced Puritanism, a stern and uncompromising form of Protantism that would thoroughly reform the Anglican Church. Finally, a small but potent minority of wealthy and important English landowners and court officials favored a return to Roman Catholicism.

Through the sheer force of her personality and prestige, Elizabeth suppressed these problems during the last years of her life, but she never solved them. That task fell to her successor, her distant relative James Stuart, who had ruled Scotland as King James VI and now mounted the throne of England as James I. Neither by temperament nor conviction was James prepared for his English experience. Although James was highly intelligent and exceptionally well educated for the times, he was correctly characterized as "the wisest fool in Christendom." Already viewed by his subjects with suspicion because of his foreign origin, James antagonized the English further with his unabashed enthusiasm for absolutism and his utter contempt for his subjects. James extolled the virtues of uninhibited monarchy and took to lecturing an unreceptive Parliament on the topic. His court was rife with corruption, immorality, and extravagance, and the monarch seemed to go out of his way to insult English sensibilities. In matters of money, James consistently circumvented Parliament, thereby threatening Parliament's control of the purse strings, something the capable Tudors had been very careful to avoid. Even one of James' great triumphs, peace with England's traditional enemy Spain, backfired. The English animosity toward Spain was so great in the early seventeenth century that James' peace was seen as a sellout rather than a signal triumph. Worse still, it seemed to confirm the rumors that James, despite his position as head of the Anglican Church, was in fact a Roman Catholic sympathizer. The Puritans in particular disliked James, and he loathed them in return.

James' death in 1625 brought his son, Charles I, to the throne. While Charles was considerably more charming than his father, he was no less a believer in absolutism. Early in his reign he clashed with Parliament over finances. His demands for more money met with resistance, and in 1628 Parliament presented the king with the Petition of Right that catalogued royal abuses and demanded that the king follow the law. Charles reluctantly accepted the Petition of Right because he desperately needed money, but when Parliament renewed its demands in 1629, Charles shut it down without any intention of ever recalling it.

Charles' high-handed behavior antagonized the country. Not only did he dismiss Parliament, but he also resorted to extralegal measures to secure funds necessary to keep his government afloat. When opponents filed suit against Charles for imposing illegal taxation, the king subverted the legal system to gain favorable verdicts. Moreover, Charles aroused enmity with his religious policy. Married to a Roman Catholic princess, Charles himself displayed Catholic tendencies that alarmed his subjects. His archbishop of Canterbury, William Laud, complicated matters when he tried to impose rigid doctrinal interpretations and ceremonial forms on the Anglican Church and harassed the Puritans, whose popularity in the country had continued to grow. Laud seemed to be leading England back to Roman Catholicism with the king's approval.

Charles' religious policy proved to be his undoing. When Laud tried to impose his ideas on the Scots (and, remember, Charles was king of Scotland as well as England), they rebelled. Unable to defeat the rebellious Scots with a hastily gathered force of aristocratic irregulars, Charles reluctantly recalled Parliament in 1640 in order to secure money to fight the Scots. When the recalled Parliament refused to fund Charles without significant concessions, Charles dismissed the body. But his needs were so pressing that he reconvened Parliament again, and this Parliament officially sat for twenty years—hence, its name, the Long Parliament.

At this juncture Parliament asserted itself. Before acceding to Charles' requests for money, it forced him to bow to its will. Charles' chief ministers, including Laud, were overthrown and in some instances executed; royal courts, including the Court of Star Chamber, were abolished; Parliament's right to control the levying of taxes was reaffirmed; and a bill was passed that required the king to call Parliament every three years and severely limited the monarch's right to dismiss Parliament. Charles reluctantly agreed to these initiatives; but when the unified Parliament split in 1642 over the religious question, Charles moved to reassert his authority by arresting Parliament's leaders. This was tantamount to a royal declaration of war against Parliament, and it touched off the English Civil War.

Charles' forces, known as the Cavaliers, came chiefly from northern and western England and consisted mainly of aristocrats and those who supported Laud's version of the Anglican Church. His opponents, known as the Roundheads because of their haircuts, drew support from townsmen, lesser gentry, and Puritans. Their base was in the south and east of England. Oliver Cromwell, a Puritan landowner, led the Roundheads. He constructed an effective fighting force, the New Model Army, and defeated the Cavaliers at the Battles of Marston Moor (1644) and Naseby (1645). The civil war officially ended when the victorious Roundheads executed Charles I in January 1649.

Oliver Cromwell and the Puritans now controlled England. Despite good intentions, Puritan rule proved to be too puritanical, and the civil war victors rapidly lost popularity. Unable to persuade Englishmen to support his policies, Cromwell resorted to force, and his rule degenerated into little more than a military dictatorship. With Cromwell's death in 1658, the way was clear for a restoration of the monarchy, and in May 1660 Charles II, son of Charles I, claimed the throne of England.

The vast majority of Englishmen heaved a sigh of relief with the passing of Cromwell's Protectorate government and welcomed the new king enthusiastically. Charles, pleased to be back in England after exile in France, let it be known that he did not wish "to set out on my travels again." However, the problems that provoked the civil war in the first place still remained, and they quickly resurfaced.

Beginning in 1661 and continuing until 1665, Parliament passed a series of laws on religion that collectively became known as the Clarendon Code. The Code had the effect of reestablishing a uniform brand of Anglicanism and discriminating against all those, but especially Puritans, who did not comply. Charles, a Catholic sympathizer if not yet accepted into the Church, feared that this religious intolerance would inevitably turn against Roman Catholics. Consequently, in 1672 he issued the Declaration of Indulgence that provided for a form of religious toleration for all Christians. A year later a hostile Parliament forced Charles to rescind the Declaration of Indulgence and passed the Test Act, which effectively barred all but Anglicans from holding office.

The issue of governance, which focused on finances, also reappeared. Although the restoration Parliament granted Charles a handsome sum of money, the revenue was not entirely adequate. When Charles demanded more, Parliament hesitated. The king managed to make some progress, thanks to a group of loyalists within Parliament derisively called Tories by their opponents, the Whigs. (The forerunners of modern political parties, the Tories and Whigs received their unsavory names from their opponents; a tory was an Irish bandit, whereas a whig was a Scottish Presbyterian who murdered bishops.) Nevertheless, as his relations with Parliament deteriorated, Charles required greater funds. In 1670 he signed the Treaty of Dover with Louis XIV, which placed him on the French king's payroll. In return, Charles secretly promised to join France in war against Holland and to reestablish Roman Catholicism in England. Word of the treaty leaked out, and England was outraged; however, the politically skillful, if lazy and cynical, Charles survived and died peacefully in 1685 despite increasingly poor relations with Parliament.

The ascension to the throne of Charles' brother, James II, brought matters to a head. Not only was James a convinced absolutist; he was also a practicing Roman Catholic. James' stupid, arrogant, and obnoxious behavior soon alienated virtually everyone. England barely tolerated James, and then only because he was old and the throne would soon pass to his daughter, Mary, a Protestant married to the Protestant William of Orange, stadtholder of the Netherlands and a man accustomed to sharing power with others. However, when James' second wife unexpectedly gave birth to a son, the calculus was upset. The child was born Catholic and undoubtedly would be raised Catholic in an atmosphere strongly supportive of absolutism. The prospect of continued conflict alarmed the English. James found himself bereft of support and in December 1688 he fled the country for refuge at the court of Louis XIV. Yet another revolution had taken place in England; this one, the Glorious Revolution, unlike the first one, was virtually bloodless.

INTERPRETIVE ESSAY
William T. Walker

The Glorious Revolution of 1688–1689 was a defining moment in British history. Not only were the long-standing religious and dynastic issues related to the English Civil War resolved, but the revolution also noted new historical forces that foreshadowed a modern age. These developments were evident in politics, economics, foreign policy, and the realm of intellectual achievements. The revolution itself contributed to the beginnings of an age of parliamentary dominance that witnessed the establishment of the cabinet system of government, the decline of the monarchy during the eighteenth century, and the setting of the stage for the democratic reforms of the nineteenth and twentieth centuries.

During his three-year tenure as monarch (1685–1688), James II alienated many significant sectors of British society. However, both Tory and Whig leaders had supported James' accession to the throne upon the death of Charles II. The Whig parliamentary leadership did not allow the exclusion question—which questioned the right of the Catholic James to sit on the throne of Protestant England and which had been a major issue during the later years of Charles II's reign—to resurface, nor did they oppose the majority Tory action in renewing the standing appropriations for the royal court. So at the beginning of the reign James II enjoyed the overwhelming support of the Tories (country gentry) and the acquiescence of the Whigs (commercial and urban interests).

James mistook the nation's acceptance of his Catholic kingship for support; he failed to recognize that British society, values, and priorities were quite different than what they had been at mid-century. In 1685 the support of the nation in suppressing the revolts of the Duke of Monmouth (Charles II's illegitimate son) and the Scottish Earl of Argyll against James II was not based on love and loyalty to the king but rather on the general recognition of the need for stability in the government. Neither Tory nor Whig leaders were interested in rekindling the fires that had led to the English Civil War in the middle of the century.

In 1686, after reorganizing his court, James II initiated policies that were designed to alleviate the impact of the remaining penal laws that curtailed the religious and political activities of the small English Catholic community. Using the questionable dispensing and suspending powers of the monarchy that supposedly allowed the king to ignore or "suspend" the law, James II appointed Catholics to offices of state and removed other officeholders whom he viewed as undesirable. In 1686 James II's appointment of the Catholic Sir Edward Hales resulted in a test case that the monarch won. In the same year James successfully suppressed anti-Catholic sentiment among Anglican leaders in London and at Oxford's Magdalen College. While the king prevailed in these instances, public opinion, particularly in London, began to turn against him.

James further estranged himself from the English majority in April 1687 when he issued his first Declaration of Liberty of Conscience. This decree granted religious freedom to all Christian sects—including Catholicism. During this same year, James II initiated steps to pack the Parliament with friends and supporters of his plan to repeal the Test Act. While his popularity continued to decline, there was no general support for removing him. However, it was James II's policies that renewed the fears associated with the Popish Plot (1678) and the rumors of a Jesuit conspiracy to overthrow the government.

During the first six months of 1688, three developments transformed public and political sentiment, and a consensus emerged that held that the king's tenure must be terminated. First, in April 1688, James issued the second Declaration of Liberty of Conscience (in content almost identical to the earlier statement), which he ordered to be read in all churches. William Sancroft, Archbishop of Canterbury, and six other bishops refused to comply with the directive to read the Declaration publicly. They were arrested and imprisoned in the Tower of London. The second development was the birth of a son to James and his second wife. James named his son Prince James and baptized him a Roman Catholic. This development altered the very basis of the political arrangement upon which English political leaders, both Tory and Whig, had accepted James II as king in 1685. It was anticipated that James II would have a relatively brief reign and then would be replaced by one of his daughters, Mary or Anne, both devout Protestants. Thus, the phenomenon of having a Catholic king over a Protestant nation would be short-lived and an acceptable alternative to a resumption of the civil turmoil that had been so disruptive to British life. Now, with the birth of a Catholic son who had priority to the throne over his half sisters, the nation faced the likelihood of a prolonged period of leadership by Catholic monarchs; that was not acceptable. The third major development also occurred in June 1688; the trial of William Sancroft and the other bishops resulted in their acquittal and a public demonstration of dissatisfaction with James II.

On June 30, 1688, the leadership of the Tory and Whig parties, acting on the authority of Parliament, issued a joint invitation to William of Orange to intervene to save the British nation from Catholicism. William was married to Mary, elder daughter of James II. William and Mary considered the matter carefully for several months, and it was not until September 30 that William accepted the invitation. While William's primary consideration was in gaining English support in his struggle with France's Louis XIV, he recognized the long-range impact of his decision to align Britain with the fate of the Netherlands. After a futile attempt that was foiled by weather, William of Orange arrived in England on November 5, 1688. James II's rule quickly evaporated when most of the nation welcomed William and Mary as liberators. The defection of the leaders of the army, the Duke of Grafton and Sir John Churchill, sealed James II's fate. By the end of December 1688, James and the other members of the royal family, including his son, had fled to France; Louis XIV emerged as the protector of the exiled Catholic Stuarts.

The parliamentary leadership established a provisional government and did not rush to name William and Mary as the new monarchs; the Glorious Revolution of 1688–1689 was to be more than a simple transfer of authority from one monarch to another. In January 1689 a Convention Parliament was convened to deal with the crisis. On January 28, 1689, the House of Commons declared that James II had fled the country and that his action was an act of abdication that left the throne vacant. Further, the Commons declared that the nation could not be governed again by a Catholic monarch. After some negotiations between the House of Lords and William and Mary, Parliament agreed to offer the throne to William and Mary as joint monarchs.

Recognizing a historic opportunity to advance the rights and concerns of Parliament, a Declaration of Rights was developed by parliamentary leaders in February 1689. This document, later modified to become the Bill of Rights, constitutes one of the most important statements in the development of representative government; it paved the way for the later democratic reforms of the nineteenth and twentieth centuries. Among its most salient points were the following: No monarch can make or suspend law without the approval of Parliament; the traditional dispensing power of the monarchy was abolished; ecclesiastical courts and their proceedings are not acceptable; taxes not authorized by Parliament are illegal; petitions to the monarch are legal; a standing army must have the approval of Parliament; the private holding of arms is legal; parliamentary elections must be free from coercion; Parliament's right to freedom of debate and speech is guaranteed; unreasonable bail should not be required; the right to a jury trial is recognized; seizure of land and holdings prior to conviction is illegal; and Parliaments should be convened frequently. William and Mary accepted the Declaration of Rights, and they were declared the monarchs; William was recognized as the ruler-administrator. Parliament also specified that the direct children of William and Mary would succeed them; in the event that they were childless at the time of their deaths, the succession would pass to Mary's sister, Princess Anne of Denmark, and her children. On February 13, 1689, William and Mary became the king and queen of England. Nine days later, Parliament and the clergy took oaths of allegiance and supremacy recognizing the new monarchs.

In addition to the issues addressed in the Declaration of Rights, Parliament established a procedure that distinguished between the civil and military aspects of the monarch's budget. Court or personal needs would be provided by a general act of Parliament; all other needs, including military expenses, would be handled through specific, short-term appropriations. Also a new Toleration Act was passed in 1689; Protestant dissenters (Puritans, Baptists, Presbyterians, etc.) were exempted from the penal laws associated with the Test Act as long as they took an oath of allegiance to the crown and declared their vehement opposition to Catholicism. Several bishops and a few hundred priests refused to take the oaths and established a separatist Anglican Church. It is of interest to note that while it appeared in law that Catholics were being effectively suppressed, the decades after the Glorious Revolution marked the steady but limited growth of English Catholicism.

With support from Louis XIV, the exiled James II challenged the new order by landing in Dublin in March 1689. While the city welcomed the old monarch, his opponents prevailed. In 1690 at the Battle of the Boyne, William III's army routed James II's forces. James fled to France but continued to develop plans for his restoration. Although James II died on September 16, 1701, his son, James Edward (The Old Pretender), and grandson, Charles (The Young Pretender), continued to advance the Jacobite or Stuart cause through the unsuccessful revolts of 1715 and 1745.

John Locke, the great political philosopher of the age, returned to England from self-imposed exile in the Netherlands after the Glorious Revolution. In 1690 Locke published two important works, *An Essay Concerning Human Understanding* and *Two Treatises of Government*. While the first work is a substantive work of philosophy that explores empirical thinking processes, the second work is directly related to the Glorious Revolution. Until recently, historians believed that Locke was commissioned to develop an intellectual rationale or justification for the Glorious Revolution. In fact, the treatises were written in either 1682 or 1683 but were not published at that time. Differing from Thomas Hobbes in his view of society and government, Locke advanced a thesis that demolished the intellectual basis for absolutism. He argued that sovereignty resided in the *citizens* and that it could not be transferred to anyone or any office. Thus, a monarch's claim to absolute sovereign power was neither credible nor defensible. The purpose of government is to protect the natural rights of its citizens; governors and governments must demonstrate their social utility or run the risk of being removed. The focus of government was the legislative power that was vested in the Parliament; the king was the executor of the laws passed by the Parliament. Thus, Locke advanced two basic principles that were essential to understanding the rationale for and the acceptance of the Glorious Revolution—the separation of powers and the right of revolution. James II failed the nation by pursuing policies and practices that ran counter to the national interests and values. Parliament and its leaders, representing the citizens, had the right to discard James II and establish a new regime.

In the instance of the Glorious Revolution and the future direction of British political development, it is difficult to overstate the importance of Locke's thoughts. Not only did the general acceptance of these sentiments effectively terminate the threat of absolutism in England, but they also accelerated the advancement of representative institutions within the government. By the 1720s, the first British Cabinet led by a prime minister would be a reality.

In many other ways, the Glorious Revolution tended to be a turning point in English intellectual and cultural life. The new *mentalité* that contributed to the resolution of the crisis of 1688–1689 was a reflection of a new, more rational and scientific way of thinking that was emerging within English culture. During the seventeenth century, English intellectuals such as Francis Bacon, Robert Boyle, Thomas Hobbes, John Locke, William Harvey, and Isaac Newton made substantive contributions to the scientific and intellectual revolution that was occurring in Europe. While their individual achievements need not be addressed here, it is important to recognize that these thinkers were in the vanguard of a cultural era known as the Enlightenment. During the last decades of the seventeenth century, English intellectual life was being transformed by the new thought. Scientific thinking and rational methodology gained acceptance in the universities and the public intellectual life of London. During the 1670s the Royal Academy was established, peer-reviewed journals appeared, and the naturalists gained in respect. These developments shaped the cultural milieu in which the Glorious Revolution occurred. English leaders responded to the challenge not by reverting to the failed and divisive methods of the past but with responsible measures that preserved the unity of state and society.

European diplomacy constituted a major factor in bringing about the Glorious Revolution in 1688, and the impact of the revolution transformed European diplomatic history. In addition to safeguarding his wife's claim to the English throne, William III's willingness to embark on an English military operation was based upon his need to bring England into his coalition, which was directed against Louis XIV's France. The ascendancy of French power in Europe paralleled the Thirty Years' War (1618–1648). From the 1620s to the early 1640s, Cardinal Richelieu served as Louis XIII's principal minister. Though a prelate of the Roman Catholic Church, Richelieu pursued a national foreign policy, supporting Protestant leaders against the Catholic Habsburgs. Cardinal Mazarin served as the principal minister during the minority of Louis XIV and continued Richelieu's policies. By 1660, when Louis XIV began his personal rule, France was unquestionably the strongest state in Europe.

The continuing development of French power during the 1660s threatened the European state system, and French dominance of the Continent became a real concern. This threat became more manifest when Louis

XIV launched a series of aggressive foreign policy initiatives. The War of Devolution (1667–1668) and the Dutch War (1672–1678) jeopardized the recently (1648) independent Netherlands. While Spain paid the price of these early ventures by Louis XIV, William of Orange, leader of the Netherlands, recognized that his country would be an easy prey unless it was aligned with other states. England's Charles II recognized the danger to the balance of power but was unpredictable because of his personal fascination with Louis XIV; Charles was enamored by the spectacle of the French court.

In 1685 Louis XIV revoked the Edict of Nantes (1598), which had granted religious toleration to French Protestants. In the wake of revocation, thousands fled France and took refuge in England, the Netherlands, and Prussia. Louis XIV's action enraged the Protestant leaders of Europe who were confronted at the same time with a succession crisis resulting from the death (1685) of Elector Charles of the Palatinate who died without an heir. Louis XIV asserted his claim to the Palatinate, an important German-speaking province located on the west bank of the middle Rhine River, but in 1686 William of Orange declared Louis XIV's claim unacceptable and formed a diplomatic coalition (the League of Augsburg) directed against France. In addition to the Netherlands, members of the anti-French alliance included Sweden, Spain, Bavaria, Saxony, and the Palatinate. The War of the League of Augsburg began in 1686, but hostilities did not become extensive until 1688. It was at that time that William III (William of Orange) and his wife replaced James II on the English throne and brought England into the conflict. With England a member of the coalition, William was able to successfully resist French efforts to seize the Netherlands. He led the alliance against France, winning significant victories at the Battles of La Hogue (1692) and Namur (1695). In 1697 the war concluded with the Treaty of Ryswick. Signatories included England, France, Spain, and the Netherlands. While France received favorable terms (largely at the expense of Spain), William III had succeeded in maintaining the independence of the Netherlands and in preventing French hegemony in Europe.

The next diplomatic obstacle was the issue of the forthcoming Spanish succession. Spanish king Carlos II was very ill and believed near death. In 1698 and 1700 William entered into two secret agreements with Louis XIV on the Spanish succession and the partition of the Spanish Empire. In entering into these agreements, William was more interested in avoiding another struggle with France than in acquiring Spanish colonies. Nonetheless, Carlos II's death in 1700 rendered these treaties meaningless. His will transferred the Spanish throne and all of its holdings to Louis XIV's grandson, Philip of Anjou, who became Philip V of Spain. Once again William III forged a coalition against France and in 1701, the War of the Spanish Succession commenced.

Even though William III died in 1702, England continued in the war until its conclusion in 1713. With the Peace of Utrecht, England emerged as a world power, winning Newfoundland, Gibraltar, Minorca, and valuable commercial rights to trade in Spanish America. More important, England entered the eighteenth century as the determining force in restraining France from dominating the Continent and with a reinforced national identity. It would be England that would assist Prussia against France in the mid-century War of the Austrian Succession; and in the 1790s, England would be instrumental in forming the coalitions against the French forces of the revolution and Napoleon. These policies are direct manifestations of the Glorious Revolution through which England became France's primary rival. At the same time, the English commitment to the open rivers of Europe via the Low Countries became a cornerstone of English policy.

Perhaps of greater importance was the transformation of the English nation's sense of identity. English national interests were now identified with world trade, imperialism, and colonial acquisitions. After the Glorious Revolution, England became a world power, no longer limited to the regional issues that dominated European politics. Indeed, increasingly English statesmen and political leaders came to view England as apart from Europe. These sentiments were supported by England's commercial revolution, the eighteenth-century Industrial Revolution, and the subsequent debate between the neo-mercantilists and the advocates of free trade.

The Glorious Revolution was a turning point in British history that witnessed the triumph of national interests over a regime that was centered on a religious identity. It was the victory of a new, modern approach to governing over the remnants of Reformation sectarian politics.

SELECTED BIBLIOGRAPHY

Beddard, Robert, ed. *The Revolutions of 1688: The Andrew Browning Lectures, 1988.* Oxford, U.K.: Clarendon Press, 1991. Sixteen perceptive essays that provide a valuable introduction to the Glorious Revolution.
Bradshaw, Brendan, and John S. Morrill, eds. *The British Problem, c. 1534–1707: State Formation in the Atlantic Archipelago.* New York: St. Martin's Press,

1996. A series of ten useful essays that treat the Glorious Revolution in the context of the emerging British state and a new British identity.

Clark, J.C.D. *Revolution and Rebellion: State and Society in England in the Seventeenth and Eighteenth Centuries*. Cambridge, U.K.: Cambridge University Press, 1986. A solid analysis of the Glorious Revolution in light of the English Civil War and the subsequent shifts in English politics during the eighteenth century.

Dickson, P.G.M. *The Financial Revolution in England: A Study in the Development of Public Credit, 1688–1756*. London: Macmillan, 1967. An important study that focuses on the fiscal and economic ramifications of the Glorious Revolution.

Gregg, Edward. *Queen Anne*. London: Routledge & Kegan Paul, 1980. The standard biography of Queen Anne; useful for understanding the Hanoverian succession.

Greli, Ole P., Jonathan I. Israel, and Nicholas Tyacke, eds. *From Persecution to Toleration: The Glorious Revolution and Religion in England*. Oxford, U.K.: Oxford University Press, 1991. A collection of fourteen essays that focus on the Glorious Revolution as a defining moment in the emergence of religious toleration in England.

Harris, Tim. *Politics Under the Later Stuarts: Party Conflict in a Divided Society, 1660–1715*. London: Longman, 1993. A reliable political history of the period with excellent chapters on the Exclusion Crisis and politics and ideology under William and Anne.

Hoak, Dale, and M. Feingold, eds. *The World of William and Mary: Anglo-Dutch Perspectives on the Revolution of 1688–89*. Stanford, CA: Stanford University Press, 1996. A series of provocative essays that examine the diverse impact of the Glorious Revolution during the 1680s and 1690s.

Holmes, Geoffrey, ed. *Britain After the Glorious Revolution, 1689–1714*. New York: Macmillan, 1969. An older but still useful volume on the political, constitutional, and diplomatic consequences of the Glorious Revolution.

Israel, Jonathan I., ed. *The Anglo-Dutch Moment: Essays on the Glorious Revolution and Its World Impact*. Cambridge, U.K.: Cambridge University Press, 1991. An outstanding series of sixteen essays relating to the global importance of the Glorious Revolution.

Jones, J. R., ed. *Liberty Secured? Britain Before and After 1688*. Stanford, CA: Stanford University Press, 1992. An important reevaluation of the Glorious Revolution.

———. *The Revolution of 1688 in England*. London: Weidenfeld & Nicolson, 1972. A comprehensive history of the Glorious Revolution by one of the eminent authorities in the field.

Kenyon, J. P. *Revolution Principles: The Politics of Party, 1689–1720*. Cambridge, U.K.: Cambridge University Press, 1977. An analysis of postrevolutionary politics in England with emphasis on the institutionalization of political parties and the growing importance of electoral politics.

Miller, J. *The Glorious Revolution*. 2nd ed. London: Longman, 1997. An excellent introduction to the Glorious Revolution; in addition to a comprehensive narrative, forty-five documents are included.

————. *James II: A Study in Kingship*. London: Wayland, 1977. A critically acclaimed biography of James II.

Monod, Paul K. *Jacobitism and the English People, 1688–1788*. Cambridge, U.K.: Cambridge University Press, 1989. An excellent account of the continuing troubles with the Catholic Stuart pretenders to the dawn of the French Revolution.

Ogg, David. *England in the Reigns of James II and William III*. Oxford, U.K.: Oxford University Press, 1955. A detailed political history of the two reigns focused on the Glorious Revolution.

Plumb, J. H. *The Growth of Political Stability in England, 1675–1725*. London: Macmillan, 1967. A dated but seminal analysis of the emergence of the parliamentary electorate as a force for stability in early eighteenth-century English politics.

Schwoerer, Lois G., ed. *The Revolution of 1688–1689: Changing Perspectives*. Cambridge, U.K.: Cambridge University Press, 1992. A thoughtful series of diverse essays that challenge the Whig interpretation of the Glorious Revolution.

Speck, W. A. *Reluctant Revolutionaries: Englishmen and the Revolution of 1688*. Oxford, U.K.: Oxford University Press, 1988. A persuasive argument that the Glorious Revolution was indeed revolutionary and that it eliminated the threat of an absolute monarchy in England.

Trevelyan, G. M. *The English Revolution, 1688–1689*. Oxford, U.K.: Oxford University Press, 1949. An excellent presentation of the Whig interpretation of the Glorious Revolution.

Appendix A

Glossary

Allah. The name given to God in the Islamic, or Muslim, religion.

Aristotle (384–322 B.C.). Aristotle was an ancient Greek philosopher based in Athens. When Aristotle's ideas about human beings and the world in which they live were rediscovered in the twelfth century, they greatly influenced the course of subsequent European history.

Balance of Power. One of the dominant concepts of international relations, the balance of power holds that preventing the dangerous growth of power in one nation or combination of nations is desirable. An effective distribution of power among nations often can be accomplished through alliance and counteralliance.

Balkans. Derived from mountains and peninsula of the same name, this seemingly eternally restless southeastern corner of Europe includes the contemporary countries of Greece, Romania, Bulgaria, European Turkey, Albania, and the countries of the former Yugoslavia.

Bourbon. The name given to the ruling house of France from 1589 until 1793. Louis XIV was the most famous Bourbon ruler.

Chinggis Khan (1162?–1227). One of the world's greatest conquerors, this Mongol chieftain overran much of northern China, central Asia, Persia, southern Russia, and the Middle East during the early thirteenth century. His name is often spelled *Genghis Khan*.

Confucius (551–479 B.C.). Confucius was a Chinese teacher and philosopher whose ideas dominated Chinese life and greatly influenced Japan's culture. Confucianism placed great emphasis on righteousness and restraint in order for people to achieve harmony with nature.

Counter Reformation. In response to the Protestant Reformation of the early sixteenth century, the Roman Catholic Church launched the Counter Reformation, an aggressive campaign to win back those who had converted and to destroy Protestantism.

Dutch East India Company. Established in 1602 by the Dutch States-General, the Dutch East India Company was given the exclusive right to handle Dutch trade with the Far East. The company proved to be exceptionally successful, turning huge profits for a number of years and cementing the Dutch presence in such places as the Cape of Good Hope (South Africa), the East Indies (Indonesia), Japan, and Malaya.

English East India Company. Chartered by Queen Elizabeth in 1600, the English East India Company gained a monopoly over English trade in Asia. Shut out of the East Indies by its rival, the Dutch East India Company, the English East India Company concentrated on India, where it made initial inroads in the seventeenth century.

Enlightenment. Emerging from the seventeenth century's Scientific Revolution, the eighteenth-century Enlightenment profoundly affected Europe with its call for reason above all else. Subjecting all human existence to rational thought, the Enlightenment inspired a vast number of literate Europeans; but its message also brought it into conflict with the status quo including organized religion, hidebound monarchies, and a benighted social system.

Estate. An estate was a social class. Prior to the 1789 French Revolution, Europe was generally divided into three estates: the clergy; the nobility; and the commoners, or all those who did not fit into the first two estates.

Feudalism. The social, economic, and political system of medieval Europe. The term is often used to describe any system whereby weaker landowners pledge allegiance to stronger landowners, whereas landless (and generally powerless) peasants are bound to the land that they work for a small share of the harvest.

Gupta Empire (320–c. 500). The Gupta Empire was a unified state comprising much of northern India. It was strong, prosperous, and united; its cultural outpouring has given rise to its reputation as India's classical period.

Habsburg. The Habsburgs were the ruling house of Austria from 1267 until 1918. They also served as Holy Roman Emperors from 1438 until Napoleon destroyed the Holy Roman Empire in 1806.

Han Chinese. The name given to ethnic Chinese who are born in China proper. They trace their origin to the Han dynasty of pre-Christian times.

Harem. The name given to both the wives and concubines of the Ottoman sultan and to that part of the palace where they lived. It was believed that too much time in the harem weakened the ruler of a warrior state like the Ottoman Empire.

Hobbes, Thomas (1588–1679). Hobbes was an English philosopher and author whose most famous book, *Leviathan*, supported the concept of strong monarchical government as the only means to control the unchecked and often conflicting ambitions of individuals.

Hohenzollerns. Originally from southern Germany, the Hohenzollern family ruled over first Brandenburg-Prussia and then a united Germany (1871) from 1415 until 1918.

Hundred Years' War (1337–1453). A seemingly interminable series of wars fought on French soil between the English and the French. The Hundred Years' War resulted in the ruin of England and its expulsion from France except for the port of Calais.

Industrial Revolution. The Industrial Revolution began in Great Britain in the middle of the eighteenth century. It was the transformation of producing goods by hand to machine production. The Industrial Revolution is regarded as one of the most important events in the history of the world.

Islam. Founded by the prophet Muhammad (570–632), Islam is the newest of the world's great religions. There are more than 1 billion Muslims (followers of Islam) worldwide, many of whom reside in North Africa, Turkey, the Middle East, Iran, Pakistan, and Indonesia.

Jesuits. The Jesuits are a Roman Catholic religious order founded by Ignatius Loyola in 1540. They were known for actively combatting the Protestant Reformation and for aggressively spreading Roman Catholicism to non-Christian peoples.

Le Tellier, François (1641–1691). Also known as the Marquis Louvois, Le Tellier was Louis XIV's minister of war. He is given credit for professionalizing Louis' army, thereby making it the most effective fighting force in seventeenth-century Europe.

Little Ice Age. During the seventeenth century, global temperatures were consistently below average. The cold weather played havoc with agricultural production and gave rise to the term "Little Ice Age" to describe the period.

Magnate. Magnate denotes the largest and most important landowners or aristocrats of eastern Europe, especially in Poland and Hungary.

Mandate of Heaven. The Mandate of Heaven is a complex Chinese theory of statecraft derived from the works of Confucius. According to the theory, God (heaven) bestows upon a righteous family the right to rule. However, God's blessing is not in perpetuity. If the ruling dynasty turns from the upright path, God can and will revoke the mandate to rule by allowing "righteous rebellion." If the rebellion succeeds, God will invest the victors with the Mandate of Heaven; if the rebellion fails, it is because God did not deem the rebels worthy of the mandate.

Metropolitan. The title given to the Orthodox Christian archbishops of major Russian cities including Moscow.

Mongols. A warlike, tribal people from central Asia; in the thirteenth century under the leadership of Chinggis Khan they built an empire that stretched from the Ukraine to the Pacific Ocean and included Russia and much of China.

More, Thomas (1478–1535). English statesman and author; his most influential work was *Utopia*, which envisions a near-perfect society.

Morea. A large peninsula in southern Greece, formerly called the Peloponnesus.

Muhammad (570?–632). Muhammad, an orphaned Arab boy of the Arabian peninsula, who as an adult founded Islam, one of the world's great religions.

Muscovy. Muscovy is the name given to the central Russian principality that between the fourteenth and eighteenth centuries expanded to become the Russian Empire.

Orthodox Christianity. Christianity is divided into three main branches: Roman Catholicism, Protestantism, and Orthodoxy. Orthodox Christianity is popular in Russia, the Ukraine, the Balkan countries, and the Near East.

Plato (c. 427–c. 347 B.C.). An ancient Greek philosopher, Plato's influence on the development of the Western world has been profound. He argued that ideas are superior to tangible things and that the idea of "good" is the most important idea.

Polis. Polis is the ancient Greek word for city or town. The Greeks considered life in the polis as the most civilized form of existence, and they spent considerable time and energy debating how to create the perfect polis.

Pontic. Pontic is an adjective describing the area around the Black Sea.

Popish Plot (1678). In a time of great sensitivity over religious matters in England, an unreliable character named Titus Oates announced that he had discovered a conspiracy to overthrow the English monarchy with French and Irish support and place on the throne a Roman Catholic who would then return England to Catholicism. No evidence was produced to confirm Oates' story, but panic swept England nevertheless.

Price Revolution. During the sixteenth century, an influx of precious metals from the New World combined with a notable increase in Europe's population to send prices for goods and commodities, but especially for food, steadily upward. In turn, this caused severe social and economic dislocation.

Pythagoras (c. 582–c. 507 B.C.). An ancient Greek mathematician who concluded that mathematics held the key to understanding the universe.

Sikhs. First evident in the sixteenth century, the Sikhs began as a Hindu religious sect but soon evolved into an independent religion that rejected the caste system of the Hindus. The Sikhs also resisted the authority of the Mogul rulers.

Sinicization. Sinicization is the process of becoming integrated into Han Chinese cultural, intellectual, social, and political life.

Tilly, Count Johann (1559–1632). General of the Catholic League and commander of the imperial forces during the Thirty Years' War, Tilly was victorious at White Mountain (1620) and Magdeburg (1631) but defeated at Breitenfeld (1631).

Tory. "Tory" is the name given to one of the two major English political parties. Its members tend to be more resistant to change, and in earlier centuries they were inclined to support royal prerogative.

Whig. From the end of the seventeenth century until the middle of the nineteenth, "Whig" was the name given to one of the two major English political parties. Its members tended to favor change, and they were inclined to restrict the power of the monarch.

Wienerwald. The forested heights overlooking the city of Vienna.

Appendix B

Timeline

1600	English East India Company founded
	Battle of Sekigahara
1601	Matteo Ricci travels to China
	Tycho Brahe dies
1602	Dutch East India Company founded
1603	Elizabeth I of England dies
	Tokugawa Shogunate established
1605	Miguel de Cervantes publishes *Don Quixote*
	Akbar of India dies
	Boris Godunov of Russia dies
	Dutch traders appear in present-day Indonesia
1607	English found Jamestown colony
1608	French found Quebec colony
	English arrive at Surat
1609	Dutch traders arrive at Nagasaki
1610	Henry IV of France assassinated
	Vasily Shuisky, tsar of Russia, abdicates
1611	King James version of the Bible

1613	Michael Romanov crowned tsar of Russia
1614	El Greco dies
	Siege of Osaka castle
1616	William Shakespeare dies
	Tokugawa Ieyasu of Japan dies
1618–1648	Thirty Years' War
1619	First African slaves arrive in Virginia
1620	Battle of White Mountain
	Wanli, emperor of China, dies
	Pilgrims found Plymouth colony
1625	James I of England dies
1626	Francis Bacon dies
	Nurhaci dies
1627	Jahangir dies
1628	William Harvey publishes *On the Motion of the Heart and Blood in Animals*
	Cardinal Richelieu defeats the Huguenots
1629	Shah Abbas I of Persia dies
	Ferdinand II issues the Edict of Restitution
1630	Sweden enters Thirty Years' War
	Johannes Kepler dies
	Puritans found Massachusetts Bay colony
1631	Battle of Breitenfeld
1632	Battle of Lützen
	Construction of the Taj Mahal begins
	Galileo publishes *Dialogue on the Two Chief World Systems*
1634	Battle of Nördlingen
1635	France enters Thirty Years' War
1637	René Descartes publishes *Discourse on Method*
1638	Height of anti-Christian persecution in Japan
1639	Japan effectively closed to the outside world
1640	Peter Paul Rubens dies
1642–1648	Civil war in England
1642	Galileo dies

	Cardinal Richelieu dies
1643	Louis XIII of France dies
	Hongtaiji dies
1644	Manchus gain control of China
1645	Battle of Naseby
1648–1653	The Fronde in France
1648	Peace of Westphalia
1649	Charles I of England executed
1650	Population of world estimated at 500 million
	René Descartes dies
1651	Thomas Hobbes publishes *Leviathan*
1652	Dutch East India Company founds the Cape Colony
1656	Mehmed Köprülü named grand vezir of Ottoman Empire
1658	Oliver Cromwell dies
	Aurangzeb rules India
1659	Treaty of the Pyrenees
1660	Monarchy restored in England
	Royal Society of London established
1661	English gain control of Bombay
	Kangxi crowned emperor of China
	Mehmed Köprülü dies
	Cardinal Mazarin dies
1662	Blaise Pascal dies
1664	Battle of St. Gotthard
1666	Shah Jahan dies
	The Great Fire devastates London
	French Royal Academy of Sciences established
1667–1668	War of Devolution
1667	Russia absorbs eastern Ukraine
1668	Treaty of Aachen
1669	Rembrandt dies
1672–1678	Dutch War
1673	Molière dies
1674	John Milton dies

1676	Kara Mustapha appointed grand vezir
	Ottoman Empire reaches its maximum extent in Europe
1678–1679	Treaty of Nijmegen
1678	John Bunyan publishes the first part of *Pilgrim's Progress*
1680	Ashanti Kingdom founded in West Africa
1681	William Penn receives grant of land
1682	Louis XIV moves to Versailles
1683	Turks besiege Vienna
	Qing dynasty captures Taiwan
1685	Charles II of England dies
	Louis XIV revokes the Edict of Nantes
1687	Isaac Newton publishes *Principia*
	Second Battle of Mohacs
1688–1689	The "Glorious Revolution" in England
1688–1697	War of the League of Augsburg
1688	Frederick William of Prussia, the "Great Elector," dies
1689	English Bill of Rights
1690	John Locke publishes *Two Treatises of Government*
	Robert Boyle dies
1691	Massachusetts Bay colony absorbs Plymouth colony
1696–1698	Peter the Great of Russia visits the West
1696	Russia seizes Azov
1697	Battle of Zenta
	Treaty of Ryswick
1699	Peace of Karlowitz
	English establish trading post at Canton
	Williamsburg founded

Appendix C

Ruling Houses and Dynasties

AUSTRIA

House of Habsburg

Rudolph II	1576–1612
Matthias	1612–1619
Ferdinand II	1619–1637
Ferdinand III	1637–1657
Leopold I	1658–1705

ENGLAND

House of Tudor

Elizabeth I	1558–1603

House of Stuart

James I	1603–1625
Charles I	1625–1649

Interregnum

The Commonwealth	1649–1653
The Protectorate	1653–1660

House of Stuart (Restored)

Charles II	1660–1685
James II	1685–1688
William III	1689–1702
and Mary II	1689–1694

FRANCE

House of Bourbon

Henry IV	1589–1610
Louis XIII	1610–1643
Louis XIV	1643–1715

HOLY ROMAN EMPIRE

House of Habsburg

Rudolph II	1576–1612
Matthias	1612–1619
Ferdinand II	1619–1637
Ferdinand III	1637–1657
Leopold I	1658–1705

PRUSSIA

In 1618 the elector of Brandenburg added the Duchy of Prussia to his holdings and began to call himself the duke of Prussia.

House of Hohenzollern

George William	1619–1640
Frederick William, the "Great Elector"	1640–1688
Frederick III	1688–1713

RUSSIA

House of Romanov

Mikhail	1613–1645
Alexis	1645–1676
Fedor III	1676–1682
Ivan V and Peter I	1682–1689
Peter I, "The Great"	1689–1725

SPAIN

House of Habsburg

Philip III	1598–1621
Philip IV	1621–1665
Carlos II	1665–1700

OTTOMAN EMPIRE

House of Osman

Mehmed III	1595–1603
Ahmed I	1603–1617
Mustapha I	1617–1618; 1622–1623
Osman II	1618–1622
Murad IV	1623–1640
Ibrahim	1640–1648
Mehmed IV	1648–1687
Süleyman II	1687–1691
Ahmed II	1691–1695
Mahmud I	1695–1703

INDIA

Mogul Empire

Akbar	1556–1605
Jahangir	1605–1627

| Shah Jahan | 1628–1658 |
| Aurangzeb | 1658–1707 |

JAPAN

Tokugawa Shogunate

Ieyasu	1603–1605
Hidetada	1605–1623
Iemitsu	1623–1651
Ietsuna	1651–1680
Tsunayoshi	1680–1709

CHINA

Ming Dynasty

Wanli	1573–1619
Taichang	1620–1620
Tianqi	1621–1627
Chongzhen	1628–1644

Qing Dynasty

| Shunzhi | 1644–1661 |
| Kangxi | 1661–1722 |

Index

About the Editors and Contributors

JOHN T. ALEXANDER is professor of history and Russian and East European studies at the University of Kansas. He received his Ph.D. from Indiana University. He is the author of *Autocratic Politics in a National Crisis* (1969), *Bubonic Plague in Early Modern Russia* (1980), and *Catherine the Great: Life and Legend* (1989).

ROBERT K. DeKOSKY is associate professor of history at the University of Kansas. He received his Ph.D. from the University of Wisconsin. He is the author of *Knowledge and Cosmos: Development and Decline of the Medieval Perspective* (1979) and has written extensively on the history of science.

JOHN E. FINDLING is professor of history at Indiana University Southeast. He received his Ph.D. from the University of Texas. Professor Findling is the author of *Dictionary of American Diplomatic History* (Greenwood, 1980; 1989) and *Chicago's Great World's Fairs* (Greenwood, 1995). With Kimberly D. Pelle, he co-edited *The Historical Dictionary of the Modern Olympic Movement* (Greenwood, 1996). With Frank W. Thackeray, he is the editor of *Statesmen Who Changed the World* (Greenwood, 1993) and other volumes in the Events That Changed the World and Events That Changed America series. He and Professor Thackeray are also series editors of the Greenwood Histories of the Modern Nations series.

RICK KENNEDY is professor of history at Point Loma Nazarene University. He received his Ph.D. from the University of California at Santa Barbara. He is the editor of *Aristotelian and Cartesian Logic at Harvard* (1995).

GARRETT L. McAINSH is a professor of history at Hendrix College. He received his Ph.D. from Emory University. He has contributed to *Statesmen Who Changed the World* (Greenwood, 1993), *The Journal of Peace Studies*, and *The World Encyclopedia of Peace* (1986).

JOHN McLEOD is assistant professor of history at the University of Louisville. He received his Ph.D. from the University of Toronto. He is the author of *Sovereignty, Power, Control: Politics in the States of Western India* (1999) and is currently working on a biography of Sir Mancherjee Merwanjee Bhownaggree.

LOUIS G. PEREZ is professor of history at Illinois State University. He received his Ph.D. from Indiana University. He is the author of *Japan Comes of Age: Mutsu Munemitsu and Treaty Revision in Japan* (1999), *The History of Japan* (Greenwood, 1998), and *The Dalai Lama* (1993).

YU SHEN is assistant professor of history at Indiana University Southeast. She received her Ph.D. from the University of Illinois. Her chief research interest is twentieth-century Sino-American relations, and she has contributed to *The Journal of American-East Asian Relations*.

DAVID STEFANCIC is professor of history at St. Mary's College/Notre Dame. He received his Ph.D. from the University of Wisconsin-Milwaukee. He is the author of *Robotnik: A Short History of Polish Labor* (1992).

FRANK W. THACKERAY is professor of history at Indiana University Southeast. He received his Ph.D. from Temple University. Professor Thackeray is the author of *Antecedents of Revolution: Tsar Alexander I and the Polish Congress Kingdom* (1980). With John E. Findling, he is the editor of *Statesmen Who Changed the World* (Greenwood, 1993) and the other volumes in the Events That Changed the World and Events That Changed America series. He and Professor Findling are also series editors of the Greenwood Histories of the Modern Nations series. Professor Thackeray is a former Fulbright scholar in Poland.

ANDREW P. TROUT is professor of history emeritus at Indiana University Southeast. He received his Ph.D. from the University of Notre Dame and is the author of *City on the Seine: Paris in the Time of Richelieu and Louis XIV* (1996) and *Jean-Baptiste Colbert* (1978). Professor Trout has co-authored numerous articles on public finance.

WILLIAM T. WALKER is vice president for academic affairs and professor of history at Chestnut Hill College. He received his Ph.D. from the University of South Carolina. He has contributed to *Statesmen Who Changed the World* (Greenwood, 1993) and *Great Lives in History, British and Commonwealth Series*.